D0871248

THE THUNDERING SCOT

The
THUNDERING
SCOT

A Portrait of JOHN KNOX

by GEDDES MacGREGOR

Philadelphia
THE WESTMINSTER PRESS

Library of Congress Catalog Card Number: 57–6850

PRINTED IN THE UNITED STATES OF AMERICA

TO THE KIRK
knawen onelie to God,
quha alane knawis
whome he hes chosen

CONTENTS

FOREWORD

Surely few figures as dramatic as John Knox have so much escaped the attention of American writers. It will be some compensation for the shortcomings of the present biography if it should stimulate other writers in this country to do better.

My aim is to be sympathetic to Knox, without ignoring his faults. That is why I have generally tried to see things as much as possible through his eyes. Like all great men, he is very susceptible to caricature. The conventional one promulgated by his detractors is singularly unpleasant: a dwarfish bore, long-bearded, long-faced, and long-winded; narrow-minded, obstinate, and infinitely rude. As in every caricature, there is an element of truth in this. Sir Winston Churchill has been immortalized as a bulldog; but while there is an element of truth in this too, the symbol surely fails to convey the grandeur of his achievement and his unique place in the history of human freedom. Nor does the conventional caricature of Knox give any idea of the immensity of his contribution to the liberation of mankind. What he did was no less important for being only the foundation that others have covered up by their more plainly visible achievements.

Knox was no rabble rouser. On the other hand, he was no great theologian or distinguished scholar. He was, above all, a preacher and a leader of men. Apparently a radical and a plebeian, he was nevertheless, more than most men, impressed by the striking differences in quality between man and man. Of such differences he was no leveler. He believed he was a harsh trumpet for the Word of God in which he put all his trust; but he knew that God could heal and hallow even the poorest instrument of His choosing. It is impossible to understand Knox if we fail to remember that it was a profound appreciation of this circumstance that drew forth his extraordinary genius. What can captivate us in Knox is chiefly his intense sincerity in the role he plays in fascinating, dramatic situations. We may not like his kind of eloquence, nor care for the way he went about his work. But perhaps it is hardly for us to complain. We do not always care for the language of a trooper; yet if his gallantry is decisive in securing victory against evil forces, it is surely churlish on our part to boggle at the indelicacy of his language on the field, or to complain of the cut of his mustache. Knox was not an unkindly man. He had a sense of humor; a dry one, perhaps, but in view of the hardships he endured it would not be surprising if he had had none at all. As in the case of many others, suffering developed in him, rather than destroyed, that invaluable defense against the absurdity and wickedness of the world.

In Scotland, the name of Knox later became to many a symbol of severe religious orthodoxy. Robert Burns, in the eighteenth century, could write:

> "Orthodox! Orthodox, wha believe in John Knox,
> Let me sound an alarm to your conscience."

For inevitably many were by then giving lip service to Knox while parodying his spirit. In the hearts of Scotsmen his place, however, was secure. He became the Moses of the Scots; more indeed, for he was their Amos and their Isaiah too, even their Washington and their Lincoln — all rolled into one. But his importance extends far beyond the little nation he both tamed and inspired. It took many generations of determined struggle to give the Western democracies such protection against despotism as we today enjoy. Neither Knox nor any other single individual could have built the elaborate system of safeguards against tyranny with which we are familiar. But he was one of the pioneers. The conditions in which he and other foundation builders had to do their work were harsh. It is not always pleasant to inspect them, for they can be ugly. The men who worked in them, however, deserve our remembrance, and of these none is a more romantic figure than John Knox.

The scope of my work is modest. This book is intended for the general reader rather than for the specialist. Nevertheless, an explanation is due to those whose reading may be more than casual. While I have consulted some manuscript sources and have made use of all the important existing biographies from M'Crie to Percy, the source to which I am most indebted is Knox's own *History*. The materials appended to my work are partly for the guidance of those unfamiliar with the historical background, and partly for the more scholarly readers who may wish to pursue the study of Knox beyond the compass of this book. I have sometimes modernized the old Scots spelling, while elsewhere, for the sake of its flavor, I have kept it. Knox himself Anglicized both his spelling and his speech, but his scribes wrote Scots. Historians will recognize that I have modernized the calendar. For the sake of beginners, it ought to be explained that the " old style " year began on March 25, so that Patrick Hamilton's martyrdom, for instance, which by our reckoning fell on February 29, 1528, is given in the old records as falling on February 29, 1527. In Scotland the change to the " new style " took place on January 1, 1600. Elsewhere it came into use earlier, as at Geneva, for example, in Knox's time. Such technicalities need not trouble the general reader, who may read the whole story without looking at a footnote — a pleasant feat that scholars are usually unable to accomplish.

Nobles, gentry, and other persons in the story are not always easily identifiable. The index has been designed partly with a view to helping the reader out of difficulties that may occasionally arise.

GEDDES MacGREGOR

Bryn Mawr, Pennsylvania

CHAPTER

1

John Knox was born in or near Haddington, Scotland, eighteen miles east of Edinburgh, the capital, in or about the year 1513.[1] The lack of precision about the date and place of his birth reflects his humble origin. Until as recently as the beginning of the nineteenth century, the house in which, according to popular tradition, he was born, was possessed, together with a few acres of land, by a family of the name of Knox who claimed kinship with him. His father, William Knox, was a peasant. This does not mean that he was a poor man, only that he was not a grandee. He was able to give John a liberal education according to the standards of the day. He was probably quite prosperous in a modest way — a sort of small farmer. Certainly he was descended from an ancient and respected family. His wife, John Knox's mother, was a Sinclair, a clan with a reputation for much pride of race. It seems she died when John was a child, and John's father married again. But class distinctions were sharp in sixteenth century Scotland, and from the point of view of the great families and the royal courts among which it was John Knox's destiny to move in later life, he was and always remained a peasant, every inch of him. He despised the intrigues of the courts, and with peasant forthrightness boasted to the Queen of Scots that he " flattered no flesh "; yet on the other hand he deplored the excesses of the mob, the " rascal multitude," as he called it, with all the distaste for hooliganism that one would expect in a man brought up in a respectable family.

[1] See Appendix II.

A Scotsman born only some twenty years after the discovery of America by Columbus, he was dead half a century before the *Mayflower* sailed. The Scotland he knew was a small, northern land that had fought its own War of Independence against England two centuries before his birth, and won it in circumstances that ensured for the Scottish people a deep, lasting, ineradicable sense of national pride. Despite subsequent defeats in defensive engagements with its vastly richer and eight times more populous southern neighbor, Scotland had never been conquered. (Nor, indeed, has it ever been conquered since, for even under Cromwell's brief rule, when there was talk of annexing Scotland as a conquered country, terms of a voluntary union were arranged, and Scotland became a part of the Commonwealth, sending representatives to the Parliaments of the Protectorates.) Knox loved his Scotland; but, like every true patriot, he was an internationalist too. In the course of his life he learned to love other countries, England not least, and his influence on the whole English-speaking world has been incalculably great.

The East Lothian district of Scotland, in which Knox spent his impressionable childhood, was especially vulnerable to military attack, as its inhabitants had learned from bitter experience. The town of Haddington, on the highroad from England to Edinburgh, the Scottish capital, had been twice reduced by the English to smoking ruins before Knox was born. In his own day it was besieged by the French. It would have been strange indeed if the English, who descended periodically on this countryside, had not envied as they did the splendid orchards, the richness of the soil, the quiet prosperity of the people. The conditions all compared very favorably with the conditions prevalent in England at that time. It is said that one army of English invaders actually lived off the beans they gathered in the fields. The splendor of the churches and monasteries of this district is also remarked by the writers of the period. One was of such beauty that it was called " the Lamp of Lothian."

Alluding to the destruction of this beautiful church by the English, Knox's own teacher, the celebrated John Major, hints darkly at a divine judgment against the wealth of the Scottish

14

religious houses. It was not right, he said, that the Minorites, a religious order especially devoted to holy poverty, should possess churches of such splendor. John Major, though critical of the papacy and an ardent supporter of conciliar, constitutional reform within the Church, remained faithful to the old religion. Knox eventually became convinced of the need for more radical reform. Growing up in the very heart of Scotland, he imbibed from infancy both a fervent patriotism and a deep sense of the corruption of the Scottish Church. This corruption was extraordinary even in an age when the Church was, by all accounts, almost everywhere corrupted. In Scotland the Church had accumulated half the wealth of the country. It had become so powerful that it seemed as though Scotland's long struggle to keep its independence was to end by its becoming a mere pawn of the Roman pontiff, or, as the Scots called him, the " paip." While the country was politically independent, its bishops and other higher clergy had come to be in abject dependence on Rome. The outrageous morals of many of the clergy, both secular and regular, were such as to suggest to the average inhabitant a foreign army of occupation rather than a Church springing from the faith of the people. In the higher ranks of this army were exceedingly lucrative appointments, for instance, a plurality of sinecures held by one individual who customarily obtained for his own bastard sons similar ecclesiastical loot.

It is true that there were scholarly prelates and others, even in such a Church, who, laboring quietly at their studies, took no part in the intrigues of their day. But in the eyes of those who felt most sharply the sting of political injustice, such saintly souls, by removing themselves from the maelstrom of life, only played into the hands of the evildoers. The few of this better sort who tried to influence public affairs generally achieved nothing for the improvement of the nation's moral health, succeeding only in having their own fingers burned as the reward of their meddling. Such was the fate of Gavin Douglas, son of the great Earl of Angus, who, as provost of St. Giles's, Edinburgh, sat quietly at his window that commanded a magnificent view of Edinburgh and the countryside from the

Pentland Hills to the shores of Fife across the water, translating Virgil's *Aeneid* into the Scottish tongue. Embroiled in the inevitable intrigues, he was imprisoned in what he called " the wyndy and richt unpleasant castle and rok of Edinburgh." Released, he became Bishop of Dunkeld, and it is of him that Scott wrote centuries later:

> " A bishop at the altar stood,
> A noble lord of Douglas blood,
> With mitre sheen and socquet white,
> Yet showed his meek and thoughtful eye
> But little pride of prelacy.
> More pleased that in a barbarous age
> He gave rude Scotland Virgil's page,
> Than that beneath his rule he held
> The bishopric of fair Dunkeld."

A creditable prelate in a discreditable Church, he won the praise of even Sir David Lindsay, the great Scottish satirist of the day. But such men as Douglas seemed to do nothing to diminish the depravity of the Church. The movement for conciliar reform, which was strong in Scotland, likewise failed. With the ever-present menace of attack by England, the obvious hope for Scotland, from the point of view of power politics, was a military alliance with France, whose court was a spearhead of papal power. In such circumstances even the best men seemed powerless to awaken the conscience of the Scottish Church as a whole.

In this Scotland into which Knox was born, the only opening, practically speaking, for a boy whose inclinations were studious rather than mercantile or agricultural, was the priesthood. So when Knox went as a boy to grammar school to learn Latin, and proceeded to further study at the University of St. Andrews,[2] it was taken for granted that he would become a priest, as he did. For a boy in Knox's Scotland this was not a decision such as a young man is expected to make today if he enters a theological seminary to prepare himself for the ministry. Nor was Knox making the choice Luther had made a few

[2] See Appendix II.

years earlier in entering the Augustinian friary at Erfurt. The action of a boy such as Knox was more like that of a poor American lad in colonial times seeking entry to the lower ranks of the Government service. To receive holy orders was to qualify oneself for appointments that would nowadays be performed by attorneys and their clerks. In the sense that every soldier carries a field marshal's baton in his kitbag, every priest might rise to high office in the administration of the state. Knox himself never engaged, as a matter of fact, in what we should nowadays call " regular parish work "; he became a legal official, an apostolic notary, supplementing this work by teaching " grammar " to boys. Though his legal position was one of some trust, he was but a cog in the ecclesiastical wheel. There was nothing very remarkable in all this. When even bishops were feverishly competing for high state offices as well as ecclesiastical sinecures, the lower clergy naturally imitated them on a smaller scale.

Knox would enter the University of St. Andrews very young, for such was the custom. He never took a degree — again by no means anything unusual. He is described in the records in later life as " Sir John Knox," the designation of a nongraduate priest. Those who took the degree were designated, instead, " Master." The distinction was not particularly important. Even centuries later, in Presbyterian Scotland, many candidates for the ministry spent years at the university but for financial or other reasons omitted the formality of taking a degree, being ordained and becoming, in some cases, scholarly as well as respected clergymen. At St. Andrews young men such as John Knox and his contemporary George Buchanan, the future poet and humanist, pursued the conventional studies prescribed in the medieval curriculum. The renaissance of learning that was sweeping Continental Europe had at that time still left Scotland almost untouched. The one place, however, where the breath of it could just be felt was, of course, the university. From the more lively and liberal teachers, students could hear echoes of the new-fashioned ways of thought. Some of these were accounted dangerous. How dangerous they could be for young men to dabble in we shall presently discover. But such novelties of the mind attracted the interest of only the more eager and irrepressible students. The rest were content to take the more comfortable course of assimilating whatever the conventions and their teachers required as a minimum, rather than risk untried paths. Even the more vivacious young minds, though they might enjoy the thrill of intellectual exploration and the refreshing sense of new life and freedom they might occasionally receive while listening to lectures and participating in the university disputations, soon tired of what seemed to be mere fruitless exhilaration. In the traditional medieval materials there was food enough for subtle minds: was it not better to whet your mind on the old, safe whetstones than to try out those that were evidently explosive?

Moreover, student days passed all too quickly, and then, after ordination to the priesthood, there were many other things to think of, not least the prosaic business of a conventional career. The fact that Knox lived for some eight years or so the humdrum life of a dominie-notary-priest before manifesting any public sympathy with Reformation ideas is therefore not at all difficult to understand. No doubt he imbibed something of the new spirit in his undergraduate days, and looked back on these, as do most university men, with some nostalgia. He had been a promising young man. Like most of the ambitious and eager students of his time he had tried his hand at assisting as a " regent," a sort of free-lance instructor of younger men, and according to friendly sources he was a good one and his classes were popular. Whatever he achieved in those early days he did by his own merit, for he had no influence to ease his path.

Nevertheless, during these obscure years after his ordination, there were influences at work in him that must have vexed his mind and troubled his heart. He could not afford to indulge much in the thought of them. It was risky even to think thoughts that might savor of heresy. An ignorant lad could perhaps afford to think them, for he was less in danger of making himself articulate upon them in the way the authorities disliked. A young priest, on the other hand, could not be too careful. Criticism of the corrupt practices in the Church was not effectively forbidden; they were too widely known and acknowledged by learned and ignorant alike. Nor were all the ideas of the humanistic renaissance banned. John Major, the teacher who had probably most influenced Knox, had spoken of them. A man of balanced judgment, capable scholar rather than original thinker, he had sowed seeds in the minds of his students, though he had not set them on fire with the new ideas. Slowly the seeds took growth in the mind of Knox. Gradually, however, his studies took him into the forbidden paths. What was above all forbidden was free and serious inquiry into the Church's theory, which controlled all practices, good and bad.

Knox was not alone in feeling deep misgivings about the foundations of the vast ecclesiastical structure on which his career depended. There were others who, embroiled in the first few years of such a career, shared his disquiet. What was conspicuous about Knox throughout all his life was the determination to translate his honest thinking into action. As he turned his attention away from the writings of the Schoolmen to those of the old Fathers of the Church, Jerome and Augustine, for example, he found a simplicity and directness that appealed to him. Through the writings of Jerome he could hardly fail to be led to a study of the Scriptures themselves. Probably it was not long before he was deeply impressed by his reading of the Bible, and in particular the chapter that was to be most influential in all his later thought and work, the seventeenth chapter of The Gospel According to St. John, which presents the last prayer of Christ with the disciples before the betrayal by Judas:

"I pray not for the world, but for them which thou hast given me; for they are thine. . . . I have given them thy word; and the world hath hated them, because they are not of the world, even as I am not of the world. . . . O righteous Father, the world hath not known thee: but I have known thee, and these have known that thou hast sent me."

As the young lawyer-priest read these words, he believed he saw the key to all the problems that had for so long disturbed him. The True Church of Christ was a mystical community.

Christ had chosen his disciples, and was continuing to choose them. To be so chosen was the greatest conceivable privilege a human being could receive. The True Church was not the great machine he was in, but a spiritual company; a congregation invisible to the world, but known intimately to God, who had formed it and would continue to succor it, as he had promised, to the end of the world, and world without end. As he laid down the Bible on whose page were written the words of Christ that had entranced him, perhaps he whispered to himself in the Scots tongue of the day the pith of the good news he had read, that the " Kirk is invisible, knawen onelie to God, quha alane knawis whome he hes chosen." Thus was born in Knox's mind the doctrine of the Invisible Church, which is of the very essence of Protestantism. It is a doctrine that has given generations of men and women a sense of ineradicable security, joy, and assurance. Some intimations, at least, of this assurance came to Knox as soon as he had read with faith these words of Christ. Troubles in plenty no doubt lay ahead. The battle would perhaps be bloodier than his worst imaginings; but now that he was enlisted in God's army what could he have to fear?

On the other hand, what could he do? He was of no personal account. Nor would those who were of more account in the nation pay much heed to him, whatever their sympathies. If he were to get up publicly and declare his private opinions, he could count on being burned alive as a heretic. Knox was not a seeker after martyrdom for its own sake. He had too practical a mind for that. Then there was nothing to do but wait and study and pray. God must be trusted to show the way in his good time.

Knox was not only of no personal account at this time. He was also undistinguished in appearance. Rather below the average height, he was a broad-shouldered man with black hair and beard. The beard was short and wispy in those early days, though later portraits show it impressively long, in the patriarchal style. His grayish-blue eyes were deep set under ridged eyebrows and a rather narrow forehead; he had a long nose, full lips, and the usual ruddy complexion of the farmer type.

His health was not very robust; later suffering in captivity further impaired it. But it is likely that even in those obscure years before the age of thirty-three, years of which so little is known, his personality already revealed that hardheaded dourness and zest for plain speech for which he was afterward famous. Yet there was gentleness too in that hard face of his, and never in later life, even in his fiercest transports of righteous indignation, did it lack human tenderness.

There was one specific event in Scotland that haunted the minds of all at this time, a terrible scene that had occurred in St. Andrews when Knox was about fifteen: the burning of Patrick Hamilton. No man of Knox's age could efface it from his memory, and it must have vividly affected Knox's own imagination during his early years as a priest gradually developing Protestant convictions. Before letting Knox spring into the full light of history as a public figure, it will be well to re-create in our imagination the effect that this event must have had upon him as an adolescent lad. To this we shall devote the next chapter, after which the story of Knox's extraordinarily dramatic career will be unfolded. The character and personality of Knox will quickly be revealed in the course of that story. Of the virtues and shortcomings of his remarkable character, the reader will judge for himself.

2   Every night in the cold month of March, 1528, in a hundred taverns in Scotland, the tavern keepers observed a strange, fearsome look in the eyes of their customers. A stranger might not have noticed it. But it swept over the men's faces, especially over those of the younger men, as they kept turning the conversation back to the question of the hour: " Wherefore was Master Patrick Hamilton burned? "

The rest of the time the men joked and laughed and quarreled and roared, and cursed God, and blasphemed the Blessed Virgin and all the saints, and mocked the Mass, just as their fathers had done before them; and they sang the same lewd songs in which they pilloried bishop and abbot and friar. In a corner of the tavern, under the flame of a spurting candle, away from the center of the din, a group of oldish seafaring men were talking to an uncouth, blue-eyed lad who might have been John Knox. By this time he was about fifteen and was as likely as not to have ignored the watchman's call that sent the more respectable citizens to their homes for the night. The tremendous drama in which he was destined to become the leading actor was taking shape around him while he was still too young to be more than an onlooker. Nearly eighteen years were to pass before he would make his first appearance on the stage that was now being set. But he was already old enough to read the meaning of the look in the eyes of those around him when the burning of Hamilton was mentioned. It was a look that could never be forgotten.

But the look soon faded from the old sailors' eyes. Now they were only telling the lad the tale, how they had just missed sailing with Columbus on the *Santa María* thirty-five years ago. The lad was only half listening, neither believing nor disbelieving their yarn. It was good tavern talk. That was enough. The powers-that-be had said there was no land west of Portugal and Ireland. Aye, but Columbus had proved them wrong. Anything that raised a laugh against the powers-that-be was good tavern talk. Better to tell tall tales about unfamiliar things than speak of sad subjects they all knew too well.

Flodden, for instance. Flodden was a sore subject for the Scots when there was hardly a young man in the tavern who had not lost his father, nor an old one who had not lost his son, fifteen years ago on that bloodiest battlefield in Scotland's proud, sad history. Scotland had suffered a terrible defeat at Flodden after centuries of bitter, victorious struggles against the mighty English. Greater even than hatred of the foe had been the sense of national independence roused in the hearts of Scotland's people by the spirit of the brave men Wallace had led to victory at Stirling Bridge and Robert the Bruce to victory again at Bannockburn two hundred years ago.

Flodden had left Scotland still independent politically, and though Scotland's pride had been injured by military defeat, its sense of nationhood had been invigorated by this even more than it had been by its victories against England in the War of Independence. Yet the memories of Flodden tore even the toughest heartstrings. There was scarcely a man among them old enough to hold his liquor who did not sometimes see in his mind's eye the faces of the women who had haunted the streets of the town, inquiring in their agony of every chance passer-by for news of their men; who did not hear at times in his mind's ear the heartbroken sob, the desolate shriek, of one woman after another as she learned that her Sandy or her Tam was among the ten thousand who had bravely poured out their blood for Scotland and lay dead on cruel Flodden Field. Flodden was a bitter shame and a heartache; but its hurts had sunk too deep to be noticed any more.

A young man banged on the table with his tankard. The tavern keeper saw again the look in the eyes of the men as they waited, in an expectant lull, for the young man to ask once more the question of the hour: " Wherefore was Master Patrick Hamilton burned? "

He asked it in a hoarse, low voice, addressing no one in particular, yet commanding immediate interest and respect. In a moment all but those who were too drunk to do more than soliloquize were embroiled in the general discussion.

Patrick Hamilton was a young Scot of gentle birth, peaceable disposition, and scholarly attainments, who, having been carefully spied on at the instigation of the archbishop, had been burned at the stake in St. Andrews, on February 29, 1528, in the presence of a great concourse of people. The horrible execution had been aggravated by circumstances of such monstrous cruelty that the thought of the whole affair bit deep into the minds of men and sickened their hearts. Until that sad, cold day, few persons had been burned for heresy in Scotland; perhaps only two, and they both foreigners: one an English priest, John Resby; and the other, Paul Craw, a Bohemian. Both of these men had been charged with preaching

Lollard views.[3] In the fourteenth century, before the foundation of the Scottish universities, the Scots had gone in considerable numbers to Oxford, for some time a hotbed of Lollardy. But while there had been trouble here and there about students openly declaring such heretical opinions, the incidents were usually hushed up. Lollard teachings were probably sometimes mixed up with subversive social doctrines — communism and free love. They would not be always chiefly directed, as were Wycliffe's, against ecclesiastical authority. Such wild ranters were feared by more than bishops and priors; they were also ridiculed by the mob. It was not surprising that they incurred punishment.

But though the Church did fear Lollardy — the University of St. Andrews owed its foundation in 1412 partly to the Church's hope of diminishing the cause of such fears — it had been able to do surprisingly little to prevent the expression of Lollard views, which had been openly voiced, especially in certain parts of the country, with considerable influence and with remarkable impunity. Both the King and the nobles had shown themselves indifferent to the Church's protests, in spite of the fact that in a nation of perhaps half a million inhabitants it commanded three thousand clerics and others deriving their revenues directly from the Church, which owned half the wealth of the country.

During the War of Independence in the early part of the fourteenth century, the Scots had ignored the papacy, which had supported English attempts to conquer their land. With Scotland's political independence seemingly assured, the papal policy changed. The popes now entered into competition with other forces in the scramble to exploit Scotland's nationalism as an instrument of their own aims. In the early part of the fifteenth century there was little hostility to the papacy as such. Of course there never was any such hostility so long as the papacy did not attempt to exercise its authority in any very definite way, and since at that time there were rival claimants

[3] The Lollards, followers of John Wycliffe, were English precursors of the Protestant Reformation. Wycliffe died in 1384. The Lollards disseminated a translation of the Bible in the common tongue of the people.

to the papal throne, one at Avignon and one at Rome, it was natural that neither claimant should do anything to offend the Scots. From 1418, however, under Pope Martin V, Roman interference became considerable, and some years later various antipapal laws were passed. Scottish scholars were, moreover, commonly sympathetic to those who, at the Council of Constance, sought constitutiqnal restriction throughout the whole Church against the growing pretensions of the Roman see.

Patrick Hamilton was a younger son of Sir Patrick Hamilton of Kincavel and Stanehouse, a knight reputed to have been the most redoubtable of his day at the chivalrous court of James IV. Through him, young Patrick was connected with the royal House of Stuart. Having gone to the University of Paris, then the leading theological school in Christendom, he came under the influence of Erasmus. In 1519, copies of the famous disputation between Luther and Eck were circulating in Paris, and the young Scottish scholar took his master's degree from the Sorbonne the following year, having imbibed some of Luther's views [4] and departed for Louvain before the doctors of the Sorbonne had examined Luther's doctrines and judged them heretical. By 1523 he was back in Scotland and was received into the University of St. Andrews on June 9, the same day as was John Major, the celebrated historian of Scotland, who was later the teacher of John Knox. A few days earlier, James Beaton had been translated to the archbishopric of St. Andrews, Scotland's primatial see. Hamilton's gentle birth and highly promising intellect brought him at once into the public eye in the ecclesiastical capital of Scotland that was also the seat of its first university. Yet for several years Hamilton's opinions got him into no trouble. He was anything but a rabble rouser. We hear of him during this time composing music for a Mass in the cathedral, and himself acting as precentor.

In 1525, however, the Scottish Parliament passed an act

---

[4] Patrick Hamilton's doctrine is set forth in a Latin treatise commonly called " Patrick's Places." It is to be found in Knox's *History* (ed. Dickinson), Vol. II, App. I, pp. 219–229. (See Appendix III, Bibliographical Note.)

against Lutheranism, and Beaton, eager to display zeal for the papal cause, instituted throughout his archdiocese a " faithful inquisition." When Hamilton was summoned in 1527 to appear before Beaton on a charge of propagating heretical doctrines, he left for Germany, where his sincerity evidently made a deep impression on older scholars of the day at Marburg. Later that year he returned to Scotland and married. He was now treated respectfully by the ecclesiastical authorities and was allowed to give both public and private conferences in the university. But this courtesy was a cloak for a well-laid scheme against him. There is little doubt that Alexander Campbell, prior of the neighboring Dominican house, was appointed to spy on him in such conferences and inform against him. Apparently to discourage royal interference in the forthcoming proceedings against Hamilton, the young king of Scotland was encouraged to go on a pilgrimage to the Shrine of St. Duthac in a remote northern part of the country. Rejecting the advice of his friends to flee, Hamilton appeared before the archbishop and his council, and was charged with having taught various theological doctrines that were deemed to be heretical. Asked for his views on these doctrines, he said half of them were questionable but admitted his firm adherence to the others. Meanwhile, since it was learned that Hamilton's powerful brother was mustering a force at Kincavel to go to his aid, and that other friends were making similar arrangements on his behalf, the archbishop's men seized him during the night at his lodging, and forcibly took him to the Castle of St. Andrews, so that there might be no risk of his slipping out of their hands.

St. Andrews is to this day notorious for its cold, high winds, and on that twenty-ninth day of February the east wind from the North Sea was howling around the cathedral. A crowd of people were assembled when the archbishop took his place, surrounded by an impressive array of bishops, abbots, and the like. Under a strong guard, Hamilton was taken thence to be formally tried for heresy. After Prior Campbell, the Dominican informer, had presented his case and Hamilton had made his defense, sentence was delivered. Hamilton was to have his property confiscated and be handed over to the secular powers for further punishment. In view of the danger of powerful help coming to the accused, a stake was immediately erected at the gates of St. Salvator's College, and Hamilton was led to it. Asked to recant, he replied that he would not do so "for awe of your fire," for he preferred, he said, to burn in their fire for obeying his conscience than to burn in the fire of hell for disobeying it. When brought to the stake he took off his coat and gave it to his servant, saying, "This stuff will not help in the fire, yet will do thee some good; I have no more to leave thee but the ensample of my death, which I pray thee keep in mind." Thereupon he was tied to the stake.

But while the men in the tavern only muttered garbled accounts of the story of the heresy hunt, they raised their voices and clenched their fists as they recalled Hamilton's hideous end. The stake was a horrible death at the best, even when merciful smoke suffocated the victim before the fire had burned his body into its first convulsion of pain. But in the howling gale of that wintry day it was difficult to get the fire lighted. When the powder was brought and at length ignited, the fire only scorched Hamilton's left hand and the side of his face. It was relighted several times, while he went on speaking of his faith, reproaching no one except Campbell, when this friar, stung no doubt in his own conscience, taunted him and enjoined him to say *Salve Regina*. When he could no longer speak and was being asked if he held to his opinions, he lifted up three blackened fingers. His agony endured six hours, it was said, before the fire, becoming at last "vehement," ended a spectacle of excruciating torture, the like of which had never before been seen within the realm of Scotland. The University of Louvain, in a letter to the archbishop, expressed its appreciation of his zeal for the true faith, its admiration for the manner in which the sentence had been carried out, and its congratulations to the University of St. Andrews for the honor that had come to it through these proceedings.

"He must have done something to hurt Beaton's pride," suggested the knobbly-faced old man with an air of inscrutable wisdom.

But the other men in the tavern were saying that it was

Beaton's ambition that had made him so carefully engineer this plot against a peaceable young Scotsman. He was doing it all for his own advancement, all to please Rome. Some spoke darkly of having seen the archbishop's eyes glisten in selfish glee at the thought of the rewards he would win at the cost of a young gentleman's agony and death. It was an insult to the people of Scotland, shouted one man. Others said they had never thought much before about doctrines of faith, but what they had heard convinced them that the doctrine Patrick Hamilton had taught, whatever it was, must be the right doctrine.

" Aye," said one of them, better informed than the others, " they say that a friend of that bloody Beaton has told him, if he burn any more men he should burn them in *how* [5] cellars, for the *reek* [6] of Master Patrick Hamilton has infected as many as it blew upon."

" The priests will curse ye for that talk," muttered a feeble old man in the corner. The priest's curse was excommunication.

" The priests don't care about talk, it's tithes they care about," rejoined another with a harsh laugh. " It's when they don't get their tithes they do the cursing."

There was general amusement at this. The weapon of excommunication had already for long lost much of its old terror.

" Nobody cares any more for the priests' curses," said a young man. "Don't ye see that's why they had to burn Master Patrick Hamilton? They're thinking that's better than the cursing."

There was grim quiet for a moment. Then somebody started to sing an extempore ditty [7] destined for a place of fame among the popular songs of the century that were later to be collected and compiled by the Wedderburns of Dundee:

[5] Deep.
[6] Smoke.
[7] I am not suggesting that the verses quoted in the form in which they have come down to us were actually sung as early as 1528, only that songs of this kind were sung before they were written down later in the century.

> "The bishop would not wed a wife,
> The abbot not pursue one,
> Thinking it was a lusty life
> Each day to have a new one."

The crowd laughed and applauded the ribaldry. It was a welcome relief from a painful subject. The songster's tankard was filled. After the murmur of conversation, in the course of which someone mocked the Dominican friars, he was again inspired:

> "The blind bishop he could not preach
> For playing with the lasses;
> The silly friar had to fleiche [8]
> For almous [9] that he assis." [10]

It would be a good thing if every priest were to marry like other men, suggested the tavern keeper, winking provocatively at the man who was providing his customers with free entertainment. Again the songster's tankard was replenished, and once more he gave tongue:

> "For then should not so many hure [11]
> Be up and down this land;
> Nor yet so many beggars poor
> In kirk and market stand."

The songs became more and more ribald. The men continued to roar with laughter. Yet somehow there was a new uneasiness in the air. The Church had for long been the butt of tavern jokes. The subject, however, had been only half serious at the most. In a rude age and among a people accustomed to coarse village behavior, the morals of the Scottish clergy that sound so scandalous today did not offend as much as they would now. Farmers did not expect much of the priests, though even so they were sometimes scandalized. But Hamilton's death had put a more awesome complexion on the traditional theme of the tavern. It had also stirred in human hearts a vengeance less than half uttered because more than half unutterable.

---

[8] Flatter.   [9] Alms.   [10] Asks.   [11] Harlots.

And when the roars of glee had subsided; when the songster had relapsed into drunken silence; when the clamor had resumed its normal pitch; when the arguments had been carried far into the night till all but a few of the men had gone — still, even in the sleepy slits of eyes, the tavern keeper could see the ghost of the fearsome look as the last retreating voice cried hoarsely: " Wherefore . . . ? "

And young John Knox, who could not but hear of all this, must also have asked himself, with all a boy's wonderment: " Wherefore . . . ? "

3   In the dreary days of December, 1545, John Knox, the hitherto nondescript little dominie-notary-priest of Haddington, leaped from obscurity into the hard light of the street. Now in his thirty-third year, he could be seen, his gray-blue eyes glistening with the intoxication of his new-found faith, his thick lips set in unsmiling determination, as he marched through the streets, sword in hand, in front of his new master. He was among those who had fallen under the spell of George Wishart's words. To the short ministry in Scotland of this preacher of the Reformed faith, destined like Hamilton for the stake, John Knox owed much of the inspiration of his own life. The carrying of the sword was a practical expedient. Knox was acting as Wishart's bodyguard, in case of trouble with the mob, for a priest had once tried to assassinate this preacher. But the sword was also a symbol of Knox's future life.

By the time of Knox's winter with Wishart, Martin Luther, in Germany, was dying, and John Calvin, now thirty-six, had already written his great work, *The Institutes of the Christian Religion*. Reformation ideas in their Lollard form had, we have seen, long been familiar to the Scots and for a generation Lutheran ideas had slowly infiltrated. To Knox, who could not forget Hamilton's gentle, blameless life and cruel end, every breath of such doctrine from the Continent of Europe must have seemed to merit sympathetic attention. In Wishart he found the embodiment of his own deepest convictions.

What was now forcing itself on the general attention of the Scots, however, was what was happening on their doorstep. In England, Scotland's traditional foe, the papal power had been broken, evidently with the greatest of ease. The annulment of the marriage of Henry VIII, a few years after Hamilton's death, had been unpopular with the English; but the breach with Rome had been popular, for the English had for long resented the interference of a pope whose throne was a thousand miles away and whose policy seemed infinitely farther removed from England's welfare. The act passed in England in 1534 destroying papal authority in England did not go unresisted; but no seas of blood were shed over it as were to be shed in the Continental Wars of Religion. Even in the nation of king worshipers that was Tudor England, the act that made him head of Church and State could not but have met with the strongest resistance, had not the minds of the bishops of Rome been for so long cast in a very Roman mold. By the time of the breach, the dislike of foreign interference in English affairs was already an old story; of longer standing in the English mind than the American distaste for such interference was to be at the time of the Boston Tea Party in December, 1773.

During Knox's apparently dormant years there had grown up in Scotland a Protestant party, an important party, for it comprised an influential section of the Scottish nobility whose power was great enough to intimidate their king. The monarchy in Scotland was exceedingly weak in comparison with that of England. This was a potent force, indeed, in keeping the Scottish king dependent on the papacy, for he was much too weak to cope with his recalcitrant nobles without some external aid from Rome. The king of Scotland, therefore, could not but give his support to the old ecclesiastical machine, since it was the best available safeguard of the security of his own throne. On the other hand, the common people, much as they hated the elaborate, wealth-sucking ecclesiasticism, could not but suspect the policy of the Protestant-minded nobles, for these nobles were looking to Henry's England as the natural ally of their cause. The instinct of the common people was right. They saw well enough what such a policy would bring. The choice was between present subjugation to Rome and the yielding up to England, their traditional enemy, the hard-won political independence they so dearly prized. The ambitious English king was in fact already dreaming of establishing a suzerainty over the Scots without even the necessity of a war, a suzerainty that his predecessor Edward II had failed to win on the battlefield. He was proposing a marriage, first between his daughter Mary and his nephew the Scottish king; then between his son Edward and the infant Marie Stuart. By such ruses he hoped to bring Scotland within his grasp. To the common people, therefore, even the slightest flirtation with England seemed, in these circumstances, to spell only disaster, and so the Protestant cause, however attractive, bore the stigma of treason. There can be little doubt that Knox, whose patriotism at this time was still inspired and limited by the fears and emotions of his class and controlled by his native prudence, shared all these popular sentiments to the full. Adversity makes strange bedfellows, and so powerful an adversary as Henry's England could for a time keep even the future Reformer of Scotland walking at the heel of the pope, whose heel sorely needed repair.

While Knox was listening to Wishart's preaching in the streets of Scotland, a few bishops of the Holy Roman Church were assembling, far away in Trent, a little village in the Tyrol, for the council that was to last nineteen years and belatedly effect drastic moral and educational reforms within its enfeebled ranks. In his Duchy of Gandia in Spain, Francis Borgia, future Jesuit saint and great-grandson of the Borgian Pope Alexander VI, whose favorite bastard son, Cesare, was perhaps the most notorious adventurer of the Italian Renaissance, was piously building a college for Loyola's Society of Jesus, which he was to enter himself after the death of his wife the following year. But in Scotland such events were hardly less remote than the doings of a mystic in India called Nanak, who had recently founded the new religion of the Sikhs. To the

Scots, Rome's way seemed almost irredeemably rotten. Almost, for perhaps even at this stage papal repentance and some recognition of the worth of the Reformers' work (a recognition such as that actually proposed, unsuccessfully, by Cardinal Contarini) might possibly have won back Scotland's confidence in the old religion. But by 1545, the Church that had seemed so rotten in 1528 certainly seemed no less so to a people whose embarrassing political circumstances had forced them to go on bearing the rottenness.

That Wishart got a ready hearing in Scotland is therefore not surprising. He was the son or nephew of a Kincardineshire laird, and he had already got into trouble with the authorities because of his practice of reading the Greek New Testament with his pupils at Montrose, a small east-coast town to the south of Aberdeen. Cited to appear before the bishop, he had fled to England and become a tutor at Cambridge. He was a tallish man of pleasing bearing and demeanor, courteous, charitable, and above all a teacher who delighted to teach. His return to Scotland came about, however, in a curious fashion. After the death of the Scottish King James V, Cardinal Beaton (hated nephew of the hated archbishop who had burned Hamilton) claimed to have been appointed regent of Scotland by an instrument executed by the dying king. Because it was put about and widely believed that this instrument was actually forged by Beaton himself, the Scottish Parliament had him arrested as a conspirator against the realm, and nominated the Earl of Arran as regent in his stead. Arran was one of the nobles who favored Protestantism and an alliance with England, and in these changed circumstances Protestant sentiments could be more freely expressed, and copies of the Bible in the vernacular were openly displayed by such as could afford them at a time when books were beyond the purse of most people. Arran, however, proved too weak to withstand the pressure of those who distrusted his Anglicizing policy, and his own bastard brother, the Abbot of Paisley, frightened him with the reminder that the legality of his mother's marriage, and consequently the legitimacy of his own birth, depended on a papal act. Therefore, argued the abbot, if the regent cast off

33

the pope as English Henry had done, he would stand to lose more than Henry had gained, for he would be a bastard, having no legal claim to the earldom, and therefore none to the regency, nor (should the case arise, as it might) to the Scottish throne. Soon Beaton was released and again vigorously conspiring against the Protestant party. During the attempted alliance with England, lasting barely six months, the Scots had entered into a cautious agreement with the English king concerning the betrothal of the infant Marie Stuart to the future English King Edward VI, and now repudiated this on Beaton's return to power. This repudiation brought down England's wrath in the form of a military reprisal that devastated the most magnificent abbeys in the Scottish Border country.

When Wishart returned to Scotland, then, it was by the invitation of a group of gentry of the defeated Protestant party. These were naturally eager to support his preaching, for they saw in it a means of fostering their political aims. But they overestimated the number of people in Scotland who were prepared to win freedom from the pope at the cost of parleys with England. Rather than undertake such an enterprise, already proved dangerous, most people even preferred having to put up with Beaton and the ecclesiastical institution over which he was primate. Ayrshire, the home of this seditious group, was an old center of Lollardy and a stronghold of the anti-Beaton faction: the Earl of Cassilis had even hinted at assassinating him. But Ayrshire was only a small, provincial district in the southwest, and it was necessary both to test out and to stir up feeling in the capital, for which operations Wishart, an ardent Protestant preacher, would make a very useful agent.

That Wishart was used by such political cliques is incontestable. But he was himself almost certainly of a very different and finer cast: a humble, lovable man; also a scholarly preacher — no less dangerous a métier in the Scotland of 1545 than it had been in the Scotland of 1525. Since Hamilton's death several other Protestants had been burned, and many exiled. While Wishart was preaching in the east-coast towns, including his native Montrose, the plague broke out in Dundee, a town only a few miles north of St. Andrews, the ecclesiastical capital. The

34

plague-stricken were not allowed to come within the walls of the town, but Wishart preached with great zeal in the Cowgait,[12] from the archway of the east gate of the town, so that the wretched people quarantined outside and preparing for death might hear no less than the citizens the message he had to declare. To a people who knew the Roman Church only in its most degraded form, to a hard, independent, northern people, bent on freeing themselves from tyrannies, yet not knowing which tyrant needed to be tackled first, the effect of Wishart's winsome exposition of the Reformed faith must have been tremendous. The princes of this world, he was saying, were set against God's people, who must suffer for a time. If a man believed on Christ, that man had Christ in his heart and was assured of his place in God's family. The princes of this world, the Beatons and the Henrys, seemed powerful; but what was their power compared to that of God's elect? Who would one rather be: a tyrant on a throne at enmity with God, or a little man hobbling down the Stannergait assured of his calling into God's very family? His hearers generally cared no more about the theology [13] of all this than they cared for that of the Mass; but the words of Wishart were words of life to them. It was a variation of the Pentecostal miracle: each man heard the message in terms of his own personal circumstances, and to each the message spelled out the same word, " freedom." As they listened to George Wishart, the street scavengers or dirt men and the smug Hilltown bonnetmakers alike felt that it was no longer a question of choosing the lesser evil, a miserable choice between two tyrannies, but the bringing in of the Kingdom of

12 *Gait* means " walk," " way," or " road." So, " Overgait " and " Nethergait," the high road and the low road respectively. Such Dundee streets are now misleadingly spelled " gate." The archway from which Wishart preached still stands, having survived attempts at its removal during the industrial expansion of Dundee in the nineteenth century when this town became the world's center of jute manufacture.

13 Wishart, who translated the Swiss confession of 1536, had come under the influence of Huldreich Zwingli, Luther's Swiss contemporary. Zwingli lacked Luther's warm sense of the freedom obtained through divine forgiveness, and his theology was less sacramental than that of other leaders of the Reformation; he stressed conformity to the sovereign will of God as revealed in Scripture.

God. Precisely how it was to be done was not clear: but if Wishart's words were as true as they sounded, God could be trusted to make all needful arrangements.

The Ayrshire lairds encouraged Wishart to go to Long-niddry House, near Edinburgh, where he would be met by sympathizers. He was; but it was dangerous company, a band of nobles plotting thuglike action against the cardinal. These were the died-in-the-wool Anglicizers who had no notion of how public opinion had veered away from their side since the Regent Arran's defection from the Protestant cause. They failed to appreciate the strength of the opposition. John Knox was at that time tutor to one of these families, and so it was that he came under Wishart's spell. This, he felt, was the Real Thing. Whatever he might think of Wishart's patrons, he believed the man they had brought back to Scotland was the man who could save it. Knox served Wishart with all the loyalty and devotion of one who, after many long years of waiting, has found a man after his own heart, a man who is also able and willing to speak his mind. He followed Wishart about, proud to be even a sword-bearer for such a man. His position as such brought to his remembrance, no doubt, the words of the pilgrim psalmist on his way to Jerusalem, who would rather be a doorkeeper in the house of his Lord than dwell in the tents of wickedness.

Wishart was no man to toe a party line, and was not prepared to be a mere instrument of his patrons' political plans. With missionary fervor he preached wherever he determined to preach; and Knox accompanied him, sword in hand. At Haddington, large audiences were expected. But on January 15, in the morning, the audience was disappointingly meager; in the afternoon it was so small as to cause comment. The following afternoon before sermon he received a letter of apology from his patrons explaining that they could not come. Correctly interpreting the situation to be that he was now being left to his own resources, to be devoured by Beaton's men, he handed the letter to his faithful disciple Knox, saying sadly that he was weary of the world because the world was weary of

God.[14] Surprised that any letter could deflect the thoughts of so holy a man from the meditations that usually absorbed his attention before preaching, Knox took the letter to read at the back of the church. From this stance he could see Wishart pacing nervously up and down behind the high altar.

There were only a few other hearers that afternoon. And it was a strange sermon they heard. Instead of delivering the one he had prepared, he extemporized for an hour and a half, warning his sparse congregation of the wrath to come. When he bade a melancholy farewell to the household whose guest he was, Knox proposed to go with him. But Wishart declined.

"Nay," he said, "return to your bairns [15] and God bless you. One is sufficient for one sacrifice."

Very reluctantly, Knox handed over the sword he had so proudly carried and returned to the house. Wishart went on his way with some of the lairds who were supporting him, and a few servants. It was an extremely cold night and the roads were too dangerous for the horses; the party went on foot, in the direction of the capital.

Unknown to them, the cardinal himself was staying, with a strong guard, at Elphinstone Tower, about halfway between Haddington and Edinburgh. Toward midnight, Wishart was apprehended by the Earl of Bothwell in person. An hour or so later, the cardinal's men surrounded the house and arrested two of the nobles, Sandilands and Cockburn. A third, Crichton, managed to make his escape.

So far as is known, Knox never saw his hero again. Wishart was eventually taken to the Castle of St. Andrews. On the last day of February, the anniversary of Hamilton's execution, he was informed, as he lay bound in chains, that the following morning he would be taken before the Lord Cardinal to give an account of the seditious and heretical doctrine he had taught.

Knox, never restrained in his language when writing of prelates, excelled himself in the vituperative venom with

[14] Cf. Knox's dying words.   [15] That is, the boys whom Knox taught.

which he later wrote of Wishart's trial. He did not scruple to liken the proceedings to the Passion of Christ; Beaton, of course, was the high priest. By a stroke of literary genius he enlivens his narrative by first recounting a thoroughly ridiculous and disgraceful episode that had occurred in Glasgow the previous June, when Cardinal Beaton had disputed with Gavin Dunbar, archbishop of Glasgow ("proud as a peacock"), which of them ought to have precedence over the other as they entered Glasgow Cathedral. The cardinal had claimed that the precedence was his, as primate of Scotland, while the archbishop had maintained that he had the precedence in his own diocese. Their respective cross-bearers, after scowling at each other, had gone on to jostling, thence to fisticuffs, and finally to a sort of fencing with the very croziers that were the symbols of the office they claimed as shepherds of Christ's flock. When the croziers had fallen to the ground, the scuffle had developed into a kind of free fight; "rochets were rent, and tippets were torn." The absurdity of this spectacle did not escape Knox, and he relates it to drive home the weight as well as the nature of the evil forces brought down on Wishart's head. Moreover, though the feud between the cardinal and the archbishop was commonly deemed past mending, all their bragging was forgotten in their sense of the common danger they faced in Wishart's seditious preaching. Archbishop Dunbar was among the first to be invited by Beaton to assist in the tribunal appointed to try the heretic. Not only did he accept the invitation with alacrity; the two prelates eventually watched the execution together from the same window.

The trial itself was not without an element of macabre humor. Even if only half is to be believed of what the records say, the dialogue between Wishart and his accusers must have been worth hearing. One of the first accusations made against Wishart was that he had likened a priest saying Mass to a fox wagging his tail in July. To this Wishart replied: " My Lords, I said not so. These were my sayings: The moving of the body outward, without the inward moving of the heart, is nothing else but the playing of an ape, and not the true serving of God."

After the people had been removed and sentence passed, two friars enjoined Wishart to make his confession to one of them. Declining to do so, he asked instead for John Winram, sub-prior of the neighboring friary, who had preached an evangelical sermon before the tribunal that morning, and whose preaching Wishart evidently approved. Winram came readily to the shriving. Knox says that the executioner himself went down on his knees to beg Wishart's forgiveness, since he did not will the death of so holy a man. Wishart kissed the executioner on the cheek, telling him that this was a token that he was forgiven, and enjoining him to do his appointed task.

4 The character of Wishart, as seen through the eyes of Knox, is essential to an understanding of Knox himself. Knox, in his account of the proceedings, presents us at once with the mystery of his own curious make-up. He sometimes writes almost like a ruffian; yet what he holds out for our admiration are the pacific, lamblike qualities of Wishart. That the latter deserved his admiration is fairly certain. Though some have suspected Wishart of complicity in his patrons' cheap political plot, there was too much of the scholar-missionary in him for this to be credible. It is doubtful whether, even if there were any evidence that he desired such a role, he would have been fitted to fulfill it. Knox's picture, if we allow for the minor exaggerations of an admirer, is surely nearer the mark. Wishart was a saintly scholar whose thoughts were with his Greek Testament. They soared to heaven more readily than they stayed on earth. He fasted severely and gave the clothes off his back to the poor. Yet he was no masochistic dreamer in search of martyrdom. He seems to have been, rather, a zealous wandering scholar enticed back to his native land by political adventurers who hoped to use him as the spearhead of a movement to stir up rebellion. The picture, all too familiar in the political history of mankind, fits what is known of his person-

ality, and there is no sufficient reason to doubt it.

From this time onward, Knox was a marked man. But Beaton's reign was drawing to a close. Two months later, on May 29, early in the morning, while the stonemasons were hard at work as usual on Beaton's gigantic scheme to reinforce his already almost impregnable sea fortress so that he could hold it, with the help of the French fleet if need be, against all comers, a few gentlemen entered quietly and inquired whether the Lord Cardinal was yet awake. When the porter resisted their progress, he was thrown into the moat and the castle servants intimidated. One of the intruders, William Kirkcaldy, was assigned to guard the postern gate while John Leslie, James Melville, and Peter Carmichael entered the keep, where they confronted the Lord Cardinal himself in his room.

Leslie made to kill Beaton without a word. Melville, however, wanted to have the pleasure of lecturing the victim first. Terrified, Beaton reminded his assailants of the sanctity of his person as God's priest. According to an ancient medieval legal theory, a prince or other secular ruler held his appointment from God, yet only through his people and only so long as he did not flagrantly flout justice. If he did, his people — such was the theory — could rise up against him. So long as their rebellion was just, they could even kill him, without being guilty of murder. But a priest was different. A priest's person was sacred.

" Fie, fie, ye will not slay me. I am a priest," cried the Chancellor of Scotland, Cardinal Priest of St. Stephen-on-the-Caelian, Archbishop of St. Andrews, Primate of Scotland, Legatus Natus, Legatus a latere, Bishop of Mirepoix, Abbot of Arbroath.

Thereupon Melville, assuming the role of God's angel of wrath, recounted the primate's sins, enjoined him to repent of them, and especially of his execution of Wishart, and ran a sword through his body. The rebels then took possession of the castle, hoping, no doubt, to encourage sympathizers to overthrow the regent's Government, now that the Supreme Tyrant had been put out of the way.

But they misjudged the temper of their nation. Nobody shed any tears for Beaton; yet few, very few, were prepared to follow the leadership of the wild band of nobles who had seized his stronghold. On June 10, at Stirling, there was a meeting of other nobles who repudiated the work of all such factions. They took measures to have offices of power redistributed with a view to consolidating the nation. The rebels were charged with treason, a charge that Parliament confirmed on July 29, by which time an army had been mustered for the taking of the castle. It seemed the end was in sight for the rebels.

Yet not quite. Beaton's fortress was incredibly strong, and Scotland's military position very weak, too weak to enable even a whole nation to besiege the castle effectively. Beaton's body lay salted for months, dumped in an oubliette, awaiting what kind of burial no one knew. The rebels held Arran's son as a hostage. It was feared that the English would come to their aid. The castle was open to the North Sea. English help might come to their assistance more easily than could the French come to dislodge them. France and England had just concluded a truce that made hope of French help slimmer than fear of English invasion. A few score more of sympathizers joined the rebels, including some who had turned their coats since taking part in the proceedings at Stirling. A truce in December provided that the regent would secure a pardon from Rome for the assassination of the primate, and that until then the rebels would keep the castle. It need hardly be said that between such adversaries no truce could be anything more than a time-gaining ruse.

Henry VIII died the following month. The English Government decided nevertheless to make considerable grants toward helping the besieged rebels, and they appointed Andrew Dudley Admiral of the Fleet with orders to harass the Scots and intercept any French vessels bringing them aid. The English quickly repented of their action in the matter, however, being afraid to risk an invasion of Scotland lest they should annoy France. When the French King Francis I died in March, it was evident that his successor, Henry II, an ardent upholder of the old religion, had designs on Scotland himself, and was expected to send every support necessary to crush all Protestant and pro-English factions, and secure the papal interests

41

in the northern realm. But this was far from provoking English intervention. Until the beginning of that year it had not
been certain how the war between the old religion and the new
would go on the Continent of Europe. But by January, 1547,
the Council of Trent had made it clear that the Roman
Church intended war to the death against Protestantism, and
the tremendous conflict in Europe was already taking shape.
It was in England's interest to do nothing to bring that forthcoming struggle to its northern doorstep: it had enough to do
for the present within its own borders.

Knox, with his little band of pupils, followed the course of
events with a characteristically prudent desire to keep out of
them as far as he could. He toyed with the notion of flight with
them to Germany, but their besieged fathers in the stronghold
naturally had other views on the matter. They sent word to
him to bring them to the castle and continue their instruction
there. Knox could have had few illusions about his future
safety if he obeyed. Yet if he declined, his position would have
been even more intolerable, for he would become an outcast
everywhere in the Protestant camp as he was already a marked
man in the pope's. He had no doubt where his loyalty lay, and
that it lay in an exceedingly uncomfortable place was a circumstance beyond his control. At any rate, by Easter he was at
St. Andrews, and it was not long before he was lecturing the
castle garrison on their corrupt life, which, he declared, " could
not escape the punishment of God." Knox's sincerity and the
genuineness of his new-found faith now triumphed over his
natural prudence. If, in his uncomfortable predicament, he
wanted to keep out of trouble, it was plainly to his advantage
at least to keep quiet. He had done so for long. Having known
Wishart he could do it no longer. Only the smoke of Hamilton's burning had reached him; but a spark from Wishart's
fire had kindled his soul.

It was in such circumstances that Knox's powers as a
preacher inevitably came to the notice of the besieged Protestant nobles. As hope of English help waned, hope of Scotland's
rallying to the words of an eloquent Scottish patriot was
aroused. There could be no doubt that Knox was the man for

the task. He was preaching with effect both in the castle chapel and publicly in the parish church of the town. A few weeks later John Rough, chaplain at the castle, preached in the parish church. Knox impetuously offered to defend the thesis, " That the present Church of Rome is more degenerate from the purity which it had in the days of the apostles than was the Church of the Jews from the ordinances given by Moses when they consented to the death of our Saviour." Then Rough, preaching on the Protestant principle of the popular election of a pastor, proposed Knox to the people for that office. Knox, with the memory of Wishart's fate fresh in his mind, was terrified. Never was a pulpit call to a great church less welcome to the man whose obvious duty it was to accept it. According to his own account he burst into tears and fled to his room. For days he sought no company.

Within a week, however, he was preaching his first sermon as pastor of the congregation, and it was a discourse on the apocalyptic Book of Daniel, the seventh chapter, the twenty-fourth and twenty-fifth verses, in which is prophesied the coming of Antichrist. The congregation that listened to it included Knox's old teacher, John Major, and other learned men who deplored Rome's corruptions yet could not swallow the Protestant pill. Knox gave them their fill of invective against Rome, the whore of Babylon, and the " paip," the man of sin. Some of it was soapbox oratory. It was certainly all unlike the erudite disquisitions of Calvin, whom Knox did not yet know. Much in Knox at this stage was worse than Luther at his most extravagant; yet perhaps it was at the time the only medicine for Scotland, where Rome had exhibited itself in no better guise. At any rate, there was no doubt that the guiding spirits of the Protestant colony thought so.

Knox had almost no qualification for the charge of a parish. He had never held such a position, and his appointment was an anomalous one. Nor was he a man who made friends readily. He was a curious mixture — half hermit, half demagogue. He had as yet little sense of corporate meditation and worship; less still of the bond of sympathy that should grow out of the tie between a priest or pastor and his flock. Yet this is not to say that he lacked genuinely religious feeling. Nor was it that he was a mere nationalist politician dramatizing himself as a man of God. It was, rather, that he conceived of himself as a prophet who went up to Sinai to receive the commandment of God, and thence descended to give it to the people. Up and down, up and down; now up the mountain alone with God-in-the-Burning-Bush, now down on the plain again with the thunders and the lightnings for the people.

Yet there is something about the earlier Knox wilder than is found in the traditional picture of Moses. Knox's endowment was quite genuine: he was a prophet, untamed but authentic. The figure that springs to mind is, rather, that of Muhammad. There are even features in the conditions confronting him in Scotland that in some ways vaguely remind one of what Muhammad found in Arabia. Certainly his conception of God sometimes borders on the Muslim notion of Allah, and the institution he created was in several ways a sort of Westernized Islam. These appearances are superficial; but they spring from what the two men did have in common — both were born leaders as well as born prophets, and neither was trained for either leadership or prophecy. Knox also sometimes brings to mind a prima donna whose unique voice deserves the best training, gets none, and yet without a single singing lesson takes the stage by storm, spending the rest of her spectacular career with a sense of her own insufficiency and an awareness of her own genius.

It is an interesting picture, at first not very attractive. Knox is, however, infinitely more appealing than he ever looks at first sight. His worst features (though also his most amusing) are on the outside. Perhaps one of the most endearing traits in his character is his unaffected simplicity. He knew he was but a rude trumpet for God. He repeatedly made the admission. He believed that that trumpet, for all the harshness of its reeds, was chosen by God in God's inscrutable providence. If the harsh reeds sometimes conveyed the spleen of the preacher along with God's Word, what could the preacher do? His feeling is akin to that of a humble and devout Roman priest who looks down at his own clumsy, pawlike hands, feels the absurdity of them as bearers of the Very Body and Blood, and nevertheless believes. The priest could probably make his hands a little less ugly if he tried, yet never beautiful enough to carry his God. Knox could have controlled his spleen, yet never sufficiently to make him a worthy trumpet of God. He felt that like Paul he " came not with excellency of speech or of wisdom," and the fact that people were impressed when the trumpet was so harsh only confirmed him in his belief that it was God who was using it. Had his " speech and his preaching" been " with enticing words of man's wisdom," one might have doubted whether it was God or the splendor of the words and thought that got through to the people. As things were, he felt there could be no doubt. It could not be he; therefore it must be God. It is not an unedifying sentiment; yet it led him to plain speaking, and to his boast, which became almost an obsession, that he " flattered no flesh."

There was something of all that in the Knox who had now become chaplain to the seagirt castle garrison, the Knox whom the storms had not yet encompassed. He was already playing his tune; but it was life that brought the breath-taking polyphony. And for that life he was only about to begin his apprenticeship. On June 29, twenty-one French galleys appeared on the horizon, under the able command of Leo Strozzi, prior of Capua. The rebels put up a fight, and after an artillery duel lasting a couple of days it looked almost as though they were to drive out the French fleet. But the sea operation was only a maneuver in support of the land struggle to come. The regent's armies were on the march. On July 18, soldiers arrived in St. Andrews. They dug their trenches; they planted their cannon in St. Salvator's College, in the streets leading to the castle, and in the abbey steeple.

From a strictly military point of view Knox must have proved a sore disappointment. Far from upholding the morale of the rebels in their struggle, he crushed it, alike in victory and defeat. When the rebels' fortunes seemed to run high, Knox warned them that they did not see beyond their noses; when plague within the fortress harassed and terrified them, he took the opportunity of attributing it to a divine judgment on the wickedness of their lives. Who would make a hireling out of John Knox? The rebels had not wanted a chaplain with a gloomy retort to every fond hope they expressed; yet they had to put up with him and endure his endless rebukes, for the trumpet was already blowing, and who was he to stop it? Was it not the voice of God? When they turned to hope of English help, he predicted doom. When they cheered themselves with the comforting thought of the thickness of the castle walls, Knox flung their fond hopes out of the window and into the North Sea where lay the menacing French fleet.

"Egg shells," he growled, as he slapped the walls and went on with his preaching of wrath to come.

At four o'clock on the morning of July 31, a terrific battery opened up on the fortress, continuing for six or seven hours. There was a blinding torrent of rain. For some time the plague had been taking its toll of several lives a day. William Kirkcaldy conveyed a message from the rebels to the French admiral, and the castle at last surrendered. The French looted it, finding not only victuals for their ships' stores but an Ali Baba's cave of treasure, for besides the cardinal's vast personal wealth, the fortress contained practically the entire movable estate of every nobleman who had sought refuge in it. The garrison, having been taken prisoner, was carried off by the fleet. The principal nobles were conducted to France; others were sent to the galleys for the winter, and with them was Knox. It was in that nightmare of floggings and cursings at sea in a French galley that he was to learn his true vocation as the prophet of the Scots. Chained to a floating hell, he began his apprenticeship as an apostle of the liberty of the children of God.

5 During the siege, Knox had protested — with good reason — that the castle garrison was not an atmosphere to which his impressionable "bairns" ought to be exposed. Accustomed though he was to the coarse morals of Scotland at

that time, it had shocked even himself. But in retrospect it must have seemed civilized compared with life on a French slave ship.

The crew of a galley ship consisted of about a hundred and fifty, with an average complement of about three hundred slaves. To the rowing benches, these slaves were chained, four or six to each bench, the religious or political offender alongside the murderer and the thief. At night they slept under the benches, unsheltered summer or winter. During the day they sat rowing, without change of posture, while along the *coursier,* or runway, that ran from stem to stern between the benches, strode, whip in hand, the *comite,* an officer in charge of the slaves. On the bare shoulders of any man who showed the slightest inclination to slack, the *comite* brought down his lash. More serious offenders were laid out on a plank and whipped into a merciful unconsciousness. The dress of the slaves was a coarse frock or shirt open at the shoulders; their food consisted mainly of bean porridge or horse loaf and water. Mass was said at appointed times.

Knox seldom alludes to " the sobbes of my harte " during these nineteen months in his floating hell. Despite his stocky build he was not a robust man (he speaks of suffering from " stone "), and his sedentary life as a priest-notary and teacher ill conditioned him for the rigors, let alone the tortures, of the French galleys. The ignominy, no less than the physical horrors, bit into his heart. A galley slave's life was held very cheap, and to survive at all, however broken in spirit, could be accounted an achievement. Knox's spirit was not broken; it was hardened. There can be little doubt that his captivity contributed to the making of those stubborn qualities in him that especially shock and repel those who have been spared hardship. It probably made him a louder trumpet for God, certainly not a sweeter one. And it was perhaps sweetness more than any other quality that Knox lacked.

Even in the worst prison, there is generally some modest reward for what is called " good behavior," that is, for giving no trouble to the gaoler. It appears that Knox enjoyed some alleviations. He was evidently allowed, for example, to communicate occasionally with his friends in their prisons in Scotland and France — surely a considerable privilege for a galley slave. Perhaps he rowed well. It is said that the Turks on the French galleys often worked so well that they were granted positions of some slight advantage over their fellows, and that their apparent docility in the galleys was attributed to their Muslim doctrine of predestination, which enabled them to resign themselves to their lot more readily than could the average man. It may not be entirely fanciful to suppose that Knox's predestinarian theology may have already sufficiently molded his character to give him that same quality that seems to have been of some advantage to the Moors. Belief in a strongly predestinarian theology does not, as we shall abundantly see in the life of Knox, make a man passive in his response to life's demands. By a seeming paradox, it has just the opposite effect. The man who believes above all else in the will of God may turn the world upside down if only he is convinced that he is an instrument of God's will. By the same token, however, he can be as unresistant to circumstances as butter to a knife, so long as he is convinced that the knife is God's.

Knox no doubt felt implicated in the guilt of the garrison whose corrupt life he had so scathingly denounced. After all, he had of his own accord associated himself with a faction whose motives, he well knew, were at the best impure and at the worst criminal. Knox was never a lawless man. He had accepted this group for lack of better support, for while he admired Wishart's way, his strong practical sense convinced him that the deliverance of Scotland from tyranny could never be accomplished without political as well as "spiritual" effort. The way of Hamilton and Wishart was fine indeed; no doubt it had been God's will to raise up such examples. But those who, like himself, would purify a land so deeply sunk in rottenness; those who would liberate a people so chained, hand, foot, and neck, to a system that had virtually turned the land of the proud victors of the old War of Independence into a papal protectorate — such men, God's tools, must recognize the weight of the wickedness that confronted them and meet its devilish agents on their own ground. It was the vocation of some pure souls to be trampled on by Satan's forces and to be forthwith gathered up to heaven by Christ. But such was not, he believed, his own calling. In the warfare against the devil in whose clutches lay the land he loved, the soldier of God had to tramp through the devil's mire, and he could hardly escape a bespattering of the mud of battle. Nor yet could he avoid a share in the guilt of the bad company he must sometimes keep. The torment of the galleys was God's judgment on *him;* he must bear it and await his next orders from on high. His views on such questions were at that time imperfectly developed, and they were probably still very confused. But one thing was already clear to him: his calling was not to die as Wishart had done, but to live to be the spear of God against the devil who had polluted the dearest land on earth and emasculated the brave hearts of its once-proud people. Scotland must rise again. Wishart had not been able to raise it up; but he had taught Knox how it could be done by the right man using the right methods under the command of God.

Whatever may have been the reason for the mitigation of his sufferings, it was certainly not any acquiescence on his part in the religious devotions imposed on the slaves. Knox says these were at first threatened with torture if they would not give their attention to the Mass; yet none of his countrymen would. On the contrary, even when the *Salve Regina* was sung on Saturday night, the Scots covered their heads with anything they could find, as a token of their contempt for " the paip." Shortly after their arrival at Nantes, a " painted brod," that is, a picture of " Nostre Dame," was brought aboard to be kissed by the chained slaves. Knox says that one of the Scots refused. (Who could it be but Knox himself?) The lieutenant of the galley and two other officers then pushed it violently against his face and between his hands; whereupon the outraged man flung the " accursed idol " into the Loire, saying, " Let our Lady now save herself: she is light enough; let her learn to swim."

It is a remarkable story. There is no word in Knox's own account of any reprisal against him. Perhaps the lieutenant did not think the matter one of any practical importance.

There was no incitement to mutiny. So long as the work was done and discipline was being properly maintained, why seek to bring on trouble over the religious eccentricities of a few slaves? There was enough to occupy officers and crew without making a fuss over a few fanatics who would not kiss a holy picture. That such was the attitude of the officers is in fact suggested by Knox's admission that the question of kissing or not kissing holy pictures would seem to be of no great importance in itself; nevertheless he excuses the protest, likening it to one commended by Jeremiah to the Israelites during the Babylonian Exile. At any rate, Knox assures us that from the time that protest was made, no Scotsman was required to participate in devotional exercises against conscience.

How much did Knox know, as he slaved at his oar, of what was going on in Europe? It is impossible to be sure. What it is safe to say is that the less he knew the better, for the true picture would have had little in it to cheer him. In September, 1547, while his ship lay at Nantes, the English protector, Somerset, had revived dead Henry's purpose of putting Scotland to "fire and sword." The aim was still the same: to raze and destroy Edinburgh. Around the old house at Longniddry, whither Wishart had gone to his fate, an English army was now encamped. In the Firth of Forth lay an English fleet. At Pinkie, the Scots had been routed — the nation's worst defeat since Flodden. On the Solway a large invading force was attending to Scotland's western side. The port of Leith, near [16] Edinburgh, was burning. Scotland was becoming accustomed to such outbursts of furious destruction from its powerful enemy across the border. This one followed the usual pattern — a train of destruction and then a retreat south — except that this time the English left a token force in Broughty Castle at the mouth of the Tay, near Dundee, and next spring they returned again with fresh devastation of the Lothians. Scotland's position was precarious. But still its independence was maintained.

[16] Since 1920, within Edinburgh. Leith became a parliamentary borough in 1833; but the nineteenth century expansion of Edinburgh made the annexation of Leith inevitable.

The natural effect of these English onslaughts was to embitter still further the hearts of the Scots and render their distrust of the English virtually incurable. Worse still for Protestant hopes, the Scottish nobles had been frightened into accepting French protection at any price. The French King Henry now believed he could use Scotland as a northern base for a future war on England. He would willingly lend Scotland both a fleet and an army, and accept into custody at the French court the five-year-old Queen Marie Stuart. If he played his cards well, he could, in due time, make the attack on England on two fronts. Already he could see the French empire extending from the Mediterranean to the Arctic.

That summer of 1548, as Knox's galley passed the familiar coast of Scotland, his health was at its lowest ebb. The ship was lying between St. Andrews and Dundee, and the steeple of the parish church where he had preached was in sight. One of the Scotsmen rowing at his side asked Knox whether he recognized the landmark.

"I knaw it weall," replied Knox, adding that it was the place where God had first opened his mouth in public to His glory. And he predicted that, despite the great physical weakness he was suffering as the result of his long privations aboard the galley, he would, before his life's end, again give tongue to "glorifie His godlie name in the same place."

An idle boast it must have seemed at the time. Who could tell how long he would slave in the galley, or whether indeed he would ever be unchained from it alive? Death seemed closer than did hope of escape. And even if he had been freed that night, what chance had he, in the political conditions then prevailing, of ever setting foot in Scotland again, let alone of preaching his Protestant doctrine in one of its pulpits? Nevertheless, the astonishing truth is that, many years afterward, his prediction was fulfilled.

As Knox's galley passed by the familiar shores of Fife and the Lothians, he may have noticed a few ships sailing out of Leith. There would be nothing remarkable about them, except their mission, which he could not know. They sailed out as if bound for a French port, which was, indeed, their ultimate destination. Well out of sight of land and other ships, however, they veered sharply north. Passing Dundee and Aberdeen, they moved beyond Caithness in the extreme north of the mainland; then westward and south to the port of Dumbarton, where they took aboard a precious cargo indeed: the infant queen with her two governors, four " young virgins of the special nobility," and the sixteen-year-old half brother of the queen, James Stuart, a royal bastard and prior of St. Andrews.

Still Knox rowed on, chained to his bench. Kirkcaldy and three others among his former associates had been imprisoned in the Benedictine Abbey of Mont-Saint-Michel in Normandy. They communicated with Knox, and he replied. Later, on the eve of the Feast of the Epiphany which the French gaolers were celebrating with much wine, the prisoners took advantage of this by binding the gaolers and making their own escape, eventually reaching safety in England. From another of his associates at St. Andrews, Henry Balnaves, Knox even received a treatise on the Lutheran doctrine of justification that Balnaves had composed in prison at Rouen, which Knox's galley was then visiting. Knox not only read the treatise but wrote a brief commentary on it.

For some time the measures against Scottish captives had been relaxed. French Henry had learned from the follies of his English namesake. This was no time for ill-treating anyone whose support he could use in his struggle for the conquest of England. A few weeks later Knox was released. But he dared not, of course, return to his native land. He betook himself instead to England.

6 In popular legend, Knox has become so much identified with Scotland that the period of his English exile is almost forgotten. England was enemy territory in Knox's day, and this was an inescapable fact for even the least patriotic

Scotsman. The Scots distrusted the English as much as the French of a later century were to distrust the Germans. Knox was certainly the embodiment of Scottish patriotism; a patriot by temperament, upbringing, and choice. Nevertheless, obliged by circumstances to seek refuge in England, where he spent five years, he found it very congenial indeed, feeling a deep sympathy with the English in their troubles, enjoying his exile among them, and even leaving his imprint on some English institutions. England, in turn, influenced his thought and even his speech,[17] and from England also he took his first wife.

The truth is that England was a revelation to Knox. It was his first taste of the world beyond his little native land (for the slight contacts he had made in captivity with one or two French ports are not to be counted), and it was in many ways surprisingly pleasant. The conditions prevailing south of the Border at the time were both encouraging and challenging to a reformer. The English Reformation under Henry VIII had been a mild thing compared with Continental movements of the same kind; but the definite breach with the pope had prepared men's minds for more positive Reformation ideas. The pulse of London, then (as now) important in estimating English opinion, had the beat he liked to hear. The great country families, though generally less radical, were glad to consider any ideas that would confirm the breach with Rome and keep the pope out of English affairs. Somerset, the protector, and Cranmer, Archbishop of Canterbury, the two most powerful men in the kingdom when Knox arrived, were both decidedly Protestant-minded.

Better still, for a man of Knox's temper, there was much in England that cried out to be done. The general trend of English Church polity suited him, yet its accomplishment fell short of his aim. The first Book of Common Prayer had recently been published, and it was a negative piece of work in the sense that while it abolished much ancient ceremonial and use of the Latin language, it introduced no positive doctrinal

---

[17] He was thought by his contemporaries to have " an English tongue." In writing, his spelling also was Anglicized, though that of his scribes was not.

change. To a radical Protestant it gave the impression of being just the same religious furniture without the beauty of the old patine; the Mass with the gilt scraped off. The bishops and clergy were for the most part conservative in matters of doctrine and liturgy, so conservative that the Protestant-minded leaders of England dared not directly enforce their ideas on them. But they could give privileges to those bishops whose doctrine they liked, and they could invite foreign Protestants to assist in the indoctrination of the English Church. It was among these that Knox found a place. He was just the sort of man that the rulers of England could use in their campaign, and by April 7, 1549, he was recorded as having been licensed for the work.

Knox's first commission, under this license, was in Berwick, a Border town that had been taken from Scotland by the English in 1482. From one point of view it was a tough assignment, for the north of England generally was conservative and disinclined for the new religious ideas. On the other hand, Berwick was an exceptional town, the natural refuge of Protestant-minded Scots who had been obliged to cross the Border. Very soon, Knox had gathered a flourishing congregation. He was bound by law to the use of the recently issued Book of Common Prayer, which had left intact the Mass with all the old doctrine of transubstantiation that was repugnant to Protestants because it implied that the consecrated wafer must be worshiped as God. But in modifying the official Prayer Book along more radically Protestant lines, Knox had the full support of Cranmer, who had always regarded the Prayer Book as but a step toward more fundamental change. Knox was not alone in violating the letter of the law. He celebrated the Eucharist according to the Genevan pattern: a sacramental meal, not a sacrificial act like the Mass; no " adoration of the consecrated elements." In the pulpit Knox preached Protestant doctrine to his heart's content, evidently also with great effect. For there seems little doubt that in a restless Border town full of foreign mercenaries (Germans and Italians and Spaniards as well as English and Scots soldiers), a town in which looting and brawling were nightly occurrences, he did as much as any single human being could have done to improve the moral climate and tame the hearts and the habits of a wild, coarse crew. He neither expected nor got credit for this from partisans of the old religion; even so, he seems to have underestimated the force of the prejudices ranged against him.

Knox was radical in his religious views, which meant that he was also politically opposed to despotism. Such radicalism is often associated with ranting oratory. Knox did not rant. His earliest attempts at preaching were probably crude. But the pulpit style he acquired was as different from the tub thumper's as is chalk from cheese. It had many faults. By modern standards it was intolerably long-winded, and the most patient congregation would groan at it today. Even in the sixteenth century it must have seemed prosy and heavy-going, with its involved sentences and elaborate gestures, all grandiloquently constructed. It was the " preachiest " of preaching, a verbose, parliamentary style. Knox could never have been a permanent success at street-corner stuff. He lacked the slick raciness of the rabble rouser. But neither was his preaching an invitation to devotionally minded souls to share with him the deep meditations of his heart. Its appeal was akin to the appeal that parliamentary eloquence was to have to a later age. His aim was not so much to inflame his hearers as to argue them into accepting the thesis he defended before them. As a rule the argument was supposed to be conducted according to the canons of medieval logic; he thought like the medieval Schoolmen, and his scholasticism was a scholasticism on its last legs. After he had proved his point he would often go back to check and recheck it with a new syllogism, categorical, hypothetical, disjunctive. He *lectured*. The Scriptures spoke plainly enough; but precisely what conclusions could be drawn from them in interpreting and solving the problems of the day? The preacher could not be too careful; he must use all the resources of the brain his Creator had given him.

Listening to Knox was a little like listening to evidence at a murder trial. At times you wearied of the long-drawn-out evidence for a conclusion you might have reached already in some shorter way; nevertheless, you admired the way he reached it, and, above all, the process had the fascination of a modern detective story. As you listened to the Scots preacher you took part yourself in imagination in the exciting chase after the workers of iniquity, the pope and all the denizens of his domain, till at last, it seemed, you had got the devil by the tail. But no: you just missed . . . so, on with the chase. From time to time you asked yourself a Watsonian question, only to receive a masterly reply from the broad-shouldered, long-fingered, keen-eyed, bearded Sherlock in the pulpit. Not the least attractive part of the chase was that, unlike Dr. Watson, you didn't have to voice your own stupidity; you could keep it to yourself and enjoy watching the preacher win the case without making a fool of you in public. And then at last, the peroration. Now Satan himself must see that the game is up. Only a question of time, and . . . *there!* The devil is cornered and you have a part in putting on the handcuffs. At last it's over, and you come back next week to see the whole performance repeated again on fresh terrain. In such circumstances the length of the sermon is no more against it than the length of the story is against *Gone with the Wind.* So long as the chase is exciting, what does it matter that you should have to wait half an hour longer for your dinner?

It was during his ministry at Berwick that Knox met Mrs. Bowes. Her father was a Yorkshireman of property and her husband the younger son of Sir Ralph Bowes of Streatlam Castle. Knox was by this time a man of about thirty-seven, though perhaps poor health and the trials of captivity made him look older than his years, while she was over fifty and the mother of fifteen children. Some years later Knox married her fifth daughter, Marjorie.

Evidently Mrs. Bowes was a conscience-troubled counsel seeker, inclined to religious melancholy. In Knox she found a patient counselor after her own heart, so much so that, in spite of the disparity in their years, tongues wagged about the frequency of their meetings. Their lifelong association gave rise later on to rumors for the truth of which there is no historical evidence despite the lengthy and sometimes almost absurd correspondence between them that has been preserved. It is really not very remarkable that a bachelor cleric in exile, engaged in a difficult and peculiarly lonely task, should have welcomed the friendship of a middle-aged parishioner, a gentlewoman and *sympathique*.

The tradition of a love affair between them is not only unauthenticated, it is unlikely, not to say preposterous. When Knox met Mrs. Bowes, he had no real previous experience of the cure of souls. In his brief pastorate at St. Andrews he would have had little opportunity of dealing with conscience-troubled matrons. It would have been remarkable if he had not taken her endless questions of conscience overseriously. Almost every earnest, inexperienced clergyman in such circumstances so errs. Nor is it remarkable that the relationship developed into a lasting friendship. Scandalmongers have sought materials in his letters; but the very ingenuousness of these makes a love affair improbable. Knox could never stop preachifying, and even in private conversation he often lectured as if he were in the pulpit. But he could hardly have made a whole series of love letters read almost like pulpit discourses. Compared with the letters of Francis of Sales, the letters of Knox are sentimentally clumsy — so clumsy that it is difficult for anyone with an impish sense of humor, let alone a religious enemy's ax to grind, to resist sniffing out impropriety. But the kind of impropriety to be suspected in such a relationship is quite incredible in this one.[18] A reader on the lookout for scandal between spiritual director and penitent could worm it out of the letters of Francis of Sales as well as out of those of Fénelon. But in the absence of evidence all such conjectures are as foolish as they are base. Every priest and pastor is likely to be besieged by women in his congregation who consciously or otherwise seek to mother him; yet even though it be a religious melancholic in her fifties who mothers an awkward pastor in his thirties, scandalmongers will read an affair into their correspondence, not least when the scandalmongers are sworn enemies of the pastor's religion.

[18] It was perhaps less incredible formerly, however, when Knox's birth was placed at 1505 rather than the now commonly accepted later date. (See Appendix II.)

But Knox had much else to do besides explore the labyrinthine conscience of Mrs. Bowes, and consider the innumerable, interminable, and insoluble problems she so unfailingly disembogued. Early in 1551 he was sent by the authorities to Newcastle. Somerset's fall in 1549 had done nothing to halt the progress of Protestant ideas in England. The religious policy of Dudley, his successor, had been no less after Knox's heart. A new ordinal was issued; a ban on images had been followed by a ban on altars; Cranmer and his episcopal household had openly eaten meat in Lent. All this was, of course, agreeable news to Knox. But Knox seldom underestimated the power of the forces against his cause; perhaps it was his realism in this as much as his eloquence that eventually secured his success. In England, at the moment, the tide was with him, and he would make the most of it while it lasted. But his uncanny gift for scenting storms ahead always made him an uncomfortable skipper to those who could contentedly enjoy favorable weather.

His gloomy forebodings made his friends often see him before the event as an alarmist and after the event as a wizard. He was neither. There was nothing magical about Knox's powers. What distinguished him from the less farsighted was, rather, his extraordinary insight into the hearts of men. And in the hearts of the political leaders who favored his cause he saw not only the power of God working to free men from the bondage of superstition and fear, but also all sorts of wickedness, time-serving, and greed. Knox was never under the illusion that all men are by nature disposed to goodness and charity. He believed, indeed, that charity and goodness existed only by the miracle of God's intervention. Left to themselves, men were a fallen race. Knox's own experience of the greed and cruelty of power-invested men had inclined him to a ready acceptance of Augustine's doctrine that mankind is a mass of perdition: a man's only hope lies in God's redemptive power. He found in some of the great men of England who were officially on his side in what he took to be the war against Antichrist, "insatiable covetousness, filthy carnality and voluptuousness, intolerable ambition and pride, ungodly

58

loathesomeness to hear poor men's causes and to hear God's words." In these feelings Knox was not alone. English churchmen such as Ridley felt much the same.

Despite his natural prudence, his moral courage seemed to be growing. He had acquired it in a hard school, patiently enduring as well as beholding oppression and tyranny and wrong throughout the long, bitter years of his youth when he had felt powerless to affect the course of events. Now that he had a hearing and, for the time being, the support of men in high places, his life was easier. In this Knox scented danger. Now as never before he must be courageous in his preaching. He dared not continue to expect God's guidance if he shirked this duty. Perseverance in obeying the call of duty was the token of being God's chosen instrument. He believed that God especially called him to " fear no flesh." That his life had well prepared him to relish the task of exhibiting a fearlessness that did not come to him by nature was, in his eyes, only one of the signs of God's commissioning of His prophet. The fact that a brave soldier enjoys fighting does not put his bravery in question. It is, rather, a necessary part of his soldierly endowment. So we need not be shocked that Knox enjoyed the role of denouncing political corruption. More than that, and well he knew it, was needed for his work. When, in December, 1551, he became one of the six royal chaplains appointed for the furtherance of the Government's religious policy (a notable mark of the speedy recognition of his usefulness) , what he saw in high places did nothing to improve his opinion of human nature. It served, rather, only to increase his sense of mankind's dependence on the mercy of God.

Besides preaching at the court of the fourteen-year-old King Edward VI, the mentally precocious son of Henry VIII by Jane Seymour, he was required to visit and preach in churches up and down the country. His labors taxed his strength. He could not spare himself. Like every soldier he longed at times for peace, yet knew he could not escape the battle. Writing from Newcastle, he complained that " the pane of my heid and stomock trubillis me greitlie; daylie I find my brain decay, but the Providence of God sall not be frustrat." Whatever " decay " he may have felt in his powers at the time, he evidently continued his labors with unrelenting determination. To his political fears and embarrassments were added the complaints of some of his old Berwick friends who, when they heard of his continual hobnobbing with the grandees of the realm, asked whether he was perhaps getting too uppish. Was not he who had enchanted his old flock by his invective against prelates becoming something of a prelate himself? To this Knox frankly replied that he was now less in his own eyes than ever he had been when his feet were chained to the galleys.

The influence he exerted on the English Church during his five years south of the Border was such that its effects are still to be found in the English Prayer Book. Knox disliked the old practice of kneeling at Communion because of its association with the worship of the consecrated wafer in the Mass. Desiring to show that the Eucharist was not a priest's sacrifice, but the sacramental meal of all Christ's people, he recommended sitting as a more suitable posture. By 1552, partly through his influence, the practice of sitting at Communion had become frequent. There was opposition to any such change of posture being officially written into the English liturgy; nevertheless, a rubric was inserted by way of compromise declaring that kneeling implied no adoration. This, later known as the " Black Rubric," has been shown to be almost certainly Knox's work. In the original draft of the Articles of Religion, moreover, there was one endorsing the ceremonies of the Prayer Book. Knox disapproved of these, and eventually all reference to ceremonies was omitted. A friendly Flemish resident in England, writing in 1552, comments on the remarkable influence that Knox " wrought upon the minds of many." More hostile observers grumbled that one man's authority should " so much prevaile." It is certainly an astounding fact that a little peasant-priest from Scotland who three years earlier had been chained to a French slaveship, never having set foot in England in his life, should be directing the ecclesiastical policy of the English Church with such a sure hand that his work has even left an imprint on the official liturgy of the Church of

England to this day.[19] Knox was a vigilant alien whose eye nothing escaped; whose outspoken tongue spared no custom, however seemingly innocuous, that might lead weak men back into the clutches of the pope.

It did not need the observant eye of Knox to notice also the corrupt transactions taking place under a Government purporting to liberate England from the papacy's pestilent tyranny and greed. What was now going on in England had already been the subject of ridicule on the Continent of Europe. The English ambassador in Paris had been humiliated by the gibes of the French court at the Philistinism of the English politicians who, while the schools and universities were falling into decay, were buying and selling offices with the proceeds of the foundations of piety and learning they had despoiled. These gibes hurt because, alas, there was much truth behind them.

In fact, if Knox liked England as much as he evidently did, his love for it must have been deep, for he was seeing it under probably the worst rule it had ever so far known. But then he loved his own Scotland best of all, and he had never seen it but in the hands of even baser men than were now at England's helm.

Knox " flattered no flesh." But neither was he himself susceptible to flattery. And perhaps this was a qualification even more needful for the work he had to do. Had he been readily caught in the flatterer's net he would have become bishop of Rochester and sunk into oblivion. He valued independence above a mitre. When Dudley offered him the bishopric in 1552, Knox correctly interpreted the proposal as a face-saving attempt to silence him, and refused it. Confined to his diocese, he would have been less troublesome to vested interests. As a matter of fact, before the proposal was made, it had been very thoroughly discussed at a high level, with a view to silencing Knox's thunder. A few weeks later, from the pulpit of St. Nicholas, Newcastle, on Christmas, 1552, he preached a fero-

[19] The rubric is omitted from the American Episcopal *Book of Common Prayer*.

cious sermon against those who, while professing the Reformed faith, were secretly opposed to the changes it involved. These wicked men were "secret traitors to the Crown and Commonwealth of England," thirsting after the king's death, "which their iniquity would procure." The boy king died on July 6, 1553. In April of that year Knox had preached his last sermon before him at Westminster on the words Christ spoke of Judas, "He that eateth bread with me hath lifted up his heel against me." It was a trenchant sermon. His hearers were left in no doubt of his meaning.

By this time he had had abundant pulpit practice, having been preaching every day of the week so far as his strength allowed, or, as he put it, "if the wicked carcass will permit." Now, with the gloomy clouds lowering again over England, there was little time left. Soon they might descend on the land where the spring sunshine of the Reformed faith had shone briefly through the old, dark clouds. Soon that land he had grown to love might be immersed once again in what he called "the puddle of papistrie." It was no time for ambiguous language; no time for a preacher to soften the thump of his fist. Knox had resolved to denounce those in high places in England who (worse than the children of Antichrist at Rome) supported the right faith for the wrong reasons.

Imagine the faces of the courtiers as they listened to the prophet, their own nominee, trouncing them in a patent allegory from the Bible. Imagine the faces of those who identified themselves or their friends as Knox spoke words such as these:

"Of Achitophel it is written that his counsel in those days was like the oracle of God. Great indeed was his authority under the most godly prince David, the anointed of God, a prince of great gifts and experience. . . . Yet was not David abused by his wicked counselor? . . . Shebna, that crafty fox, had likewise high office under Ezechias, and God had granted to this prince also the choicest endowments. . . . Yet did he not also suffer from the counsel of one who showed such a fair countenance to his king but was in his heart but a dissembling hypocrite? . . . Finally was not Judas the traitor purse bearer to Christ Jesus the Lord himself? . . . What wonder then in this present time that a young and innocent king should be deceived by crafty, covetous, wicked, and ungodly counselors?"

Knox was not alone in his estimate of the rulers of England. The English chaplains were saying much the same, and in language just as forthright. Grindal, for instance, who was to become Archbishop of Canterbury, and Haddon, one of the most erudite scholars of his time, were no more polite about the state of the English court than was Knox. After the boy king's death, events took the course they had all feared. Knox himself was in London on July 19 when Mary Tudor was proclaimed queen. All the Protestant developments for which he had labored were repudiated by Parliament, which, in November, 1554, passed an act forbidding any form of service other than that which had been in use in the last year of Henry's reign.

But infinitely worse was to come. With the daughter of Spanish Catherine of Aragon on the throne, whose education had been a brooding over her mother's wrongs and her mother's religion, disaster was assured. Mary, lacking English pride herself, had no feeling for the wishes of either Parliament or people. Her policy of attempting, at this late date, to put England into a state of submission to Spain and the pope would have been sufficiently insulting to her subjects to ensure her everlasting contempt among them, even if she had not, within four years, caused three hundred Protestants, men and women, to die in agony at the stake, against which fanatical stupidity even her own Spanish husband advised her. In Spain one might do such things; but in Tudor England even a Spaniard could see the folly of it. When, after leading England to a humiliating defeat by the French at Calais, in a war waged to please Spain, Mary Tudor died in 1558, the best there was for her subjects to say of her was that she was childless.[20]

Clearly, Mary's England was no place for Knox. Shortly after she came to the throne, his friends, anxious for his safety, advised him to flee. Though conscious that his flight would be interpreted by some as evidence of cowardice, he eventually

[20] A Roman Catholic writer, however, attributes the brevity of her reign to God, who " would not suffer her to reign long, either on account of the sins of her father, or on account of the sins of her people, who were unworthy of a princess so holy, so pious, and endued with such divine and rare dispositions." (Laing, *De Vita Laer.*, fol. 28.)

decided upon it. His health was poor, and after five years of struggle he felt, for the time being, unable to face further conflict. " By God's grace," he wrote, " I may come to battle before all the conflict be ended." Nothing had any terrors for him now; but he knew, as always, how to distinguish between a fight that was profitable for his cause and one that was not. " My prayer is," he said, " that I may be restored to the battle. . . . I am ready to suffer more than either poverty or exile for that doctrine whereof it has pleased His merciful Providence to make me a witness bearer."

In the summer of 1552 Knox had been betrothed to Marjorie Bowes. The engagement was commonly supposed to have been engineered by her mother, with little enthusiasm on the part of either Knox or Marjorie. His earliest extant letter to the girl is certainly not romantic. After all, an awkward bachelor cleric of forty who has known little of the sweetness of life, who has been embittered by years of hardship, and whose intense zeal for a high cause is being hampered by ill-health, is not likely to be much of a Romeo. Yet in the long run the marriage was evidently a happy one, much happier than many that have begun in a blaze of romantic passion. It is not surprising that the girl's father, who did not even share his wife's enthusiasm for Knox's cause, let alone for Knox himself, should have opposed the betrothal. There would certainly be strong opposition from many other quarters also, not least among those in whom the conventions of the old religion died hard despite their infidelity to its doctrine. There is no one more confirmed in religious prejudice than a man who has ceased to believe the doctrines of his faith but, lacking the courage (or, it may be, the grace) to accept a new one, clings to the outward shell of the old. The notion of clerical celibacy, for instance, is notoriously difficult to eradicate, and prejudice against Knox's proposed marriage would be strong among many who, dissatisfied with their traditional faith, were only halfheartedly attracted to the new ideas. Knox's flight meant that he had further to postpone his marriage to Marjorie; but it is no indication that he cared little for her at the time. On the contrary, had he stayed in England he would have put her as well as himself in the gravest danger. There is evidence that his conscience deeply troubled him at the time: he was well aware that he appeared to be fleeing from the arena; but decision had to be made quickly, and he knew in his heart that he was fleeing only to return later to the thick of the battle. He spoke at the time of his future wife with deep, though characteristically restrained, affection. He was to be separated from her for a while; but he would return and marry her, as indeed he did.

As for pastoral responsibilities, he had none. His royal chaplaincy had been taken away from him. He had made use of it while it lasted, in the interest of the Reformation cause. A reformer had to use what opportunities he could get; exile and flight were among the hazards of his life. Knox's flight from England was a strategic retreat. As Muhammad, pursued by enemies, fled to a cave on Mount Thaur, so Knox fled to Dieppe. As Muhammad, when the pursuit died down, mounted camel and made his withdrawal to Yathrib, so Knox betook himself to Geneva. Yathrib was later named Medina, "the city of the Prophet," and Geneva was to become, at any rate in the popular imagination, the place where Knox prepared himself for the eventual triumph in his native land. Perhaps the campaign as a whole looks, in retrospect, as though it had been conducted with the military precision and skill of an able general, carefully planning defense and attack; as able to bide his time as to fling himself into the fray, according to the exigencies of the moment. But Knox never thought of himself as a general, making the plans and giving the orders. He thought of himself, rather, as a soldier entrusted with a commission. At times he could believe he understood what his divine Commander was up to. At other times he had, like any other soldier, to carry out his orders whether he understood their wisdom or not. Like any other good soldier he felt humiliated when he got orders to retreat; but he knew that in obeying such orders he was not deserting. In God's as in any other army, it is the disobedient soldier who is guilty of desertion. It was from such disobedience that Knox ever prayed for deliverance, and it does not look as though his prayer went unheard.

7 When Knox crossed to France and arrived in Dieppe, he was a man past forty with less than ten groats [21] in his pocket. Everything he had fought for years to achieve seemed to have gone for nought. His letters to English friends, to whom he took the opportunity of writing at this time, show that he felt deeply discouraged. His heart was, he tells us, "sore trubillit." The French, because of their hostility to Spain, could give reluctant asylum to refugees from a Spanish-dominated England; but France, even with its growing Huguenot underground, was a precarious refuge for a Protestant. Knox could find refuge, however, in Geneva, Calvin's stronghold, and thither he went, after no more than a month's stay in Dieppe. What troubled him more than fear of personal danger was his sense of the defeat of his cause. It looked to him almost as though victory lay with Satan's armies. To a man of Knox's temper it was a poor consolation that there were still oases in the desert, a few havens in Europe where a man of his opinions might live in peace. In England he had found great favor for a time for the Reformation cause; yet now it seemed doomed there. If this could happen in England, it could happen also on the Continent, where Protestant ideas had taken root in certainly no more promising soil. In writing to Mrs. Bowes, whom he addresses as "beloved mother," he questions whether they would ever meet again on this earth.

Had Knox thought of religion as a purely individual affair between a man and his God he could never have accomplished his mission. He would perhaps have gone the way of the humanists, the way of Erasmus and Reuchlin and Knox's own compatriot and contemporary, George Buchanan. That is to say, he would outwardly have maintained an indifference to

[21] A groat was fourpence, which today is worth about a nickel. In Knox's time it was the price of a dozen eggs.

the existing state of the Church (an indifference that never gets one into serious trouble with Rome) , while cultivating a private religion of his own. But that, to Knox, was a coward's way. To him it seemed hardly less reprehensible than the way of the tyrants themselves, for such passive submission was just what the tyrants wanted. Popes were always tolerant of individualists so long as these did not seek to make their individualism effective in this world. But it is in this world that the battle between God and Satan is waged. In the Day of Judgment you would not be able to shelter yourself under the plea that, though you had done nothing to resist the enemy, you had nevertheless secretly disliked him all the time. You would not be able to plead that, conscripted on Satan's side, your heart had always been privately set against him, in spite of the fact that you could not show you had ever committed a single act of sabotage. No: in Knox's view, the question the Supreme Judge would ask of men was, rather, " What did you *do* in the battle against idolatry and corruption? " Increasingly, Knox's conscience demanded action. If he was to be worth his salt in God's army, he must use all his strength and every resource of his mind and body to secure the *overthrow* of tyranny and the *establishment* of a Reformed Church. It was a glorious vision. To Knox, it went without saying that religion must have political consequences. He maintained that, partly at any rate, this is what religion is for. If it is a bad religion the political consequences will be bad; if good, they will be good. A religion is known by the fruits it bears in society as much as by the change it works in the individual human heart.

Such were Knox's thoughts when he reached Geneva. He arrived at an unfortunate time, for Calvin's hands were already too full of trouble to allow him to attend properly to the inquiries of a sympathizer from a remote land, who seemed inclined for revolution. Before the end of that year, Calvin was to attain great personal authority in Geneva; but he did not have it yet. In Geneva, the Reformed Church was still, as he himself had said earlier, like Noah's ark, tossed in the flood. At the moment, with almost all Switzerland and many of his own former friends against him, Calvin's authority was precarious. It was no time to lend his official support to a Scottish firebrand. After some informal conversations with Knox, he sent him to Henry Bullinger, patriarch of Zürich, to whom Knox put certain very definitely political questions, with a request for written replies.

" 1. Might the son of a king, upon his father's death, though unable by reason of his tender age to conduct the government of the kingdom, be regarded nevertheless, by right of inheritance, as a lawful magistrate, and as such to be obeyed as of divine right?

" 2. Might a female preside over and rule a kingdom by divine right, and so transfer the right of sovereignty to her husband?

" 3. Is obedience to be rendered to a magistrate who enforces idolatry and condemns true religion; and are those authorities, who are still in military occupation of towns and fortresses, permitted to repel this ungodly violence from themselves and their friends?

" 4. To which party must godly persons attach themselves, in the case of a religious nobility resisting an idolatrous sovereign? "

Bullinger replied with caution and skill. Where regents and female sovereigns came into power through lawfully established law or custom, no godly person could legitimately challenge their rule. To Knox's inquiry about resisting idolatrous sovereigns, Bullinger replied more cautiously still. True, no Christian could obey a command that was against God's law plainly set forth in Scripture. There might even be circumstances that justified rebellion; but this would be a course to be pursued only after the deepest soul-searching and earnest prayer; only when every other way had been tried. Bullinger thought Knox's questions so important that he communicated both them and his own answers to Calvin himself, who approved them, indicating that he had already discussed the subject with Knox in more general terms, and had given him much the same advice as that contained in Bullinger's formal answers.

Though Knox, as we shall presently see, recognized the soundness of their counsel, he doubtless felt that neither Calvin nor Bullinger had faced the existential situation he had in mind. And once again, Knox, practical rather than doctrinaire, turned out to be right, in the sense that Calvin himself was later constrained by circumstances to modify his opinions about the rights of the people against their rulers, and come to conclusions nearer Knox's heart. Temperamentally, Calvin favored aristocratic rule, government by an elite; but in face of the practical situation that developed with the growth of Protestantism in France, he was also obliged to consider more seriously the old theory of the political sovereignty of the people.

Taking their admonitions to heart, Knox wrote to his English friends counseling forbearance, patience, and hope. Nevertheless, he reminds them that " all is not lawful nor just that is statute by civil laws, neither yet is everything sin before God, which ungodly persons allege to be treason." He did not feel satisfied that any queen had the right to hand over any part of the sovereign power to her husband. Mary Tudor had engineered Parliament's approval of her marriage without any genuine regard for the wishes of her people, whose distaste for foreign interference at court had already long been abundantly plain. Her action, on Knox's view, amounted to treason against the realm, since " under an English name she beareth a Spaniard's heart." What had just happend in Scotland gave every promise of a re-enactment of the English tragedy there. The regent Arran had relinquished the regency in favor of the queen mother, so that the way was now open to make Scotland France's vassal as England now appeared to be Spain's.

In May, Knox returned to Dieppe, now the resort of crowds of refugees from England and the hatching place of revolutionary plots against Mary Tudor. The following month Knox wrote a pamphlet, inevitably in the form of a sermon. For his text he chose the fourteenth chapter of Matthew: the feeding of the five thousand and the walking on the water. Essentially, this pamphlet was a call to repentance and a promise of hope for the godly. Christ was in the midst of the storm that was raging: the storm would cease and the people would be delivered. The faith of the people had faltered under the terror, as Peter's had faltered when he tried to walk on the sea to meet his Lord. But in spite of their failure, the people would not be allowed to perish. Would not Christ, who had saved the sinking

Peter, save also the people of England? The situation called for great patience on the part of the godly. The wicked must be allowed to fill their cup. At the same time, however, Knox bluntly charges Mary Tudor with treason. She had become " an open traitress to the Imperial Crown of England, contrary to the just laws of the realm, to bring in a stranger and make a proud Spaniard king — to the destruction of the nobility, to the spoil of them and theirs, to the utter decay of the treasures, navy, and fortifications of the realm; to the abasing of the yeomanry, to the enslaving of the commonalty, to the overthrow of Christianity and God's true religion; and finally to the utter subjection of the whole public estate and commonwealth of England." Her advisers are likewise guilty of treason, not least Gardiner, a bishop, " son of Satan, brother to Cain and fellow to Judas the traitor."

The pamphlet, printed on July 20, 1554, contained some violent language. Knox does not spare those bishops who helped to bring Mary to the throne: " wily Winchester," " bloody Bonner," " dreaming Durham." Treasurer Paulet (the Shebna of his last great sermon at the English court) is singled out for special invective:

" Who was judged to be the soul and life of the Council? Who but Shebna? Who could best dispatch the business, that the rest of the Council might hawk and hunt? None like unto Shebna. Who was most frank and ready to destroy Somerset and set up Northumberland? Was it not Shebna? Who was most bold to cry ' bastard, bastard, incestuous bastard, Mary shall never reign over us '? Which of the Council, I say, had these and greater persuasions against Mary, to whom he now croucheth and kneeleth? Shebna the Treasurer."

He also repeated a thrust which, in his famous sermon, he had made against the Holy Roman Emperor: " no less enemy to Christ than was Nero." This proved, we shall see, to be a fateful quotation. But the modern reader would get an exaggerated notion of the violence of Knox's tongue and pen if he did not bear in mind that in the sixteenth century even men of the most gentle dispositions and scholarly tastes sometimes resorted to language that would now be accounted socially offensive. Parliamentary restraint is admirable when you have

70

secured a free parliament in which to exercise it. When you are still fighting to obtain one you cannot afford to be so squeamish. Moreover, the limits of decency and convention are relative to particular societies. What one society accounts sufficiently polite another may regard as exceeding all the bounds of propriety. In Knox's Europe even kings and queens could sometimes talk more coarsely than would be tolerated today in the better sort of tavern. Scholars of that age, such as Melanchthon and Cranmer and Erasmus and Thomas More, all used language for which a modern writer might be expelled from a good social club. Knox's language was, as a rule, by no means remarkable, and was accepted according to the standards of the day.

Knox did fail at this point of his career, however, in understanding the English people. It is, at the best, and always has been, a peculiarly difficult task for the foreigner, the Scot not excepted. Knox, who saw that the pope could gain control of even the best-ordered Protestant land as soon as a queen was on the throne and disposed to marry a French or Spanish prince, felt that all England must be ripe for civil war. Such was not the case. Characteristically, Englishmen were for the most part more ready to sacrifice their private opinions than endanger the unity of their country. Historically, this has been both England's weakness and its strength. It is this quality in his compatriots that Chesterton expressed thus:

" In foam and flame at Trafalgar, on Albuera plains,
    We did and died like lions, to keep ourselves in chains."

It is this quality in the English character that has so often been miscalculated abroad. Even Knox, for all his uncanny insight into political situations, failed to understand English insularity. All Protestant sympathizers in Knox's day needed to be more or less cosmopolitan in their outlook. Events and circumstances forced this attitude upon them, and it was an attitude that was generally intensified in time of trouble. In England, however, trouble always intensifies nationalism, which generally is already intense enough without it. Knox loved England, but it was a foreigner's love, and England has always

71

been indifferent and unresponsive to this. The Englishman in the street felt himself in no need of being told by a Scot in France that England was in a bad way; he felt he was likely to know that better than Knox. Already Knox was thinking internationally, as every Reformer had to think; and no cosmopolitan can really understand insularity, however much he may try. Knox's five years in England had been a success in their way, as much of a success as ever they could have been for a man of his temper. He had left his mark on it, even on the English Prayer Book; but his work in England was finished, and the rest of his sojourn there would be only an episode in his own life. The English would work out their own salvation; they neither deserved nor needed a Luther or a Calvin or a Knox. Too independent for subjugation by Rome, they were at the best too temperate, too patient in trouble, and at the worst too indolent in mind, to be stirred by a squib from a Scots refugee, sometime chaplain to their late boy king.

But though his work in England was a closed chapter of his life, a mere unit of preparation for his *opus maximum,* the English abroad had still a use for him. Having left Dieppe for the second time to go to Geneva, he had hardly arrived there when he received a letter, dated September 24, 1554, from Frankfurt, Germany. The congregation of English exiles there were inviting him to be one of their ministers.

In the course of the Marian terror, about a thousand English Protestants had sought asylum in Europe — a considerable number in those days, for in relation to England's population then it was as ten thousand would be today. Crossing the Channel, they betook themselves to the Netherlands, Switzerland, Upper Germany, and elsewhere, throwing themselves upon the charity of Protestant congregations. Among these exiles from England was a French-speaking group that had settled in England at Glastonbury Abbey during the reign of Edward VI. Forced now to flee from the land that had sheltered them, they went, with their pastor, Vallerand Pullain, to Denmark. But the Danish Protestants did not wholly approve of their views; nor did the Protestants at Hamburg, whither they next went. After further journeyings they eventually settled in Frankfurt, a city that had been for some fifty years exposed to the turmoil of religious controversy and subjected to both Lutheran and Zwinglian influences. It was predominantly Lutheran when, on April 19, 1552, Pullain, with his Calvinistic views on the Eucharist, arrived, escorting his flock.

This French-speaking congregation had been settled for just over two months when a group of English exiles arrived. These, on Pullain's advice, petitioned the City Council for permission to stay and be granted a place where they might worship in English. They were allowed the use of the building already being used by Pullain, on condition that they subscribed to the French Reformed Confession of Faith, so that there might be no grounds for dissension between them and their Walloon companions in exile. This meant that they had to modify their English Prayer Book: no surplice, no litany, no responses. They did so in order to comply with the conditions imposed on them; but the course was one they took willingly, for they were mostly representative of the radical wing of English Protestantism. One of their leaders, William Whittingham, had that cosmopolitan experience that made him more naturally sympathetic to Continental Protestantism than was the average English Protestant of his day. What the latter most valued was the Prayer Book that Mary Tudor forbade; what the Continental Protestant sought was theological unity.

On August 2, 1554, the English exiles at Frankfurt had sent a letter to their compatriots in places such as Strassburg, Wesel, Emden, and Zürich, urging these to join them. They felt that Frankfurt had much to offer: it had a cosmopolitan flavor, and twice a year there was a great fair much frequented by students in their everlasting search for books. But the invitation was not so tactfully worded as the situation demanded, and the recipients gave a doubtful, inconclusive reply.

Knox, whose mind had busied itself for some time with thoughts about England and its Prayer Book, had come to the conclusion that the latter was a stumbling block to the full reform of the English Church, and no sooner had he arrived among his new flock than he found himself involved in strife.

Richard Chambers, a man of some wealth, and Edmund Grindal, later Archbishop of Canterbury, came from Strassburg on November 28 to negotiate with the Frankfurt congregation. Both they and Thomas Lever from Zürich, who had been appointed Knox's colleague at Frankfurt, favored a much more conservative attitude to the Prayer Book. Lever tried to mediate between Knox and the Zürich delegates, and when he had failed in this, he came out in support of the English Book. The Frankfurt congregation did not agree, however, and further attempts to settle the question failed. Knox and Whittingham appealed to Calvin, explaining the reasons for their own dislike of the Book, and not neglecting to emphasize the points they knew Calvin would dislike. While waiting for a reply, Knox wrote to Calvin's colleagues at Geneva, urging them to make him see how regrettable it was that the peace of the Frankfurt congregation should be endangered for the sake of some ceremonies of merely human invention. He concluded with the ominous request that they should ask Calvin whether he, Knox, might in good conscience resign from the Frankfurt pastorate, since his presence there seemed to be disruptive. Calvin's reply is dated January 20, 1555. Steeped in Paul, he gave an admirably Pauline counsel: avoid contention and seek conciliation. Yet he did not disguise the fact that much in the Book seemed to him odd and insular.

On February 6, Knox agreed on a compromise with his colleague: they would try out an experimental order until Easter. On March 15, however, came another batch of refugees, and among them one of the chief authors of the contested English Prayer Book, Richard Cox. Naturally he did not like what had happened to it at Frankfurt. Fresh from an England where men were being martyred for their love of this Book, he was in no mood to listen to those who belittled it abroad. Besides, he was by temperament an autocratic man. As chancellor of the University of Oxford he had been nicknamed "the Cancellor." He had always been among those who disliked Knox. With a copy of Knox's pamphlet in his pocket and his heart set against the Scotsman, he immediately began a vendetta against him with an organized campaign by his supporters to

74

interrupt the services with their litany. Next Sunday afternoon, Knox, being due to preach, gave the English roisterers a trouncing that was hardly undeserved. He had once, he said, thought well of the English Book, though he thought less well of it now; but in any case it ill became them to bring strife deliberately when in a difficult situation a compromise had been devised in the interests of peace and Christian forbearance. Knox was no sooner out of the pulpit than he was "verye sharplie charged and reproued," and that night there was a bitter meeting.

What makes the conduct of Cox and his friends even more remarkable is that at the time of their troublemaking they had not yet even been admitted to membership of the congregation. When this question came to be considered by the latter, the majority were naturally opposed to their admission. Knox insisted, however, on their being admitted, and carried his proposal. But his generosity was wasted. Cox immediately took full advantage of it by stirring up hostility to Knox and rallying support for himself, until eventually a motion was passed forbidding Knox to preach. Whittingham retaliated by going to the city magistrates, who forbade any sermon that day; and while some further discussions were in progress, one of Cox's party visited Knox in his lodging and tried to secure his acquiescence in Cox's wishes by offers of fair promises together with hints at ugly consequences should he decline. These were, of course, the worst tactics to employ for winning Knox to anything. His dour countenance only toughened at the words. The magistrates seem to have favored Knox's side, and eventually, under their influence, Cox not only had to abandon the Book but accept the forms in use in the French congregation.

But Cox had not yet used his best weapon. Now he flourished it, and it was indeed fatally poisoned. He went to the magistrates, and taking out of his pocket his copy of Knox's pamphlet, he pointed to the unfortunate phrase in it about the emperor. In all, he made nine charges of treason out of the document. Knox's language about Philip, king of Spain, for instance, was hardly respectful, and Philip was, after all, the emperor's son. Whatever the Frankfurt magistrates may have felt about the matter personally, they could not overlook such language against their emperor, especially as he happened to be in the neighborhood, at Augsburg, at the time. They were therefore forced to forbid Knox to preach.

It had shocked Knox when the strangers had behaved in such an outrageous fashion in church, for he had strong convictions about seemliness in such matters; but that fellow Protestants in exile should carry their complaint to secular magistrates and denounce him to them as a traitor for reasons which, rightly or wrongly, he believed to be merely spiteful, evoked a deep resentment in his generous heart. When next he entered the congregation, Cox and his supporters ostentatiously left the building. The magistrates, gravely concerned about the whole matter, persuaded Knox's friends to use their influence with him to leave the city. He took their advice, and on March 25, 1555, some fifty persons gathered in Knox's lodging, each dolefully aware of what was in every heart. In what they had believed to be a congregation of the Church of God, ruffianism had triumphed over law and order within a fortnight. Yes, Antichrist in Rome would laugh. Knox addressed the company on the Passion and resurrection of Christ, telling them of the joys that were in store for God's elect, who in this life must suffer sorrow and persecution. No cross, no crown. The following day, some of his hearers accompanied him a few miles of the road. In spite of his sermon of the previous night, there were tears in their eyes as they bade him farewell, earnestly committing him to the care of their Heavenly Father.

On he went to Geneva. Henceforth, this city on the lake was to be his headquarters until the way should be opened up for the final struggle and triumph in his native Scotland. In his darkest days in the galleys, Knox had confidently predicted that he would once again preach in the old church on the Scottish coast. Surely, as he now fled from Frankfurt, he must have questioned his old prediction. Scotland, England, and even the English in exile had all, in turn, cast him off. The whole of Europe seemed set against the gospel of Christ and the joyous liberty this could bring to believing hearts. Where

Europe was not in the clutches of the pope it seemed to behave worse than if it were. Geneva was still a refuge for his weary body and soul, but it offered no promise for his work as a Reformer. Surely, it seemed, his work as a Reformer was over and done with, finished and fast to be forgotten. He had failed in every mission, failed and failed and failed. The clouds in his sky were at their blackest, too black for even a prophet like himself to penetrate.

8 Knox's first visit to Geneva had been made at an unfortunate time, while Calvin's position there was unassured. When Knox returned in April, 1553, Calvin was at the summit of his power. Knox saw Calvin enjoying the fruits of his struggle in Geneva; he saw little of the methods Calvin used to obtain them. Despite the opposition of those who had wanted to keep Genevan citizenship closed to outsiders, Calvin had succeeded in turning the city into an international Protestant commonwealth, almost the United States of Europe in miniature. A month after Knox's arrival, Calvin's enemies had made a last bid for rebellion. This bid failed and its failure reinforced Calvin's policy of making Geneva into a cosmopolis of exiles and refugees. The Calvinists had never had any qualms about the treatment of insurrection. To quell and punish those whom they arrested they freely used banishment, gaol, torture, and execution.

Of Calvin's pogroms, however, Knox saw almost nothing. He probably saw little of Calvin himself. Geneva, as Knox knew it, in the calm after the storm, seemed to him " a school of Christ." Knox did not mean, of course, that it was a theological school or a university: as a seat of learning it did not at that time compare with other Swiss centers such as Lausanne and Basel. He meant that it was one place where, in a storm-tossed world, a man might see Christians gathered together visibly in a communion whose peace and joy seemed to reflect the very bliss of heaven itself. Geneva, as Knox saw it, was a foretaste of the Beatific Vision.

The spirit of Geneva was indeed, at that time, very remarkable. A contemporary Scotsman wrote of it that it was the miracle of the day. The harmony impressed everyone. It was due, in part, no doubt, to the rigorous tests of admission and the legalistic discipline imposed; nevertheless it was an extraordinary achievement on Calvin's part to collect such a motley crowd and make visitors remark less on the striking differences of their costume, speech, and personal habits than on the unity of their purpose and the harmony of their will.

On June 10, the small English colony at Geneva formally petitioned Calvin for a place to worship. Calvin ordered that one be found, and Knox was to be their minister. Meanwhile, however, Mrs. Bowes had written Knox, informing him of her husband's death. She proposed that Knox return to Scotland and join Marjorie. It cannot be doubted that this proposal appealed to Knox's heart. But it did not appeal to his judgment; it was, he said, " most contrarious " to this. The temper of Scotland had, in fact, greatly changed in the eight years since Knox had left it, and there were now many there who were ready to welcome him. But Knox did not know this. The few remaining supporters he had from the old days were mostly dispersed. So far as Knox could guess, his prospects in the land he loved were bleak indeed. Evidently heart triumphed over head, however, for by the end of August he was on his way north.

Knox married Marjorie immediately on his arrival in Scotland " in the end of the harvest." Marriage in the sixteenth century was often very much a matter of convenient arrangement, so that, even apart from the peculiar circumstances in which Knox was placed, the long period of betrothal was not remarkable. Nor was Knox's attitude to it, however unromantic it may seem to us in our own day. To us, the prevalent attitude of sixteenth century husbands to their wives seems inconsiderate, to say the least; but it fitted in with the general pattern of life, and Knox, now well over forty, looked on his marriage to Marjorie as would most men in their forties four hundred years ago. There is no good reason to doubt he was happy in the step he now took. Marjorie helped him in his work: he called her, in later years, his " left hand," and when she was ill his papers evidently got out of order. He spoke of her as " my own flesh."

What filled Knox's cup of happiness to overflowing at this time, however, was the new spirit he found in his native land. The younger folk were ready for fresh ideas. The whole atmosphere, very different from that which had prevailed in the dark days when he had been carried off in a galley in 1547, surprised and delighted him.

" Gif I had not sene it with my eyis in my awn contrey, I culd not have beleivit it," he wrote.

In the earlier days, Knox's message to his compatriots had been too negative. It had been all an endless diatribe against the old corruptions. Nobody could really disagree with his attacks on Rome. But what had he been able to offer as an alternative? Perhaps he had known himself; perhaps he hadn't. Certainly his average hearer had no clear notion of any positive plan he might have had, and it is doubtful whether he had ever so far been clear about one in his own mind. At any rate, to the average man or woman it is neither convincing nor inspiring to be told over and over again to stay away from Mass and find your own path to heaven somehow or other with the help of a Bible of which perhaps you cannot very readily obtain a copy.

So the time had now come for a more positive message. Knox set himself at once to preach it. It was not enough, he now said, to boycott the Mass and the sacraments and all the rest of the Roman paraphernalia. You must put something in their place. Not just a substitute, for want of something better. No, you must replace the discarded trappings by the Real Thing. God does not give you the priceless gift of election, does not make you his chosen servants, just so that you may have the opportunity of registering your protestations against corruption. Have not even abbots and friars protested for centuries against this? No, even the most indefatigable Protestantism is not enough. Knox was now telling his hearers that their calling was to nothing less than the restoration of the True Church of Jesus Christ. The True Church, whose only Head is Christ, must be firmly and fully established in Scotland in place of the Babylon of Antichrist that had so long usurped the Church's rightful place. He was telling his hearers that they *were* the Church. The pope's Church had been a parody of the True Church. In the rebuilding of this they must see that there was nothing missing of what had been parodied.

The Mass, for instance. It is an abomination. But why is it such an abomination? Not simply because it is a vain imagining of man, a futile attempt to propitiate an angry God. If this were all, it would be less odious; it would be merely foolish. What makes it so evil, so Satanic, is that it is *idolatry*, and what makes it idolatrous is that it is the shamelessly blasphemous substitute of wicked men for the Blessed Feast of Christ's Love. It is not because it is wholly *unlike* that mystical Supper that the Mass is a filthy abomination; it is because it is so *like* it. It is a diabolical caricature of it, as Satan himself is a caricature of God; as the Lord Pope is a caricature of the Lord Christ.

It was this vision of the sacramental character of the Church that gave Knox the power he now needed. It had been a grave weakness of Protestantism on the Continent that the sacraments tended in practice to be regarded as ordinances useful to the health of the Church, but not absolutely essential to it. In theory, the Reformers never underestimated the importance of the sacraments, perhaps not even Zwingli; least of all Calvin. Calvin had taken a high theological stand on the doctrine of the Eucharist. He had wished for a weekly celebration of it and he ordered his Genevan service on the Eucharistic pattern. Knox likewise hoped for the establishment in Scotland of a fully organized Church celebrating the Lord's Supper weekly.[22]

22 For the text of the form of service used by Knox at Geneva and its relation to other liturgies, English, Roman and Lutheran, see William D. Maxwell, *John Knox's Genevan Service Book* (Oliver and Boyd, 1931). This form was used in some Reformed congregations in Scotland by 1560, if not earlier, while others used the English form. In 1564, Knox's service book, which had been modified and enlarged, was printed in Edinburgh

Was not Scotland the perfect terrain for such a restoration of the wholeness and fullness and purity of the Church of Christ on earth? In Scotland, independent little Scotland, the old medieval dream could come true. In Scotland, whose people now seemed to be but waiting for the signal, Jesus Christ would be lifted up as head of his Kirk, and would draw all men unto him. His reign would displace that of Antichrist; his Supper would displace the Mass, the idolatrous sacrifice of Antichrist.

Early in November, Knox went north with Wishart's old patron, John Erskine, to the latter's house at Dun, a few miles inland from Montrose, where Wishart had begun his teaching of Greek. To Erskine's house resorted the nobility of that part of the country, and Knox addressed them daily. Then he journeyed south into Lothian. There, at Calder, he could exercise his influence on the grandees of the capital itself. He did, and among those who listened to him here were two future regents of Scotland, the Earl of Moray and the Earl of Mar. The latter was at the time governor of Edinburgh Castle.

During the winter, Knox made various excursions, including one to Ayrshire among Wishart's old friends there. Shortly before Easter he visited the house of Alexander Cunningham, Earl of Glencairn, in the region of the river Clyde. Everywhere he went he seemed to be welcome. By Easter the atmosphere was so propitious that he revisited the various congregations he had already gathered together, celebrating the Lord's Supper among them wherever he went.

On this second tour, Knox preached openly — " in greater liberty." News of his activities reached the ears of the queen regent, Mary, herself. Mary had no inclination to take action against Knox; but the Scottish bishops, understanding him better than she and no doubt well aware by now that Knox was bent on nothing short of the complete overthrow of their authority, determined to get him out of the way. During his second visit to Dun, Knox was summoned to appear in the

---

and enjoined by Assembly for the use of all ministers and readers. See George W. Sprott and Thomas Leishman, *The Book of Common Order of the Church of Scotland commonly known as John Knox's Liturgy* (Blackwood, 1868).

Church of the Blackfriars, Edinburgh, on May 15, 1556.

He duly arrived in Edinburgh. But to the consternation of the bishops, he was not alone. He had brought with him an impressive company of important persons who were all obviously ready for action if as much as a finger should be laid on him. The bishops hastily withdrew their summons, and Knox now preached openly in Edinburgh to a greater audience than ever. Among those who attended his meetings was a great noble, William Keith, the Earl Marischal, who, though he came cautiously at first, under cover of night, was so impressed that he and Glencairn urged Knox to write a letter to the queen regent. It was known that she had no love for the bishops, and it was erroneously surmised that she had already halted their pressure on Knox. Perhaps, Glencairn and Keith suggested, she might now be ready for even friendlier action. It was a groundless hope; the fact that Mary disliked her bishops did not mean she cared for Knox.

It was never difficult to persuade Knox to compose a sermon. Readily enough, he sat down and began a letter to the queen regent. It was a remarkably reasonable one, and showed that he knew something of her state of mind. She was eager to affirm the authority of the Crown and bring Scotland under a just and orderly rule. Knox warmly applauded her desire. The morals of Scotland did need reforming, and she was right to seek a reformation. But, he argued, " vain is it to crave reformation in manners where the religion is corrupted." He was not unaware of the dangers attending religious reformation; but it was for her, a dutiful ruler, to attempt it. The tone of the letter was respectful, even courtly. No doubt Knox still felt he was not " flattering any flesh "; yet he was uncommonly polite. "Superfluous and foolishe it shall appeare to many that I, a man of base estate and condition, dare enterprise to admonische a Princesse so honorable, endewed with wisdome and graces singularly." Nor, though he naturally expressed hope of favor for his cause, did he seem to have any delusions about the opinion she might have been led to hold of him personally. " I doubt not but the rumors whiche came to youre Grace's eares of me have bene suche, that if all reportes were trew, I were unworthy to lyve on the earth. . . . I am traduced as an heretyke, accused as a fals teacher and seducer of the people, besides other opprobies, which, affirmed by men of worldly honor and estymation, may easely kyndle the wrath of magistrates when innocency is not knowen. But blessed be God, the Father of oure Lorde Jesus Christe, who by the dewe of hys heavenly grace, hath so quenched the fyre of displeasure in youre Grace's harte. . . ."

Glencairn delivered the missive in person to the queen regent. Though Mary had felt it best to let Knox preach his head off, she had never taken him seriously. That he should lecture her on her duty to overthrow the hierarchy amused her. She took the letter as a joke, and when the Archbishop of Glasgow was present a few days later, she handed it to him, saying laughingly: " Please you, my lord, to read a pasquil." [23]

Mary's mockery of the letter did not reach Knox's ears for some time. When, two years later, he sent her a revised version of it, he did not conceal the hurt her levity had caused him. The tone of the second version shows Knox at his fiercest: " The avarice and crueltie, as well of yourselfe as of suche as be in authoritie, may be known by the factes. . . . The conspiracie and conjuration of your false prophetes is knowen to the world, and yet is none founde so faithfull to God, nor mercifull to your Grace, that freelie will and dare admonish you to repent before that God rise hymselfe in judgement."

It was shortly after he sent the first version of this letter, the one that Mary laughed off as a " pasquil," that Knox suddenly announced that he felt his duty lay for the present, not in Scotland, after all, but in Geneva. Historians have puzzled about the motives that led him to leave Scotland just at the point when he seemed to be at the height of his influence with the nobility and in no immediate danger from the regent or the ecclesiastical authorities. In the existing state of affairs, it was plain that all hope of religious revolution lay with the nobles. Why, then, did he leave Scotland just as he had secured their support?

[23] A lampoon, satire.

Knox is such a controversial figure that his motives are sometimes made unnecessarily difficult to understand. May it not be that, with his caution and his extraordinary sense of the national pulse, Knox scented greater personal danger than any modern historian could now detect in the situation? He may have felt, for it is in keeping with his calculating determination, that

> " He who fights and runs away
> May live to fight another day."

But a scrutiny of the situation shows that it was, at any rate, not mere fear of personal danger that now took him back to Geneva. The nobles who were so eager to support his cause were too involved in the vicious circle of Scottish politics to espouse it with the religious fervor and singleness of purpose that he demanded. They were not yet fully awakened to the gravity of the situation; they could not yet sufficiently understand the root of Scotland's disease. What Scottish patriots at that time needed above all, in their struggle to maintain and make secure their country's independence, was a strong leader. The welfare of Scotland could not be otherwise promoted. The country was ruled by a band of lawless nobles whose dissatisfaction with the existing state of affairs was grounded in an unconscious dissatisfaction with themselves. They were eagerly urging the need for reform without being ready to pay the price of it. Under a weak, absentee ruler, Scotland could never escape its own bonds. Popes and regents had not and could not have any real interest in Scotland's national welfare.

Knox, peasant that he was, saw his country's need more clearly than his aristocratic supporters dared to see it. The queen regent's Council, mainly French, had little understanding of either the virtues or the vices of the Scots, and therefore they could neither sympathize with Scottish aspirations nor take account of Scottish weaknesses. The Council was actually proposing to raise a standing army of mercenaries, mainly French, maintained by public taxation in Scotland, as a means of bringing law and order to a people who had suffered oppression too long and were not made of the stuff that tyrants find congenial. The nobles wanted to uphold the old feudal system which, though decaying, had much to be said for it, since at its best it still fostered a natural, kindly relation between landlord and tenant. Why could not the old, trusted feudal system be revived by the power of the new faith? Were this to happen, what should it matter that Scotland had no strong king? There were some nobles who had a vision of themselves enhancing their own power and confirming the old ways by means of the new religion. There was no need, they felt, to smash scepters and overturn thrones. The royal house could stick by its traditional papalism and play its old games of intrigue as old men play cards for lack of anything better to do. The nobles could go ahead in spite of the court; they could reform the country their own way, to suit their own interests. In other European countries, so far, there had been no need for a Protestant revolution. The decadent forces of Rome had been allowed to die out gradually. They were dying everywhere except in Spain, and there was no fear of a Ximenes or a Loyola reviving the Roman Church in Scotland. That Church had never been healthy enough to revive and was now so weak that many of its buildings were standing empty, all ready for Protestant preachers to walk in and take over. Meanwhile, the queen regent was writing her brother, the Cardinal of Lorraine, to explain that there were many things in Scotland she had to put up with for the present that she hoped to put right by and by. Not that she had a definite plan of action. She was but hoping that sometime, somehow, some intrigue or other would save the old religion.

Knox must have known that nothing could be done until his associates recognized more clearly what they had to face in supporting the Reformation cause. He could compromise in some things; but he believed he knew a ruthless enemy when he saw one. And when it came to " damnable idolatry " there was no question: either the old religion or the new must win. Did not the Scriptures say that " all plantation that my Heavenly Father hath not planted shall be rooted out "? His terms for the enemy were simple: unconditional surrender. So long as his supporters cared to tinker with policies of appeasement

85

and conciliation, it was plain they did not understand the situation. Therefore the time to strike was not yet. Knox could not forget, as we are apt to forget, that in the sixteenth century the Roman doctrine of transubstantiation was no merely academic question: it was the basis of the power of a foreign Church over the people of Scotland. If the people's independence were to be guaranteed, that power must be completely destroyed. To say that a few Masses did not matter was like saying that a few enemy posts in your island do not matter when your island is at war for its very life.

The ancient palace and abbey of Holyrood House form a group of gray-stone buildings that nestle at the foot of the most romantic by far of the many hills among which Edinburgh is set. The abbey was founded by the Scottish King David I in 1128. David had a reputation for extravagance in building and endowing religious houses, and this one henceforward played a role of extraordinary importance in national affairs. The Parliament of King Robert the Bruce, Scotland's great hero, assembled in the abbey in 1326. Both the marriage of King James III to the Scandinavian Princess Margaret in 1469 and that of James IV to the English Margaret in 1503 took place there, and by the time of the latter wedding, at any rate, there was already a royal residence of some kind associated with the abbey and afterward, in Knox's own lifetime, greatly enlarged. Above this picturesque cluster of buildings rises the gaunt traprock ridge of Salisbury Crags that reveals a whole panorama of geological splendor: a columnar arrangement of porphyritic greenstone with veins of compact and crystallized prehnite between the columns. Beyond and above that great ridge, separated by the valley of the Hunter's Bog, rises the hill of Arthur's Seat, in the form of a couched lion, the symbol of Scotland's pride. From the summit of this hill, which, though less than a thousand feet, gives the impression of a great mountain, you can see spread out all around and below you the glories of the city of Edinburgh. In Knox's day, when the town was much smaller, Knox could have climbed Arthur's Seat and looked down on Holyrood and all his beloved Edinburgh, remembering the temptation of Christ,

86

when "the devil taketh him up into an exceeding high moun-tain, and showeth him all the kingdoms of the world, and the glory of them." Might not the devil now be showing him, John Knox, a way of becoming the people's leader without first fully converting the people to God? Might this not be Satan's last ruse to impede the work of God? Knox took his mission very seriously. Perhaps it was that, while hitherto he had been fighting Satan's armies, now Satan himself (as later on the eve of his death he expressed it) was wrestling with him. Surely Satan had taken him to the summit of Arthur's Seat and had spoken the wily words of the supreme tempter: "All these things will I give thee, if thou wilt fall down and worship me. . . . Fair Edinburgh and all the Lothians; yea the whole land is thine, if . . . if. . . ." And Knox, who feared no flesh, trembled in his heart until he had the courage to make what he believed was the only reply that was not total surrender to the infernal foe: "Get thee hence, Satan: for it is written, Thou shalt worship the Lord thy God, and him only shalt thou serve." The congregations must learn the hard way, as the Israelites had learned in captivity, by first purifying their own hearts. God would teach them, and when they were ready, so was he. When they were ready, he, God's minister, would be at their disposal.

So, having sent his wife and mother-in-law ahead to Dieppe, Knox left Scotland in July, 1556. Before his departure he left " A Letter of Wholesome Counsel " to his supporters. " Within your own houses . . . ye are bishoppes and kynges; your wyfe, chyldren, servauntes, and familye are youre bishopryke and charge; of you it shalbe requyred howe carefullye and dyly-gentlye ye have always instructed theym in Goddes true knowlege, how that ye have studied in them to plant vertue and repress vice. And therefore, I say, ye must make them par-takers in readyng, exhorting, and in makyng common prayers, which I would in every house wer used once a day at least." Herein lay the very core of Scotland's spiritual liberation and the beginning of a tradition of family worship that became a source of immense strength to Scotland's people. The Refor-mation did not break down the Church in order to exalt the

87

individual; it was rather that the individual had to learn to work alone before he could partake in the Church's rebuilding. The new enterprise was such that it could not be undertaken by slaves: the last remnants of past bondage must therefore be entirely destroyed.

Knox arrived in Geneva with his wife, his mother-in-law, a servant, and a pupil called Patrick. Scarcely had he entered Geneva when he was summoned a second time to appear in Edinburgh to answer charges against him by the ecclesiastical authorities. Because he was unavailable, these burned him in effigy at the Mercat Cross. But letters from his friends streamed into Geneva, and he conducted a considerable correspondence, answering also the innumerable conundrums that conscience-ridden women in the Edinburgh congregation put before him. One of these, probably the wife of the Dean of Guild, wrote to him complaining of her husband. With some gentleness and tact, and not without some sense of humor, Knox told her that her husband was dear to him, not only because he was a man of some good gifts but because he was her husband. Her husband, she had said, was cold, and his coldness might justly be called infidelity. But as for himself, Knox would promise nothing that it was not in his power to perform. She must stick to her man, for he was the husband appointed her by God. She must determine to win her own independence of soul even in her apparent bondage, and in so doing she would find her tears turned into joy.

Even when the questions were about much more trivial matters, such as dress, Knox showed the same patience as a pastor. He took the point of view that while it is true, on the one hand, that matters of dress should be of little concern one way or another to those who enjoy Christian liberty, nevertheless one must bear in mind the effect that extravagances may have on those who are still partly in bondage. Cloths of velvet, silk, and gold, for instance, are good in themselves; but since some women do in fact abuse them, either to catch the eye of men or because they are the slaves of fashion, he could not wholly approve the indiscriminate use of such fineries by women who profess to be godly. In his judgment, he said, all affectation, all

88

efforts to excel, either in the dressing and embroidering of the hair, or the decking of the body, or the correction of natural beauty, or any slavish following of fashion, offended against the precept of Scripture. Since the Scripture enjoined that a woman's hair be modestly covered, surely it could not be a good thing for a woman to dye it. But there was no great severity in Knox's recommendations on the subject: he was, rather, simply urging his inquirers, who were women of some position and wealth, burgesses' wives and the like, to think much less about dress. Christian women should not be thinking about whether this or that fad of the moment, these or those buttons or bows, were allowed or disallowed to a Christian. A Christian woman would dress modestly and neatly and so would always appear graceful without resorting to extremes of fashion. Her attention would be occupied with more important matters. She would dress inconspicuously. All this was good, fatherly counsel, and shows how unfanatical Knox could be in matters that he thought relatively unimportant.

9   Knox lived a busy life in Geneva. As pastor of the English congregation there, he preached three sermons a week, and every sermon lasted well over two hours; some almost three. This was in accordance with the usage of the time. He applied himself also to the discipline and encouragement of the flock, and in the time left over he pursued the study of Hebrew, Greek, and the Scripture that he so loved. There was probably no period of Knox's life in which he felt happier. Yet there was a tug at his heart from the north. He knew that if he had a destiny worthy of the name it lay in Edinburgh.

Edinburgh has an extraordinarily haunting quality that is not easy to convey to any but those who have lived there. The city is, of course, remarkable for the splendor of its situation and the spectacular grandeur of its sky line, a pageant of many centuries. The diversity of the buildings and the magnificence of the streets impress even the most fish-eyed modern tourist. The Edinburgh streets Knox knew were much less splendid than those of the " New Town " built in the eighteenth century; but some of them were then as famous throughout Europe as Princes Street was to become. In Knox's day one of the most fashionable streets in Paris was the now quaintly narrow little Rue St. Jacques, so that it is not surprising that French visitors to Edinburgh cried out in admiration at the spaciousness of the High Street of Edinburgh that is now but a romantic medieval curiosity. The Castle that today dominates the great garden slopes of the city, casting a magic spell of the past by day and conveying, when floodlit at night, the fairyland enchantment of a scene from an opera, is breathtaking. It was no less striking to the sixteenth century visitor, but for a very different reason. What impressed such a visitor was not its picturesqueness but its impregnability. " I have seen," wrote one traveler of that time, "many strengths in Germany, the Netherlands, Spain, and England, but they must all give place to this unconquered castle, both for strength and situation." Others remarked on the fruitfulness of the soil of the surrounding country, the delightful air, and the abundance of the springs of sweet water. But beyond all, that the uniquely haunting character of the town has always made Edinburgh live in the hearts of her sons, wherever they have gone and however long they have stayed away. To those who have fallen in love with Edinburgh, all other cities look tawdry. For a man with a mission such as Knox's, this peculiar nostalgia must have been extremely acute. Even in his happiness in the lovely Swiss city on the lake, Knox's thoughts inevitably turned again and again to the stately enchantress of the north.

But in Knox's view, Edinburgh was not yet converted; Geneva was. Writing to Mrs. Locke, a London merchant's wife who was among his innumerable counsel seekers, he commended Geneva as the most perfect school of Christ since the days of the apostles. Elsewhere Christ was being preached, no doubt; yet nowhere else had religion and manners been so sincerely reformed. It was more than curiosity, however, that brought not only Mrs. Locke but also Edinburgh's Dean of

Guild and another Edinburgh burgess to Geneva in May, 1557. These two gentlemen were the bearers of a letter signed by Glencairn and the three nobles who had listened to Knox at Calder: Erskine, Lorne, and James Stuart. It was an invitation to Knox to return once again to Scotland. They reported that though the political situation was unchanged, the Roman Church was standing even more unfavorably than before in the eyes of the nobility and also, it seemed, of the queen regent herself. The messengers evidently also brought proposals not put in writing, probably for renewed efforts to obtain complete freedom of worship for the Protestant congregations and fresh petitions to Regent and Parliament for the reform of the Church.

Knox conferred about these proposals with his colleagues in the Genevan consistory of clergy and with Calvin himself. These all held that he was bound in conscience to accept the call to Scotland. His Scottish friends could hardly, however, have chosen a more inconvenient time. Knox's first son, Nathaniel,[24] was born the month the visitors arrived. Mrs. Locke, his guest, had brought her son and daughter with her, and when her daughter died a few days after arrival in Geneva, she was grief-stricken. Knox had her to console as well as his own wife and child to care for. But there were other impediments. News, for instance, of war. France was evidently planning an invasion of England; Picardy and Normandy were said to be full of cavalry, and the Channel ports in France were reported

[24] Nathaniel died at the age of twenty-three, eight years after John Knox's own death in 1572. Both he and Knox's younger son, Eleazer, born the following year, 1558, also in Geneva, were educated at, and later became Fellows of, St. John's College, Cambridge. Eleazer, who was made one of the University Preachers, died in 1591, at the age of thirty-two.

That the sons of the Scottish Reformer should have become clergymen of the Church of England is not so remarkable as it may seem to some modern readers. Knox had no fundamental antipathy to the English Church. If his sons went to Cambridge, it was to be expected that they should take holy orders in the Church of England. Ordination was a qualification for all college fellowships at both Oxford and Cambridge until comparatively recent times.

Knox's three children by his second wife were all daughters, so that his family became extinct in the male line.

crowded with ships ready for the fray. The king of France had requested the pope to establish an inquisition on the pattern of the notorious Spanish one, with the Cardinal of Lorraine, brother of the Scottish regent, as the Grand Inquisitor. Because of the opposition of the French Parliament, nothing came of this; nevertheless, an edict against heretics was issued by the French king on July 24. Finally, the regent was doing her best to involve Scotland actively in war with England.

In spite of these difficulties, Knox at last set out, arriving in Dieppe on October 24. To his consternation he now received word from friends in Scotland referring to a change of situation there and questioning whether the time was, after all, opportune for his coming. Knox was furious. He had seen enough on his way to Dieppe to be in no doubt about the risks he had taken in crossing France, and he did not relish the discovery that he had gone on a wild-goose chase. He sat down and wrote an ill-tempered letter. Pointing out that he had arranged to come to Scotland with the first ship from Dieppe, he referred to the " anguish and sorrow " he had felt on learning of the change in plans. He had regarded the invitation as a most serious challenge to him, and had therefore taken the best advice he could get as touching his duty. Either he had taken the matter too seriously or else the Scottish nobles had not taken it seriously enough. " Either it shall appear that I was marvellous vain, being so solicitous where no necessity required, or else that such as were my movers thereto lacked the ripeness of judgment in their first vocation." Was it a light matter that he had left his own family fatherless and his flock shepherdless? True, he bitingly admitted, it was a small flock; yet it was no less dear to God for that. To worldly men such things might appear of little account; but they did not so appear to the flock he had left in Geneva, who had wept as he had wept himself in taking his leave of them. What was he to say to them at Geneva on his return, if perchance he should reach it again in safety? He took care to make it clear that his rebuke, skillfully peppered with broad hints about the plagues and punishments that God can send the wicked even on this earth, not to mention the everlasting torments of hell — that his rebuke applied to all the nobility without exception. " God open your eyes, that ye may espy and consider your own miserable estate." He knew that his words must seem " sharp " and even " indiscreetly spoken"; but he reminded his readers that there are times when a true friend, who is never a flatterer, must sometimes speak uncomfortably.

Even under great provocation as he certainly was, Knox should not have written such a letter. It was an outburst of passion that does not show him at his best. The nobles could not be held responsible for the unfortunate worsening of the situation. Gradually, in the months following, Knox showed by his writings that he had now more fully grasped the situation himself; indeed, these writings demonstrate once again Knox's uncanny gift for doing so. Meanwhile, a group of nobles, in response to Knox's fiery letter, made and signed a " Common Band " in which they solemnly charged themselves to strive for their cause even unto death. So, after all, even the original letter had had its effect.

Knox's supporters in Scotland had very good reason to reconsider the wisdom of their invitation. The bishops were engaged in a feeble attempt to reform the Roman Church from within at the eleventh hour. In Spain, Queen Isabella and Cardinal Ximenes had accomplished the much-needed reformation with success sufficient to make that country comparatively invulnerable to Protestantism. But Scotland was not Spain; nor was there anyone in the least like Ximenes among the Scottish hierarchy. All that resulted from the deliberations of their Provincial Council was an indication that they were not unmindful of the necessity of reforms. This was far from enough, and indeed they succeeded only in further exhibiting the irreformability of the Roman Church in Scotland. In a curious document, which the people came to call " The Twopenny Faith," [25] they made some enactments such as that no cleric should put his own son in his own benefice in the

[25] There is a facsimile of it in the *Bannatyne Club Miscellany*, iii, pp. 313 ff.; also printed as an appendix to A. F. Mitchell's facsimile edition of Archbishop Hamilton's Catechism (Edinburgh, 1882). It was easy for Knox to poke fun at it; nor did he neglect the opportunity.

Church; that no one should enjoy the emoluments of a Church benefice without having been ordained; and that any priest found in open adultery should, for the first offense, lose a third of his benefice, for the second, half of it, and for the third, all of it. They also made regulations about the proper form and use of caps, tippets, and the like.

Plainly, they had no idea of the gravity of the case. Knox's friends wanted to let them have time to condemn themselves out of their own mouths, and to try, if possible, to play them off against the regent and the regent against them. On the other hand, there was even more serious trouble among the Protestants themselves. As elsewhere, there was a left wing of extremists among these who were intoxicated by Luther's cry of " Freedom from the Law," and interpreted it to mean that God's elect need neither confession nor forgiveness. Liberty is a heady wine, and it was no doubt inevitable that it should have intoxicated many on their first taste of it. These thought they were the very saints of God. But they did not stop there. They would be gods themselves. " Ye shall be as God " was Satan's promise to men, and there was indeed something Satanic in the spiritual pride of these extremists. Much remained to be done before Scotland would be ready for the orderly sort of revolution that Knox at present had in mind. But perhaps, thought his friends, it could be done more quickly than appearances suggested. The first step was to get the regent out of the way at all costs, and some sinister plans were laid for this end.

Knox, when he heard of these plans, did not approve of them. He had seen, and was now more than ever before aware, that the Reformation must be accomplished not by the overthrow of the secular authorities but by a patient winning of these to the Protestant cause. Of course, he would gladly have seen the succession pass to a monarch or other ruler who would act rightly, according to Knox's own beliefs; but the transformation must be constitutional, so that it might never be said that the Reformation was built upon political anarchy or rebellion. He believed that the princes of the world were blind to the essential loyalty of their Protestant subjects. They must be converted, or, if they would not convert, they must be overthrown by the practice of the established principle of popular sovereignty. There must be no disorderly shooting. An unworthy prince, such as one who was willing to keep his subjects in the thraldom of the pope, should be deposed, but the will of the people must first plainly assert itself; it would not do for the ruler to be murdered by a few thugs or even intrigued out of his throne by such shady characters.

Once again he addressed the Scottish Lords in a letter. One of his boldest and firmest utterances, it was at the same time full of common sense. He had heard, he said, rumors of rebellion. He *commanded,* " in Godis feir, and by the assurance of his trewth," that no one seek to promote Christ's cause by any wanton disobedience to the established civil authority, which must be obeyed in all lawful matters. " But in the bowellis of Chryst Jesus I exhort yow, that with all simplicitie and lawful obedience, joynit with boldnes in God, and with open confessioun of your faith, ye seik the favours of the Autoritie that by it (yf possibile be) the cause in whilk ye labour may be promotit, or at the leist not persecuted." Only after every other course had failed would it be lawful to " attempt the extreamitie; " that is, the overthrow of the civil powers by force.

He was never more right in his judgment, not least from the practical point of view. He scented nastiness in the moves of some of his supporters, and nastiness there was. Had he gone to Scotland then, he would have been inevitably embroiled in it. Even if the Protestant cause achieved some sort of victory under his leadership in circumstances such as these, it would probably have been an ephemeral victory, and Scotland's last state would have turned out to be worse, perhaps, than its first. Whatever else happened, one thing must never happen. The Protestant Reformation, whenever it might take place, must not fail. Even the prevailing state of affairs, the persistence of the " abominable idolatrie " of the Mass and Scotland's miserable enslavement to Antichrist and Babylon, was less hateful than the thought of a merely ephemeral triumph for his own cause. For Knox knew that in Scotland, at any rate, there were no second chances for Protestantism. Once it really failed, the enemy would be secure for centuries. When you at last get to close quarters with such a foe, you must strike a blow to kill, else you are as good as dead yourself. So Knox's pacific counsels on this occasion were also good military tactics.

Yet Knox, like any good soldier, hated retreat. No sooner had he set his face in the direction of Geneva again, than he began writing his women friends in Edinburgh, confessing the misgivings he felt about his *reculade*. In spite of all the excellent reasons he had for not going to Scotland, in spite of the near-impossibility of landing in safety, let alone accomplishing his mission, he had pangs of guilt and shame. After all, was he not fleeing from the battle? True, the general of an army must sometimes stay far behind the lines to direct operations; but in God's army was not every man a foot soldier? Had not his action been bolder than his words? Arriving in this mood in Geneva in mid-March, 1558, he champed at the bit, feeling that the bit was of his own making. The repressed urge for action was agony to his heart, however plausible the reasons his head might concoct for waiting and biding his time.

Thoughts of Scotland crowded into his mind, magnified, caricatured — thoughts of the bishops and friars still smugly sauntering down the High Street at home; still muttering the Mass; still shriving such miserable souls as still cared to be shriven. The insulting scene of the burning of himself in effigy inflamed him. Not least bitter were the echoes of the queen regent's mockery: "Please you, my lord, to read a pasquil." This was a capital offense in Knox's eyes, for he took himself so seriously that when others failed to do so he had no effective comeback. In his imagination he could hear the regent's words reverberate throughout the palace, to the accompaniment of the laughter of the courtiers; he could hear them gain resonance until they echoed from hill to hill the length and breadth of Scotland, the answer of a fool of a queen to the words God had put into the mouth of His prophet.

These thoughts, which had been developing for some time, were behind the best known of all Knox's pamphlets. He published it that summer under the title *The First Blast of the*

Trumpet Against the Monstrous Regiment [26] *of Women.* In
calling rule by a female "monstrous," Knox meant that it was
"unnatural." A monster is not necessarily wicked or hideous;
but it is irregular, not according to the rule of nature. In his
impotent anger at the whole situation he was compelled to
find a scapegoat. No doubt he was feeling tired of women in
general; the possessiveness of his innumerable women admirers who, like Mrs. Bowes, sought to mother him, could be irksome. And when a woman was set in a place of the highest authority in a nation, she could become, Knox felt, a positive
evil. It was Mary Tudor who had brought his work in England to nought, and she was still on the English throne. Childless, she was about to be succeeded by Elizabeth. In Scotland,
the place of the queen regent, Mary of Lorraine, would be
taken by her own daughter, whose marriage with the French
dauphin was already in prospect. Knox thought of the sighs
and groans of the patient, righteous, and reasonable men who
had suffered under such rule. Was it not petticoat government that was in large measure responsible for stemming the
tide of Reformation in those very lands over which it ought
to have swept triumphantly long ago? Knox was anything
other than a misogynist; but in sixteenth century Europe, in
which the father of a household was set in a place of definite
authority over his family, it did seem anomalous that a nation,
which is a large-scale family, should be under the governance
of a woman. Was it not then a nation without a head, in the
same case with a family that has to struggle without a father?
Such, at any rate, were Knox's prejudices, and they were natural enough according to the temper of his day.

On the other hand, the manifesto was plainly seditious, and
Knox, well aware of this, published it under every cover of
secrecy. There was no indication of the name of either author
or publisher. Calvin could and would never have tolerated its
publication in Geneva, where he exercised a strict censorship of
books. But Knox did not submit it to Calvin, to whom it would
have been embarrassing, to say the least. Calvin afterward dis-

[26] "Regiment" means "rule."

claimed any knowledge of it until a year after its secret publication. But if the *Blast* were embarrassing to Geneva, it had to be pilloried in England as a calculated incitement to the overthrow of the existing government. At the time of its appearing there was in fact a good deal of disaffection throughout that realm, and the English authorities, therefore, could not afford to ignore so dangerous a document. In a royal proclamation it was officially condemned. Anyone found in possession of it, and anyone into whose possession it came and who failed instantly to burn it, was liable to the death penalty under martial law.

The *Blast* began dramatically. It was a wonder, Knox said, that in the Isle of Great Britain that had produced so many great minds, so many godly men, so many preachers, so many men of learning and judgment, who were now exiled by Jezebel, none were found patriotic enough to speak out against the abomination of an empire ruled by a woman who was a traitress and a bastard. Was it wisdom to conceal the truth that it is monstrous for women to rule a kingdom? Then the ancient prophets of God had been fools. He had no choice himself: either he must offend God or else he must displease the world. Very well, the world must be displeased, for he was determined to obey God. " To promote a Woman to beare rule, superioritie, dominion, or empire above any Realme, Nation, or Citie, is repugnant to Nature; contumelie to God, a thing most contrarious to his reveled will and approved ordinance; and finallie, it is the subversion of good Order, of all equitie and justice." Knox could generally find a pious reason for almost any opinion he held; yet even he himself later on admitted to John Foxe, the author of the once-celebrated Protestant martyrology, that his argument in this case had been weak. In support of his contention he drew evidences from four sources: the authors of classical antiquity, the Roman law, the Bible, and the Fathers. But beginning with a show of logical argument, he quickly lost himself in wild denunciations. Man was strong and discreet; woman was weak and emotional: was it a good thing that the passions should rule the intellect? Had not Tertullian called woman the portal and gate of the devil?

98

Had not Augustine and Ambrose pointed out that through woman sin had entered the world? Had not Paul called man the woman's head? Nor was it only the Christian apostles and Fathers who had denounced woman. Knox could quote Aristotle and other pagan philosophers to the same effect. Indeed, one need only look at nature itself: did the lion stoop down before the lioness? But the day of vengeance was at hand for cursed Jezebel of England, with all her pestilent and detestable generation of papists that were making no little brag and boast. Their time would come. Let all men be advertised: the First Trumpet hath once blown.

This was an unwise pamphlet if ever there was one. Knox himself, as we have already seen, came to regard it as such when he had calmed down and considered the whole question in the light of a more sober judgment. Nevertheless, the modern reader ought to bear in mind that there was nothing in the pamphlet that sounded as ridiculous to the sixteenth century ear as some of it sounds to ours, else it need not have been taken quite so seriously by the authorities. Knox's views on women in government were almost exactly those of Jean Bodin, probably the greatest political thinker the sixteenth century produced, who in his *De Republica* says that women ought to be removed as far as possible from the majesty of government, for the rule of women is contrary to the law of nature, which has given to men prudence, strength, greatness of soul, and force of mind to govern, but to women has denied these gifts. Bodin reminds his readers of the distaste of the Romans for the presence of women in any assembly of state, and of how they resented even the action of Heliogabalus when he invited his mother to the assembly, not to vote or take part in it, but merely in the role of onlooker. To have a woman at the head of affairs seemed to Bodin to be the deepest ignominy into which a state could fall. Montaigne likewise disparaged women. So we must avoid supposing that there was anything extraordinary in Knox's attitude. If he was prejudiced, his prejudices were those of the age he lived in. Moreover, having his mind on his Bible, Knox left a loophole that his contemporaries did not provide; there were, he said in the

Blast, exceptions to the general rule: some women who, for reasons known only to God, were exempted from the ordinary disability of women as rulers of the state.

When it came to trying to get a passport to England, however, after Elizabeth had ascended the throne, this exception availed Knox nothing. Elizabeth was deeply offended by his pamphlet and never forgave him for it. So angry was she that she showed her displeasure not only to Knox himself but to all who were in any way associated with him, including Calvin. It was of the greatest importance for the Reformation cause in Europe that Elizabeth of England should look benevolently on its promoters, who put great hopes in her as a Protestant sovereign who from every point of view should have been their friend, patron, and ally. But when Calvin dedicated his *Commentaries on Isaiah* to her and sent her a copy, she received it with coldness, and Calvin discovered from her ministers that the reason was the queen's displeasure at his having permitted Knox's book to be published when, as she believed, he might have stopped it. Calvin did not wish to quarrel with Knox, and they always remained on terms of friendship; he believed, nevertheless, that Knox's unfortunate diatribe had lost Geneva its influence in England. This was not true of course: Elizabeth had little natural sympathy with either Geneva or Rome. However much the *Blast* affronted her, her policy would hardly have been different if it had never been written.

10 The *Blast* was followed by three other publications by Knox: a *Supplication* to the regent, embodying the letter she had despised as a pasquil, but showing much less deference; an *Appellation,* addressed to the nobles, against the condemnation by the Scottish bishops; and a *Letter to the Commonalty of Scotland.* In these four documents, Knox set forth an important development in his political doctrine. He had so far been fairly conservative. As we have constantly seen, he upheld the old doctrine of popular sovereignty as he had understood it from his teachers at St. Andrews. This doctrine was dependent on another old doctrine: the test of a people's right to rebel is whether their prince has flagrantly transgressed *justitia*, the justice on which the inalienable rights of all men depend. A sense of this justice is written into the heart of everyman. But from this doctrine of the natural law Knox now turned to what he called the moral law, " the constant and unchangeable will of God " as revealed in the Scriptures. This is indeed the very law of God, which all godly men must uphold, and which no man-made law may supersede or improve upon. Not only must the moral law not be contravened by the godly; no godly man may suffer either prince or thrall to frame laws that are inconsistent with it. Now, according to Knox, the Scriptures set forth the law of God that in the ordinary course of human affairs no woman may rule over a people. Deborah was an exception. Hers was a case of special divine ordinance. God, who is the source of his own laws, may make such special legislation, as he may likewise suspend the ordinary course of physical nature and bring about a miracle. But one is no more entitled to act as if such special legislation on God's part were to be considered normal than one is permitted to expect miraculous interventions on the part of God against the ordinary course of his providence. It was consequently not only the right but the positive duty of every godly man in Scotland to remove the queen regent and to execute the death sentence on any who should come to her defense. That a subject should have taken an oath of allegiance to her was no excuse from this duty. Such an oath *ought* to be broken, for no one ever had the right to make it, since it is contrary to God's law. One might as well plead that one is bound to steal because of an oath to do so. Furthermore, since a queen has no lawful authority to reign, she cannot, of course, convey any authority to anyone else, for example, her husband. This convenient consequence of Knox's doctrine would take care of the dauphin.

The exceedingly dangerous development in Knox's teaching in the summer of 1558 shows his resourcefulness when he felt himself thwarted in fulfilling the mission in which he believed. The "extreamitie" had come. He was prepared to go as far as Scripture could be made to warrant, and he could make Scripture warrant revolution; orderly, yet with sabers flashing if flash they must.

Such a revolution needed a further doctrine, which Knox provided in his *Letter to the Commonalty*. The commonalty that Knox addressed consisted chiefly of the intelligent, growing middle class to whom, in every land, the progress of the Reformation was to be most indebted. Knox warned them that the responsibility for dealing with corruption and idolatry rested as heavily on their shoulders as on those of the nobles. They must take their part along with the nobles in *compelling* the bishops to cease their tyranny over the souls of men. For while God had indeed ordained a distinction between rulers and people in the administration of civil affairs, yet all men were equal in the affairs that pertain to eternal life. Rulers and people alike are required to follow Christ, and there is not one of God's children so poor but that he can contribute to His tabernacle, nor is there any so rich he can do more than this. Moreover, the poorest subject may lawfully demand true pastors and preachers to take the place of the Roman wolves that devour Christ's flock, and if such true preachers are not provided by the rulers of the land, then they must be provided by the people themselves, who are also required to maintain and defend these preachers against persecution.

How was this to be accomplished, practically speaking? Knox provided some suggestions. For example, one might refuse to pay the tithes. "Ye may, moreover, witholde the frutes and proffets which your fals Byshoppes and Clergie most injustlie receyve of you, unto such tyme as they be compelled faithfully to do theyr charge and dueties, which is to preach unto you Christ Jesus truely, ryghtly to minister his Sacramentes according to his own institution, and so to watche for the salvation of your soules, as is commaunded by Christ Jesus hymselfe, and by his apostles Paul and Peter."

Knox was by no means unaware that even in the sixteenth century, when men were much less readily shocked than they are today by the idea of a holy war, the turn his doctrine was taking would offend many. But he believed it could offend only those who, being " carnal," did not see, as did the godly, the terrible reality that had to be faced. For centuries Scotland had suffered wrong and injustice at the hands of a cruel, ignorant, and greedy Church. That was bad enough, but in itself it could hardly have warranted the extreme measures he now proposed. What did warrant them was the recognition that it was not merely a question of injustice and wrong in the affairs of this transitory life. That the wicked should prosper and the righteous suffer in this life was nothing new. The righteous must expect to suffer. But they were being defrauded not only of the fruits of the earth but of their spiritual food, an infinitely more serious deprivation. This was the tyranny that justified the revolution.

Extreme as were the measures he now advocated, they were still, neither in intention nor in result, nothing like mere ruffianism. Knox was too much in deadly earnest to propose wanton slaughter. Anybody who hoped for a spree of free-lance killing was bound to be disappointed in Knox's program. For no individual had the right, still less the duty, to take God's law into his own hands. Knox was not looking for a dependable hooligan to set light to the tinder. But how then was it to catch fire? Reform in Scotland was to come about by revolution: how was the revolution to start?

Knox cast his mind back to the Scriptures once again. In olden times God had entered into a covenant with his ancient people, his elect people, Israel. The people of Israel had been bound to obey God's laws under the terms of this covenant, and they were no less bound to execute them. If such were the duties of the race that God had chosen as his own before the coming of Christ, could the duties of the spiritual race of God's elect be less obvious? And if God had entered into a covenant with the Children of Israel, in times past, was there not an even more sure and splendid covenant between God and his spiritual elect in Christ? The medieval political theory had been that between prince and people there was a pact, a covenant, under God. But was there not for the godly, the elect, a covenant above all others, the covenant between them and God himself? Acting under *this* covenant, God's own law, now written in the hearts of the godly, could be established as the law of the land.

This was a tremendous doctrine, but it was an interpretation of the democratic principles that had for long been taught by the medieval canonists, and democracy is itself a tremendous doctrine, however it be interpreted. Democracy had been to a great extent latent in medieval practice, and Knox's proposal would make it patent, according to a form of his own invention. The manifestoes of 1558 make it sound theocratic rather than democratic; but as it eventually worked out after Knox's triumph, it was, due to his own practical sense as well as his own personal limitations, less theocratic than it looked on paper.

The extent to which all this revolutionary propaganda really affected the course of events in Scotland in the year that followed its publication is questionable. Probably its influence was comparatively slight. A superficial reading of some passages in Knox's missives gives the impression that he had become virtually dictator to his Scottish followers. This was far from the case. Knox could assume an imperious tone. But the authority he had over the hearts of his followers was a pastoral authority, not a coercive one. No doubt it was all the mightier for that in the long run; still, he was a binnacle rather than a truncheon to the compatriots whose respect he now so abundantly commanded. The truth is that he had already so well exercised his prophetic influence over them that by the time he wrote the manifestoes of 1558 he had no need to write these: his followers had drawn the same conclusions for themselves and were taking steps to put them into effect. On December 3, 1557, they had, without any direct injunction from him, drawn up and signed a pledge " before the majesty of God " to foster the preaching of " the most blessed Word of God and His congregation," to provide regular pastors, and to defend these and the whole congregation " against Satan and all wicked power that does intend tyranny or trouble " against it. This was the first covenant. It could hardly have been more in accordance with Knox's mind had he framed it himself; yet it was done without him. Moreover, a very definite program was put forward. The Government was to be asked outright to sanction the reading from the English Prayer Book every Sunday in every parish church. Sermons and Bible-reading would take place in certain private houses. Sandilands of Calder was directed to present to the regent, in the name of the Congregation, a petition in which the signatories humbly asked that, since they had obtained the right, after long controversy, to read the Bible in the common tongue of the people, they be free to convene publicly or privately for common prayer in that tongue, so that they might commend to God " the Church Universal, the Queen our Sovereign," and the " whole Estate of this Realm." The signatories likewise asked for freedom to interpret the Scriptures at such assemblies. " And if any think that this liberty should be occasion of confusion, debate, or heresy; we are content that it be provided, that the said interpretation shall underly the judgment of the most godly and most learned within the realm at this time." The administration of Baptism and Communion should also be in the language of the people: " We desire that the holy sacrament of the Lord's Supper, or of his most blessed Body and Blood, may likewise be ministered unto us in the vulgar tongue; and in both kinds,[27] according to the plain institution of our Saviour Christ Jesus." Finally (and this they couched in the form of a demand, not a request) , " the wicked, slanderous and detestable life of prelates " and ecclesiastics generally must be reformed. " And if they suspect that we, rather envying their honors, or coveting their riches and possessions, than zealously desiring their amendment and salvation, do travail and labor for this reformation; we are content not only that the rules and precepts of the New Testament, but also the writings of the ancient Fathers, and the godly approved laws of Justinian the Emperor, decide the controversy betwix us and them: And if it shall be found, that either malevolently or ignorantly we

[27] That is, both bread and wine. The Roman Church had already for long refused the chalice to the laity, as it does today, in the Latin rite.

ask more than these three forenamed have required and continually so require of able and true ministers in Christ's Church, we refuse not correction, as your Grace, with right judgment, shall think meet." [28]

The regent temporized. Parliament, she promised, would consider Church reform. Meanwhile yet another extraordinarily stupid action on the part of the conservative forces took place, with the approval if not (as Knox would have it) by the command of the ecclesiastical authorities. An old priest, Walter Myln, said to be over eighty, was apprehended, accused of apostasy, condemned, and burned on April 28 at St. Andrews. He was a scapegoat. The effect of his martyrdom can well be imagined. It was just thirty years since young Patrick Hamilton had been burned in that town. Now they were burning a decrepit old man whose age made him harmless to every cause, but whose martyrdom was infinitely harmful to the old religion that now seemed more decrepit than he. The people began piling up stones by way of commemorating him. The authorities threatened excommunication for anyone who laid a single stone on the pile, and Knox says that when this failed, they had to come by stealth at night to take the stones away.

By the time Knox was writing his manifestoes from Geneva that summer, his supporters in Scotland, now deeply committed to revolution, were already carrying one of their own around the country for signature by every squire and burgess they could persuade to sign. They were likewise appealing to the common people to lend their support for the protection of the godly pastors from the fate of Walter Myln. The people's anger was not difficult to rouse. They had their own, less fastidious, way of expressing revolutionary sentiments. As they gathered in the old churches where the Reformation doctrine was being preached they answered in the time-honored way of those who are more accustomed to use their hands than their tongues or pens. They smashed windows; they pulled down statues. Had not the preacher denounced idolatry? It was their way of saying amen to his sermon. And in most of the old

[28] The date on which this petition was actually presented is obscure.

churches in which they forgathered and committed these acts of violence there was no parish priest or friar to remonstrate with them, for such was the ill-health of the Roman Church that many of its own buildings had fallen into neglect. In Edinburgh the angered mob threw the image of Saint Giles into the North Loch, paying no more heed to the priest who promised them everlasting damnation in hell for it than if he had been swearing at his horse. When at last, in July, the alarmed authorities summoned the preachers for trial, the summons was answered by armed bands. The regent ordered them south to defend their country against the English, who were still giving trouble on the Border Marches. But among the armed adherents of the Reformation cause were some gentry who had just returned from there, and they forced their way through to confront her with open defiance of the hierarchy. The atmosphere was electric: " every man put on his steel bonnet." The regent promised that the summons would be withdrawn on condition that the preachers make a public recantation on September 1, the Feast of Saint Giles, at the Mercat Cross in Edinburgh. Satisfied with the withdrawal of the summons, the armed men dispersed. But when the Feast of Saint Giles came, there were no preachers at the Mercat Cross, and the mob took the opportunity of openly flinging an image down the public street. During the following months, meetings for worship were held in private houses in Edinburgh, at one of which the provost of Edinburgh,[29] Lord Seton, took part.[30] The bishops convened to determine what might be done to stem the tide against them, and came forth with the announcement that one or two of the leading preachers were declared outlaws. In spite of the establishment by James V in 1532 of the College of Justice, a court of secular judges, the ecclesiastical authorities still took the right of making judicial pronouncements, especially, of course, in all matters concerning doctrine, in which they considered their judgment absolute and their

[29] The provost of a Scottish town is the counterpart of a mayor in the United States.
[30] Seton was not, however, as will be seen later, a supporter of the Reformed cause.

powers unlimited. Sentence of outlawry meant that anyone giving a meal or a night's lodging to the outlaw was liable to arrest.

The country was on the verge of civil war, but there were hopes that the Scottish Parliament might find some constitutional way out of the impasse. When it met on November 29, it had to consider a petition for the repeal of all acts that had conferred powers on the ecclesiastical courts to try heresy cases, which they had been doing on the principle that they had an absolute right to interpret the Scriptures, the Fathers, and every other authority according to their own judgment, and for the transference of all such powers to a secular court that would try these cases in due legal form and according to " the manifest Word of God." But Parliament had also before it very important business concerning the proposed marriage of the young queen to the French dauphin. There had been the usual, endlessly complicated intrigue; but so far as the hopes of Knox's party in Scotland were concerned, it came to this: once more the regent could not afford to lose the support of the ecclesiastical hierarchy. " She spared not amiable looks, and good words in abundance," to the petitioners, but pleaded that the time was peculiarly inexpedient for the consideration of their proposal. As soon as a more propitious time would come along, she would tell them what might be done, and meantime she would give them any personal support she could. It was the customary double-dealing; nor had the regent double-dealt for the last time.

Whether the petitioners put any trust or none in what she said, they withdrew their petition, and in its place they brought forward a document called a Protestation in Parliament. In this they simply claimed freedom in religion until such time as a reform of the Church might be properly undertaken. They took care, nevertheless, to assume no responsibility for any " tumult or uproar " that might arise from the religious toleration they sought to have written into the law; nor would they be answerable for what the extremists might do, for in the circumstances, having no power to restrain these, they could take no responsibility for their extravagances.

The regent declined to have this document registered in Parliament. Meanwhile, the act conferring the " crown matrimonial " on the dauphin was passed. Confident that all would be well in the realm as soon as French law and order would be more fully imposed on it, and unruly Scotland become an outpost in the empire of the French king, she had no notion of the nature of the force that opposed her will. Neither the carefully drafted petitions of the nobles and gentry calling for the reform that in principle she acknowledged to be most necessary, nor the wild uprising of the mob, suggested to her mind anything as strong as the spirit that in fact had stirred the heart of the nation to its most awesome depths. So when a paper was nailed to the gates of all the friaries demanding, in the name of the poor of the land, that these institutions be transferred to the poor, their only lawful proprietors, by next Whitsunday, she naturally paid even less attention than she had given to the more sober requests of the highly born. However, when the bishops resorted again to a summoning of the preachers, this time for trial on Candlemas at St. Andrews, she did restrain this action, perhaps adding a hint that it would be more effective at a later date when the country was more settled and the forces at the disposal of the authorities stronger than they now were. The sincerity of her desire for the reform of the Church, according to any ideals, Knoxian or Jesuit, may be judged by the fact that when certain valuable Church benefices fell vacant at the beginning of the year, through the death of her bastard stepson, she assigned them to her brother in France, the Cardinal of Lorraine, and then, as Lent approached, issued a proclamation that death would be the punishment for defiance of the Lenten fast.

One of the reforming preachers, Methuen, was working in Dundee, which was in the vanguard of the movement. After trying without success to have him quietly arrested there, the queen regent now issued a fresh proclamation, on Holy Thursday, to the effect that he and the other leaders were excommunicated and that any persons receiving the sacraments at their hands would share in their fate. Yet another summons was issued against them, requiring them to appear at Stirling on May 10. For one reason or another, her confidence in the military forces at her disposal had grown. Misinformed, perhaps, as she later persuaded herself, by the prelates, that the military strength on which she could count was much greater than in fact it was, she made a bid to do what for a time she had thought it wise to postpone — crush the troublemakers by the sword and so bequeath to France a less unruly colony. Perhaps, on the other hand, she was only trying to bluff the opposition into subjection. But the bluff, if bluff it was, was soon called. It was not long before she received alarming news that the preachers and their supporters were ready for fight, and since she had fully unmasked herself by her recent proclamations, duplicity would no longer help her. There was nothing at the moment for her to do but wait, cursing Knox in her heart, and all his works.

A week before the preachers were due to answer the summons to appear in Stirling, the bishops were sitting at table in the Dominican friary when a messenger rushed into the room. Breathlessly he uttered his report: John Knox himself was already in Edinburgh. He had come from France and arrived the previous day, May 2. The bishops rose abruptly from the table and walked out into the yard, chattering in consternation at the news. At last their instincts were right, for they had good reason for alarm.

11 Knox had left Geneva for the last time in January, 1559. The reason that it was May before he arrived in Scotland was that he was delayed at Dieppe because of the refusal of Elizabeth to grant him a passport to travel through England. No sooner had the English refugees at Geneva received the welcome news of Bloody Mary's death in November, 1558, than they made preparations to leave their exile and return to their native land. With her Protestant sister Elizabeth safely on the English throne, the security of all Protestants seemed to be guaranteed. Having met to offer thanks to God, the Genevan congregation sent one of their number to the various other centers of the Reformed faith in Europe where there were English refugees, such as Frankfurt, praying for forgiveness of past wrongs and expressing the hope that their former differences might be quickly forgotten in the joy of returning to the homeland. When these sentiments had been reciprocated, most of the English at Geneva left, some of them bearing letters from Knox to various acquaintances at the court of the English queen, requesting permission to travel through England on the way to Scotland. Then, in January, after various honors had been conferred on him, including the freedom of the city,[31] Knox departed, leaving his wife and family behind until he could ascertain with what safety they might make the journey.

It was in Dieppe that Knox learned to his astonishment that not only was he refused the passport, but that those who had made the request on his behalf narrowly escaped prison themselves. Elizabeth regarded them as associated with the man who had written the offensive *Blast*. Knox, who knew that his old Frankfurt enemy Cox, who had preached at Elizabeth's coronation, had helped to poison her mind against him, was so enraged that only his preoccupation with matters of greater moment saved him from reopening the old controversy. In writing the *Blast*, Knox had intended no personal affront to Elizabeth, who was probably not much in his mind at the time; but not unnaturally she had been easily enough persuaded that the offense had been directed to her. In a letter dated April 6 he wrote: " The second Blast, I fear, shall sound somewhat more sharp. . . . England hath refused me; but because, before, it did refuse Christ Jesus,[32] the less do I regard the loss of this familiarity. And yet I have been a secret and assured friend to thee, O England, in cases which thyself could not have remedied."

---

[31] This was a very high mark of respect. Calvin himself, eager though Geneva was to honor him, did not receive the freedom of the city until about a year later.

[32] Knox is referring, of course, to the Marian terror.

Why was he so eager to visit England instead of sailing directly from the Continent to Leith, the port of Edinburgh? Naturally, he wanted to visit old friends, especially those at Berwick. But he had another motive. He suspected, from information he had received, that the Scottish queen regent, being all out for the old policy of the closest possible alliance with France, was planning to support France in closing in on England. This would have meant not only the destruction of all English Protestant hopes but the ruin of Elizabeth herself. That Knox was right in his suspicions is confirmed by the fact that a year later Elizabeth herself, to the astonishment of some of her friends, gave ready assistance to the Scottish Protestants of whom Knox was the leader, in order to enhance the security of her own throne.

Knox decided to make a further bid for the passport. He wrote his old English acquaintance Cecil, that he might exert his influence to get the document for him. But Cecil had been a turncoat, and Knox, whose present temper was not at its best, and who in any case could never resist an occasion for sermonizing, wrote perhaps the most tactless letter of his life. Cecil, he declared roundly, was worthy of hell for his horrible defection from the truth during the Marian terror. Let him take care now not to trouble God's servants, otherwise he would " not long escape the reward of dissemblers." This was hardly the best way to ask for a passport! But it was characteristic of Knox, who, for all his practical sagacity and uncannily profound political insight, had no more sense of diplomacy than a forward schoolboy. He even told Cecil to tell the queen of England that she held her throne only on condition of humbling herself before that of God, and warned him that if he failed to communicate that message to her, he, John Knox, would not fail to tell the world of Cecil's failure. Knox himself must have recognized the arrogance of this extraordinary letter, for he had difficulty in getting anyone willing to carry it, and no sooner was it eventually dispatched than he sailed from Dieppe on April 22, bound for Leith and arriving safely in Edinburgh on the second of May, two days before the Feast of the Ascension.

From this time onward Knox was in the thick of the battle he had so long felt it was his destiny to wage. Now the undoubted leader of the Reformation cause in Scotland, he became a national figure of paramount importance in the life of his own people. In some ways his career up to this time seems unpromising as a preparation for the decisive role he was now called upon to play. Except for brief interludes he had been away from Scotland since the age of thirty-three. He was now forty-six. If his experience during these thirteen years had been such as to place him in positions at all comparable to the one he was now to have, or if he had been aide-de-camp to some Reformer abroad who was engaged in a comparable struggle, his long exile would not seem to matter in the least. But in England he had been in a singular position, the occupant of an honorable office in the Government service, preaching at the royal court, mixing with the great English statesmen of the day, and ministering to isolated congregations. The Geneva he knew was an intellectual center, a cosmopolis with a somewhat rarefied spiritual atmosphere. The congregations he had served there and at Frankfurt were no less abnormal, specialized fields of work. The man one thinks of as suitable for appointment as pastor of a group of exiles in a foreign city will have valuable qualities of a certain kind, but he is not likely to be the sort of man to lead his own nation at home. True, if he had needed toughening, the torments of the galleys and the troubles and anxieties of a sometimes fleeing refugee on the Continent of Europe would have provided it. But toughening is the last thing Knox would seem to have needed. What he would seem to have needed is, rather, a less itinerant and more settled life with abundant opportunity to serve some sort of apprenticeship in the leadership of a whole nation.

The Scotland to which Knox returned was small, poor, and backward. Corruption and misgovernment were turning the ancient pride of Scotsmen sour, and their spirit of independence into one of aimless rebellion. Transportation was exceedingly slow in those days, and mountain ranges could be remarkably effective in isolating various parts of the country from one another, notably the Grampians, which, running from the southwest to Aberdeenshire in the northeast, practically severed the country. The important centers were mainly in or toward the east: Edinburgh, St. Andrews, Dundee, Perth, and Stirling, all within a radius of about fifty miles; but beyond the mountains stretched inaccessible tracts of land, sparsely populated, and still further lay the home waters with their numerous islands even more sparsely populated. Though the area of Scotland is small,[33] the distance from the most southwesterly point to the farthest island in the northeast is considerable — comparable to the distance between Toronto and Richmond, Va. Such a country was by no means easy to control under sixteenth century conditions. Its very inaccessibility had been one of the circumstances that had prevented the English from ever subjugating Scotland, despite their greatly superior forces, persistent efforts, and occasional victories in the field. Yet it was this land that Knox held in the hollow of his hand within little more than a year of his arrival.

In such a difficult undertaking, Knox would seem to have needed above all a thoroughly dependable body of associates to support him: men of exceptionally high principles, outstanding loyalty and zeal, and pellucid clarity of vision; men in whom he could put almost unlimited trust. He was far from enjoying any such advantage. His colleagues, apart from the preachers, consisted of the Scottish nobility and gentry, who, mainly for financial reasons, were inclined to sympathize with his cause and assist in obtaining its victory.

The preachers were sincere men for the most part, but few of them, if any, were fitted for the conduct of the revolution that now seemed to Knox the only cure for Scotland's longstanding disease. One of his friends, Erskine of Dun, was a man of fine character, cultured, moderate, and disarming. But he had comparatively little influence. Lord James Stuart was a talented man who, as the bastard son of James V, had a special but not entirely advantageous position. Brave and ambitious, he was ready to sacrifice much of his wealth to the cause, but he was too cold-blooded to be very popular except with

[33] 30,410 square miles.

those already committed to the revolution. Maitland of Lethington was perhaps the ablest man in Scotland, yet he lacked integrity. A typical Renaissance figure, intrigue came so naturally to him that he does not seem to have been able to avoid it even by accident. In some other ways he was a caricature of the less attractive elements in Knox himself, with little of the Reformer's native goodness of heart. Argyll was loyal enough to the cause, but his personal life was sufficiently discreditable to embarrass it. One of the men who, had he not vacillated, might have been an immense help to Knox, was the former Regent Arran, who had relinquished the regency in 1554 in favor of the queen mother, Mary of Guise. But it was evident that he was a man who could be bought: the bribe of the dukedom of Châtelherault, which he accepted at that time, was but an instance of his instability from Knox's point of view. His eldest son, now Earl of Arran, was too feeble-minded for the question of trust to arise at all. He eventually lost his mind. Glencairn was an asset to the cause, on the whole, as also was Kirkcaldy of Grange; but it is doubtful whether Knox ever found them really very reliable. Ruthven was a notorious, bloodthirsty scoundrel, probably a neurotic, perverted type of man, and certainly by far the least trustworthy of the Lords of the Congregation who, even at the best, were not the men that any sane leader would have chosen had there been a choice. For Knox there was none. He had to lead a people in overthrowing an old order that had rendered them quite helpless. The unruliness of the mob, their readiness to vent their rage whenever they had leadership strong enough to encourage them, was by no means enough for Knox's purpose. Without all the aid he could possibly muster from the upper classes, he could not successfully wage his war. It was not for him to complain of the caliber of the lieutenants that Providence had provided.

That Knox could work with such men at all is a testimony to his own remarkable character. He was not an arrogant man, and few great men in history have been more conscious of their own shortcomings. He repeatedly accused himself of churlishness, and begged his friends to bear with it. He was subject to moodiness and depression; his temperament and his poor health both contributed to these fits of melancholy. But the worst of him was on the outside. His tenderness breaks through his prophetic vehemence, as sunshine through the storm clouds; his humble simplicity rises up from his dour determination, as the snowdrop through the hard winter earth. It was for these qualities that his friends loved him in their hearts, and none who followed him with even a shaky loyalty found him more difficult to love than to respect. For us to love him now, we have first to think ourselves back into the very different age in which he lived: to his own friends, having no such barrier, he was congenial. No doubt even his least satisfactory associates found him so in their hearts, seeing in him what their hearts yearned for, yet could not find in themselves, the man that the Hebrew poet had dreamed of, who would " reign in righteousness " and " rule in judgment," who would " be as a hiding place from the wind, and a covert from the tempest; as rivers of water in a dry place, as the shadow of a great rock in a weary land " (Isa. 32:2). Certain it is that the effect of Knox was what that old prophet had expected of such a man when he predicted that " the tongue of the stammerers shall be ready to speak plainly " (Isa. 32:4). For whatever Knox may have failed to do, he made his countrymen articulate.

But not yet. What is most awesome about Knox in the months that followed his final return to Scotland is that all the personal timidity he had hitherto displayed was gone. " I see the battle shall be great," he predicted in a letter to Mrs. Locke, " for Satan rageth even to the uttermost; and I am come (I praise my God) even in the brunt of the battle. Assist me, sister, with your prayers, that now I shrink not when the battle approaches." He sent her " the perpetual comfort of the Holy Ghost for salutation." He was right again. This was the real battle, and it was swifter than even he could have foreseen. It was now if ever that he needed these prayers for his personal courage, and it seems they were most bountifully granted.

Knox had arrived on Tuesday. On Thursday, the Feast of the Ascension, he proceeded to Dundee, which was crammed with Protestant sympathizers determined to protect the preachers from arrest by the authorities. On Saturday, Knox was publicly proclaimed an outlaw. The preachers were due at Stirling the following Wednesday. If they went alone, they would be instantly seized and almost certainly burned at the stake, for the authorities were now thoroughly frightened. On the other hand, for them to march into Stirling with an impressive escort would signify open rebellion, and perhaps Knox was the only man in all Scotland at this time to know that the state of rebellion had already begun. Since the march on Stirling could gain no general approval, it was decided that the sweet-tempered Erskine of Dun should go ahead to assure the queen regent that the marchers intended no harm to the authorities, but only the protection of the preachers. Meanwhile the preachers and their escort would proceed from Dundee to Perth, about halfway on the road to Stirling. Perth, on the river Tay and with access to the sea, was the only walled city in Scotland. It was an ideal place for a siege, if siege there was to be.

The queen regent had at her disposal only a small French army of less than two thousand men. Using her accustomed tactics, she had no difficulty in dealing with the conciliatory Erskine. She talked with him until many of the Protestants who had come to Perth with Knox decided that no news was good news and that, since there was evidently no danger in the offing, they could return to their own homes. Then, on the appointed day, Wednesday, she outlawed all the preachers for not coming to Stirling to answer their summons. When Erskine hurried back to Perth with this news of her perfidy, those who had remained there were fired with just that kind of indignation that Knox felt they should have had in the first place. On Thursday, in the historic Kirk of St. John Baptist, they heard Knox preach furiously against idolatry. Most of the gentry, having listened attentively, quietly left the church after the sermon was over. But a few remained, and the common people were slow in dispersing. A priest, endeavoring to win these back to the Roman ways, went forward, uncovered a rich altarpiece decorated with images of the saints, and began to celebrate Mass. A lad in the crowd repeated some vitriolic phrase from Knox's sermon, and the priest cuffed him sharply on the ear, whereupon the lad threw a stone at the priest. It missed its objective, but broke an image. The onlookers, sympathizing with the lad, determined to show their support, and within a few minutes the crowds loitering outside heard the noise of images being torn down all through the church and dashed in pieces on the ground. In a few minutes more the mob poured into the church, and this time they included not only sympathizers but every idler in Perth who relished the prospect of a good row. Soon the church was gutted, and the mob, having had their appetite for destruction whetted, looked further afield.

There were two friaries in the town, the one Franciscan and the other Dominican, besides the Charterhouse. This monastery had been founded in or about 1429, under King James I, who had brought the Carthusians to Scotland. More hermits than monks, these were little known to the people. But the friars were very well known to them, and for a long time there had been a feud between them and the citizens of Perth. As early as 1543 there had been a demonstration against the Dominicans when some persons had broken through the front gate of the friary, smashed open the door on the north side the cloister, entered the kitchen, and carried off their meal pan from the kitchen fire, to parade it up and down the town.

Instinctively the mob hurried off to the friaries, smashing images, looting silver and gold, meats and wines, stripping beds of their linen, pulling up young trees by the roots, and throwing friars out on the street. Fine fun, and profitable. None of the gentry took part, and the magistrates and preachers convened to try, but without effect, to persuade or restrain the rioters. A council was held in the evening at the town bridge, where Knox prayed, summoning the Carthusian prior to forsake idolatry and live according to the will of God as revealed in the Scriptures. The prior did not hearken; nor was the mob satisfied. It sacked the rich buildings of the Carthusians. The promise to the poor had been kept after all, in

118

Perth, at any rate. The posters that had been nailed to the gates of the friaries the previous year — posters that at the time had seemed childishly ridiculous, demanding as they did the transference by next Whitsunday of these properties to the poor, the lame, the blind — these posters seemed less ridiculous now, on Whitsun Eve, when the looting and destruction had been in fact accomplished. Such was the feeling in Perth on that Whitsunday that the town council deemed it prudent to prohibit the celebration of Mass on pain of death.

The queen regent, hearing of all this, knew now, if she had not known already, that the war was on. Mustering those of the nobles who were for the present on her side, she summoned the levies of Stirlingshire, Lothian, and Clydesdale, and marched on Monday, May 22, to Perth. Politically, she had an excellent case. She could appeal to the consciences of the pious adherents of the old religion, horrifying these with accounts of the sacrilege that had been done, while appealing at the same time to those who, while favoring the new religion, could be made to feel that the attack on the Charterhouse, a royal foundation, was the prelude to anarchy that would lay all Scotland low and, destroying all law and order, reduce the land to barbarism. Her armies, under the command of Châtelherault, now numbered about seven or eight thousand. She also enjoyed, naturally, the moral support of the whole body of the higher clergy of the old religion.

The Protestants were more than ready for her. Knox had, of course, remained in Perth, instructing those who, in his own words, were "young and rude in Christ." And when news of the queen regent's intended march on Perth reached him, he speedily got word out to the supporters who had prematurely returned to their homes. The Protestants mustered every man they could get, while in the name of "the Congregation of Christ Jesus within Scotland," Knox wrote manifestoes to the queen regent, to the French soldiery (among whom were evidently some Huguenots), to the nobility (of whatsoever religious inclination), and to the prelates. In the addresses to the queen regent and her armies Knox affirmed the loyalty of Protestants to the Scottish throne: all they asked was freedom to worship. To the nobility he wrote more ominously. They who were still unready for the new faith had better stop themselves and others from persecuting its adherents until the Protestant cause should be " tried in lawful and open judgment." He did not forget the nobles who, having embraced the Protestant cause, had since deserted it and " left us in our extreme necessity ": they had best come over again to the right side or they would be excommunicated from the Reformed Church. Knox warned them that the Reformed Church had this power. " Doubt ye nothing," he said, " but that our Church and the true ministers of the same have the power which our Master, Jesus Christ, granted to his apostles in these words, ' Whose sins ye shall forgive, shall be forgiven, and whose sins ye shall retain shall be retained.' " Cleverly he also reminded all the nobles who were supporting the queen regent that she was acting on her own authority, without consulting the young queen [34] in whose stead she was ruling the country. The Protestants would appeal, if need be, not only to the young queen, but to the princes and council of every realm in Christendom. In the letter to the prelates there was no need for such delicacy. Knox knew their hearts and their enslavement to the exceedingly profitable appointments whose duties they had so ill discharged. He began the letter to them accordingly in his plain language: " To the generation of Antichrist, the pestilent prelates and shavelings [35] within Scotland, the congregation of Jesus within the same saith." If the papists persisted in their cruelty toward the children of God, they should be treated as common murderers, and " we shall begin that same war which God commanded Israel to execute against the Canaanites; contract of peace shall never be made till ye desist from your open idolatry and cruel persecution of God's children."

Such plain language was unlikely to have any effect on the episcopal ears, but its effect on those of Knox's supporters was excellent. The Protestants swore to fight to the death. Most of

[34] Marie Stuart was sixteen and a half at this time.

[35] Clerics were " tonsured," that is, they had their heads shaved before being admitted to orders.

the men put a rope of flax around their necks in solemn token
that they would either hang the enemy or be hanged by him.
Victory or defeat it might be; surrender never. Knox had made
the men feel what Robert Burns was to express two hundred
years later in lines that have become famous as Scotland's national anthem:

> " Scots, wha hae wi' Wallace bled,
> Scots, wham Bruce has aften led,
> Welcome to your gory bed,
>   Or to victorie.

> " Wha will be a traitor knave?
> Wha can fill a coward's grave?
> Wha sae base as be a slave?
>   Let him turn and flee!

> " By oppression's woes and pains!
> By your sons in servile chains!
> We will drain our dearest veins,
>   But they shall be free! "

The Protestants had five thousand men at the most, but they
were dedicated. And by the time the queen regent's army had
reached Auchterarder, on the road from Stirling fifteen miles
short of Perth, the Protestants were taking up their position a
mile or two outside their city, ready to defend it to the last
drop of the last man's blood.

12 The queen regent, for all her shortcomings, was not
foolish enough to want to unleash civil war in Scotland if it could possibly be avoided. In hope of averting it at
the eleventh hour she sent Argyll and Lord James Stuart, who
were at this time on her side, ahead of her forces to offer
Knox terms. These had a familiar ring: if the Protestants
would evacuate Perth, she would not suffer a single French soldier to enter the town. There were comings and goings. Knox
was not under any illusion about the queen regent's intent.
She was certain to break her word, he said. He thundered at
the mediators with such conviction that they promised to re-

main with the Protestants and, if Mary failed to keep her word, come over to the Protestant side and fight with Knox's men. It was an interesting offer. Knox knew that the responsibility for the impending battle was in question: in the eyes of the world, at any rate, a battle now would be at least as much his responsibility as hers. If he accepted the terms, he would be only postponing the fight, but the responsibility for the bloodshed would be entirely shifted to the enemy. Moreover, he would acquire two important, if not hitherto wholly reliable, lieutenants.

Meanwhile, news of his manifestoes had reached Glencairn and other Protestant leaders who had not been associated in the fray at Perth, having been in Ayrshire in the southwest. Resolved to bring Knox what help they could, they mustered an additional force of some two and a half thousand men and were soon in Glasgow. Since the Stirling road was blocked by the regent's armies, Glencairn's had to take the more difficult western route across the mountains. This detour had delayed them; yet by the time Argyll and Lord James had returned to Perth to conclude the arrangement Knox had decided to make, they found the supplementary forces of Glencairn already there. Knox, having promised nothing but the evacuation of the Protestant armies from Perth, saw that the forces left. Not, of course, without sermon: the war, he warned them, was not over; rather, the fighting had not yet begun. Argyll and Lord James waited to see what would happen. Glencairn and a few of the Protestant nobles and gentry also remained. Knox himself went off to preach in neighboring towns, waiting for Mary to break her word.

He had no longer to wait than he expected. On Monday evening, as the queen regent entered the town, attended by Châtelherault, her soldiers let off their muskets. A shot accidentally killed a child standing at a window. A bad start. Then, finding that the town council had forbidden the celebration of the Mass, an action she could not condone and at the same time keep the favor of the clergy on whom her power largely depended, she appointed a new town council. Since these must have a garrison of soldiers to protect them, she provided one. Not French soldiers, for that would have been against the letter of her agreement; no, they were Scottish soldiers on the French pay roll.

She need not have taken the trouble to make so fine a distinction. The presence of any of her soldiers was good enough to convince Argyll and Lord James that they were on the wrong side, and on Wednesday, May 31, they formally espoused the Protestant cause and promptly left the city, riding in the direction of St. Andrews. Mary sent after them, and they answered her with contempt: they could not, they said, be associated with " so manifest tyranny as by her was committed," or with " so great iniquity as they perceived devised by her and her ungodly Council the Prelates." Mary received this message of defiance on June 1, while the turncoat nobles, taking the lead, were on their way to St. Andrews, rousing the Protestants from the countryside around them as they went.

It was perhaps Knox himself who had suggested the lead they ought to take in the event of their seeing the light when Mary exhibited the perfidy he so confidently expected of her. St. Andrews was second only to Perth in physical advantages as a place of siege. As the ecclesiastical capital, it was second to none for dramatic demonstration. But for Knox it was more than all that. His prophecy in the galleys that had seemed such an empty boast had gone unfulfilled for eleven years. Surely now was the time to fulfill it. Though the Protestant side was still weaker than he could have wished, it was strong enough for this, if his supporters could get there in time, before the armies of the regent. Besides fulfilling his own prophecy, he would be sanctifying the air the Beatons had polluted by their infamous cruelties on two Protestant saints and martyrs, Hamilton and Wishart.

But there was no time to lose, for the regent's armies were already on the march, and by the time Knox prepared to preach in St. Andrews they were at Falkland, only eighteen miles away. Archbishop Hamilton, successor of the hated Beatons, was well aware of the kind of trouble that was brewing. Whatever else happened, Knox must be prevented from preaching. Gathering his colleagues, he and they, taking with them a hundred armed men, went to confront the Protestant Lords on the Saturday evening before the day Knox was to preach. It was the Archbishop who had ordered Knox to be burned in effigy three years before. That Knox should now preach in the Archbishop's own church was a personal affront. If he as much as showed his face near the church, the Archbishop threatened, he would be met with fire from a dozen muskets "whereof the most part should light upon his nose."

The Lords were uneasy. The Protestant supporters at hand were still scanty, and the regent's armies were rapidly approaching the town. Moreover, the sympathies of the townsfolk were as yet by no means assured: much more hostility was expected than had been met at Perth. Would it not be more prudent to delay the promised preaching? They communicated their misgivings to Knox, urging great caution and reminding him of the horrors that might befall him. Had it not seemed a piece of personal effrontery to the Archbishop, the case against his preaching might not have been so strong; but they begged him to remember that it was a question of a prelate's pride, and none knew better than Knox how dangerous it was to touch that.

But Knox could not be put off at this stage. Since he had left Perth he had been keeping his armor bright by preaching rousing sermons in the small towns of Craill and Anstruther. No man could stop him now. Very rarely did he ever allude to the tortures he had endured in the galleys, for he was too independent in spirit to seek any man's compassion; but in his reply to the Lords on this occasion he did hint at the horror of them, while observing that now was no time for a recitation of personal trials. The point was that God had, "above the expectation of many," spared him and brought him back at last to the place where He had first called him to the office of a preacher, so he begged them not to stand in his way on pretext of protecting him. Seeing that God had so plainly offered him the occasion to preach at St. Andrews, the custody of his body should be left to God. Because he felt all this so strongly, he had no fear of the Archbishop. It was for God's sake he was to preach, not to spite an enemy. "God is my witness," he declared, " that I never preached Christ Jesus in contempt of any man."

So Knox did preach that Sunday. His text was on the Gospel incident about the money-changers whom Christ threw out of the Temple. Was it not the duty of Christ's people today to follow the example of their Saviour? Were not the abominable papists worse than the money-changers Christ had ejected? Surely they ought to be expelled no less unceremoniously from the house of God which they had defiled for generations. The sermon drove straight home to the people's hearts. They were so hostile to the old religion that they needed but a fearless word to encourage them to action. The effect was much the same as that of the sermon at Perth. The people tore down everything they could; then, as before, they burst into the friaries. But the vandalism and the looting could not have been, even in the later stages, entirely thoughtless. For the people ended by choosing as the site for a bonfire of the images they had collected the place where, only the previous year, poor Walter Myln had been burned alive, a harmless octogenarian, for preaching the gospel of Christ.

Knox was not burned for what he preached; nor did one of the muskets the Archbishop had threatened light upon his nose. So skillful had been his presentation of the theme that even those magistrates and others who conservatively adhered to the old religion sat silently through his sermon and offered no effective resistance to the action that followed. The truth is that in all his campaigns Knox's hearers were already half converted before they heard him. The Archbishop, thinking better of his threat, hurried off instead to tell Mary. While Knox went on with his preachings for days on end, Mary's forces approached Cupar, ten miles off. Argyll and Lord James decided to try to hold Cupar with, at first, only a hundred horse. The state of the Protestants was exceedingly grave. The forces they had sent for throughout the neighboring counties did not seem to be coming.

Then suddenly, during the night, the musters arrived. From Angus, north of the Tay, they were pouring in as hoped for. But there were others streaming in from the south, too; many from the Lothians. Ruthven rode in from Perth. All Fife was rising, including even the Provost of Falkland, where Mary's armies had passed. "God did so multiply our number," Knox wrote afterward, "it appeared as men had rained from the clouds."

The regent and her armies, unaware of this development, were complacent. They expected to outnumber the rebels easily. Dawn came, a misty one. The regent's forces could see only some spears on the slope beyond the Eden stream at Cupar Muir. Jauntily, they edged round toward St. Andrews. Some hours later, the mist lifted. The Protestants had an impressive force, with artillery moving into position to command their line of advance. Who might win such a battle, with the forces showing no marked superiority on either side, was anybody's guess.

The commander of the queen regent's forces, D'Oysel, had hoped for a chance to harry and rout a band of insurgents: he had not bargained for doing battle with a foe of equal or perhaps greater strength than his own army. Messages came in, meantime, from France. The French king would be pleased to send as much help as possible if the rebels were really menacing the royal authority; if, however, it was only a question of religious rebellion, then . . . no promise of aid from France. In such a case the French would be for a broad policy of moderation and tolerance. Moderation and tolerance! Little did France know of what had happened to Scotland's temper. The queen regent was concerned, rather, to know whether she dare even play for time. But an armistice was arranged, an eight-day truce of a sort. The regent hoped her armies might be able to retreat from their difficult position. They withdrew toward Edinburgh, leaving nothing in the north but a small garrison in Perth.

Knox's side had forces that were less manageable. It had no regular troops. The unruly Lords of the Congregation and their still more unruly musters could not be expected to sit idling while the regent looked for terrain more to her liking. Soon a party of Protestants went off to Lindores Abbey near St. Andrews and sacked it. Moving on to Perth, they easily subdued the garrison and took possession of the town. Others marched to Scone,[36] not far from Perth, and Scotland's old-time capital. But when news came that the regent was re-occupying the Forth bridges, it became plain that there was no time to lose. Argyll and Lord James sped off south to Stirling.

Meanwhile the mob fury that had been roused spilled all over central Scotland north of the capital. By Friday morning, June 30, Argyll, Lord James, Ruthven, and Rothes, followed by Glencairn, rode into Edinburgh with a force of six thousand men. The queen regent had gone to Dunbar, a coast town southeast of the capital. Her own troops were on the verge of mutiny; her counselors had no counsel left in them but to appeal to the French King Henry II to send Marie Stuart and the dauphin to see whether their presence in Scotland might alleviate the uproar. Even this was too late. The day before the Protestants had entered Edinburgh, the French king had been fatally wounded in a tournament and in little more than a week afterward he died, bringing Francis II, Marie Stuart's husband, a sickly, adolescent half-wit, to the throne of France. On Saturday, July 1, John Knox was holding forth in St. Giles's, the premier church of Scotland's capital. Lord Seton, the provost of Edinburgh, who had in the past greatly troubled the preachers and had taken upon himself the duty of protecting the friaries from the anger of the uprising poor, cleared out of the town when he heard of Knox's coming, and by the time the Protestants arrived the mob had already sacked the churches and friaries, leaving scarcely as much as a door or window in the naked walls.

13 Knox always sought to disown responsibility for the excesses of the " rascal multitude." Even his most fervent admirers, however, can hardly pretend that his self-exoneration is altogether successful. On the other hand, his de-

36 Pronounced " scoon "; it does *not* rhyme with " stone."

tractors overlook the fact that his patently sincere concern about the matter makes it difficult to believe he was a vandal at heart. Calvin, whose approval he always wished to have, never condoned the destruction or pillage of property belonging to others. A man might have the duty to destroy property belonging to himself; the duty of destroying other people's was another matter. When a French preacher at Nîmes, Tartas by name, declared that he felt bound in conscience to destroy images and the like, not his own property, Calvin told him in effect that he was talking nonsense. God imposed no such duty. Moreover, Calvin was evidently inclined to believe that a man who shows himself recklessly unappreciative of the heritage of the past reveals himself to be unworthy to exercise any authority in the present.

This was, in theory, Knox's own view. Neither did he with his own hand deface or destroy any images or other appurtenances of the old religion, nor did he directly enjoin any such action. He must certainly have known, however, that his sermons would inflame the passions of others who would have no qualms about vandalism. He might have used his eloquence to inveigh against vandalism as he inveighed so convincingly against idolatry, instead of merely commenting regretfully afterward on the wantonness of the rascal multitude; but he did not. While it is not easy to defend Knox on this score, it is not difficult to offer a plea in mitigation of his behavior. He had been brought up from boyhood to listen to endless criticism of the old religion. Disputations about the notorious and universally recognized evils in the Church were part of the regular pabulum of his training at the university. But disputations had never answered the question that had been on the lips of everyone since ever he could remember, the question how the sorely needed reformation could actually be brought about.

In *The Satire of the Three Estates,* a morality play by Sir David Lindsay of the Mount, who was about twenty-seven years old when Knox was born, Gude Counsel tells Spiritualitie (the Church) :

> " We came not here for disputations:
> We cam to mak gude reformations! "

The satire was performed at Linlithgow Palace on the Feast of the Epiphany, 1540, before James V and Mary of Guise. For all the latter's subsequent persecution of Knox, neither she nor her husband had any illusions about the shortcomings of ecclesiastics, and it is reported that James V made the performance of the play in 1540 the occasion for lecturing some of the bishops about their unedifying conduct. But it is one thing for royalty to scold pachydermatous prelates; another for a none too secure monarch to liquidate the most conservative buttress of his power in the realm. Knox had heard the Church scolded all his life; he knew that it had been scolded before he was born, in his father's day — yes, and his great-grandfather's. Nothing had come of it but an increasing cynicism. Knox himself had for years taken the passive way. Not until early middle age had he openly committed himself to even a Wishart's scholarly and moderate enunciation of Reformation doctrine. Only very gradually, in the course of the years of his suffering and trial, had these doctrines so filled his consciousness that he could steel his will to " make reformation " *at all costs*. Now he felt he must be put off by nothing, for he had come to believe that failure to achieve the reformation of the Church was the root evil whence sprang all others, whether in the body politic or in the individual hearts of men.

As the war developed he quickly recognized that it was what in our own day we have learned to call *total* war, war to the death between those who desired to " make reformation " and those who wished to impede this godly end. He no more believed that everything done by every soldier on his side was righteous in the sight of God than would anyone today pretend to defend everything that was done in the war against Hitler. But he did most earnestly believe in the essential righteousness of his cause, and the righteousness of going to war to defend a righteous cause from a centuries-old tyranny. Knox felt that if he was to hold together those who were " young in Christ " long enough to destroy the tyranny and make reformation possible, he must let the mob express its passions in its own way. The responsibility for this, though not negligible, was surely light indeed compared with the responsibility in modern times for Hiroshima, or even the release of a single torpedo. If anyone within Germany had succeeded in 1939 in overthrowing the Hitler regime at the sacrifice of some of Germany's art treasures, he would hardly have been reproached for his lack of squeamishness. All things considered, the parallel is not unfair.

These reflections are necessary for a real understanding of Knox's heart in the situation in which he now found himself. After two months of war, he had succeeded in leaving the imprint of victory on the ecclesiastical headquarters of the land whose Church he had determined to purify. He had carried the war into the very heart of the capital, and was now holding forth in the pulpit of a church within sight of the royal palace itself. But his cause was still very far from final triumph; indeed, it suffered from weaknesses that few saw as plainly as did he. In the far north and elsewhere there were considerable elements that for one reason or another might be counted upon to support the established order in some future showdown, probably not far ahead. While the extent of such possible resistance to the Protestant campaign was difficult to determine, it would have been less than reasonable for him to have felt that the war was even half won. His caution probably dictated to him a much more pessimistic estimate.

The first stage of the war had been comparatively easy. Using what aid he could get from the nobles, and reinforcing this with the violence of the mob, he had achieved a remarkable triumph for a side that had no regular troops at its disposal. But there was still no area that could be pointed out on a map as being definitely in Protestant hands. All that could be said was that there were certain important regions where sympathy had been roused and eloquently expressed. There were, however, too few preachers for the spiritual nourishment of even these areas. In the practically bloodless warfare he had conducted, Knox had been able so far to raise a very fearsome-looking force against the established authorities; but these had only to get some money and a few shiploads of mercenaries from France to massacre the Scottish Protestants as Catherine de Médicis was to massacre the French Huguenots thirteen years later on Saint Bartholomew's Day.

The regent would certainly get help from France, limited, no doubt, but adequate. Very well: Knox must get help from England. It was a pity about the *First Blast,* for he could hardly expect to have any more favor in Elizabeth's eyes now than he had had the previous year when she had refused him even a passport. On June 28, however, he wrote to Cecil saying that he knew very well how odious he had become to the queen's Grace; nevertheless he would persist in seeking her help. He got his old friend Kirkcaldy, who had defected from the Protestant side but had recently returned to it, to write to influential friends in England, explaining what had been done, what it was proposed to do, what help was needed, and how England would benefit from the reformation that was being " made " in Scotland. Kirkcaldy was honest, yet tactful. Knox was certainly no less honest. How lacking he was in the fashionable diplomacy may be judged from the fact that in a letter to Elizabeth a few weeks later he counseled her to forget her high birth and the privileges it entailed, and reflect, rather, on how she had, through cowardice, bowed to idolatry. What party could have put up with the leadership of such a man, had not his other qualities far outweighed his incorrigible forthrightness?

Knox and his friends were intriguing with the English court as victors who, though they might not be liked by all concerned, had something to offer of great advantage to England. The terms offered were in fact advantageous, or, rather, would have been had the Protestants been in a position to be offering anybody any terms at all. In fact they were not; they were bluffing. Knox's intentions were honest enough in their way. Not yet master of Scotland, he was not in a position to negotiate with England; but he hoped to be master of Scotland very quickly indeed if he could get England to negotiate with him: why cavil at the chronological order of the steps? At this stage in his career Knox reminds one of the bank clerk who wanted to marry the daughter of the bank president, who in turn would not consent to letting him have his daughter's hand until he had attained a more important position; whereupon the suitor got an appointment as vice-president of another bank on the strength of being engaged to the daughter of the president of the first. Knox has, for once, an almost Gilbertian flavor; no more unlovable because of this, but certainly a little comical.

By the middle of July, there remained in Edinburgh only fifteen hundred of the six thousand men who had entered the capital. Once again, having no regular troops, the Protestants had been unable to hold their forces together; once the emergency seemed over, many drifted away. Unhelpful rumors were circulating, such as that the Protestants were backing Lord James Stuart for the Scottish throne. Then quite suddenly, on July 23, the regent's forces, twice as strong as those available to the Protestants, marched on Edinburgh from Dunbar, under the command of Châtelherault and D'Oysel.

Leith, Edinburgh's seaport, had promised to support Knox. When the men of Leith saw Mary's army approaching, however, they fired a solitary, token shot, and surrendered. Meanwhile the Lords of the Congregation and their army took up their position on Calton Hill in Edinburgh and watched the enemy approaching along the road from Leith. Another truce, and once more gracious clemency from Mary, for clemency was still the correct card to play. She was not nearly strong enough yet for burning preachers in face of the present climate of opinion. She had accused the Lords of the Congregation of seizing the royal palace of Holyrood in Edinburgh and the royal mint. If the Protestants would kindly return the coining irons, depart from the capital within twenty-four hours, and cease inciting the mob to wreck monasteries and trouble the clergy, she would undertake to let the capital choose its own form of religion, and she would see that the preachers were not molested. Then Parliament, meeting on January 10, the following year, should consider the whole question.

The terms in themselves were generous in the circumstances; but for men who were presently offering terms of their own to the powerful English Government they were too humiliating for the Protestants to wish to see widely published. They accepted them, for there was nothing else to be done, and Knox was encouraged by his infinite trust in Mary's perfidy. But before leaving Edinburgh, the Protestants tried to whitewash the terms by publicly proclaiming them with a couple of imaginary ones added, to the effect that the old religion should not be restored where it had been already abolished, and that the French army should be sent away after a time and never allowed to return to Scotland without the consent of the entire nobility. This was not true, since Mary had not given any such undertaking; but it was not, perhaps, such a barefaced lie as it sounded. For once again two of the most important nobles supporting Mary had promised to come over to the Protestant side if the regent broke her promise. This time they were Châtelherault himself and Huntly, and Châtelherault had added that he would come over in any case if the French army was not sent away within a reasonable time. Still, what the Protestants gave out was, to say the least, an inexactitude that even their warmest sympathizers would have to call very like a lie. Knox did not believe that the end justified any means (he was too farsighted as well as too moral for that); but he was not too fastidious about the means, especially when the shadier deeds for the cause were done by men who would have been doing shady deeds in any case.

The events that followed are so complicated that their labyrinthine course is beyond the scope of this account of the story of John Knox. The men Knox worked with were, we have already noticed, by no means an exemplary crew. What they expected of him as a leader was that he walk among them blamelessly and cultivate a good deal of myopia wherever their dirtier work was concerned. There is no doubt that Knox often fulfilled this role for them. He had no great personal difficulty here: had not God allowed evildoers to fulfill his purposes in ancient times? But Knox went farther. In his own account of the history of these doings he showed no scruples against portraying the deeds of the Lords of the Congregation as all wholesome and purely motivated, as though these noblemen had kept their integrity in defeat and victory alike. The truth is that many of them had no integrity to keep. The more astonishing truth is that the characters of the nobles whose murkier treacheries and dissimulations Knox had to soft-pedal where he could and disguise where he felt he must — the characters of these nobles improved under his influence to such an extent that what he had been saying of them when he had to whitewash them became actually true in many cases. And after all, Knox was not the only man of his age to go in for pragmatistic history-writing.

In the next few months Knox was kept so busy with the intrigues of his associates that he wrote about this time to Mrs. Locke, saying that it was only with difficulty that he could snatch an hour in the whole week for personal recreation or relaxation with his friends. At the end of July he sailed to Holy Island off the English northeast coast, where he had a secret tryst with the Governor of Berwick, who was acting for Cecil. He had not been long on the island before his whereabouts were known to the queen regent. Apprised of this, Knox left for Stirling on August 3 with a companion, Whitelaw. Whitelaw took ill on the way back; Knox went on ahead, and when Whitelaw recovered and continued his journey he was chased for three miles by Lord Seton, who was evidently under the impression that he was chasing Knox. At one stage of the pursuit, Lord Seton got close enough to break a chair over what he thought was Knox's head.

As a result of the intrigues with England, which Knox's associates (especially Balnaves) managed very much better than he was able to do, the English Government gave the Reformers three thousand pounds and the promise of more. More important, however, Arran arrived in Scotland, and his father, Châtelherault, came over to the Protestant side. A thousand French troops arrived in Leith, followed in a few days by eight hundred more. Mary was feverishly preparing to fortify Leith. This was a breach of what the Lords of the Congregation had said the treaty was. Certainly her intentions were clear enough, and if the Protestants were ever going to fight it would have to be now.

Seven or eight thousand strong, their forces entered Edinburgh on October 16 and peremptorily ordered the queen regent to send the Frenchmen back. She replied to the effect that princes gave orders to their subjects, not subjects to their princes. The Protestant leaders held a meeting in the Tolbooth in Edinburgh on October 21 and invited Knox and some other preachers to be present, for they were now to consider whether it would be proper to depose Mary. Knox was not enthusiastic about this proposal. She ought to be given an opportunity to repent. But the Lords of the Congregation felt that Knox was being unduly fastidious. They took to heart, however, his reminder that the true sovereigns of Scotland, the young Marie Stuart and her husband Francis, must not be overlooked. On October 24, the Lords formally deposed Mary from the regency. From the Mercat Cross came a proclamation that by the " Nobilitie, Baronis, and Broughes convenit to advise upoun the affairis of the commoun-weall," Mary of Guise was suspended from the regency of Scotland. The grounds were her tyrannical sacrifice of Scotland to France. This was a clever device, for while there was very widespread sympathy with the Protestant cause throughout Scotland, there was a still more open dissatisfaction with the increasing subservience of Scotland to France that Mary was encouraging. It was given out that the deposition of the regent was in accordance with the wishes of Scotland's young sovereigns now in France. The Protestants even got a goldworker to forge the royal seal, and by their assumed authority they commanded such nobles as had not yet come over to their side to obey Arran, until such time as the young sovereigns could come to take their Scottish throne. To justify themselves in the sight of the world at large, they also composed a long address in Latin to the princes of Christendom, recounting the grievous wrongs done to Scotland by France under Mary of Guise.

It was perhaps the most audacious piece of bluff ever perpetrated by a band of well-born desperadoes. No wonder that Knox, still thundering daily in the pulpit, complained that he could not get time enough even for sleep. No wonder he wrote to a friend in England: " Mack ye advertisement as ye think

good, for I cannot write to any, especiall for lack of opportuni-
tie; for in twenty-four hours I have not four free to naturall
rest and ease of this wicked carcass."

14 Knox's final victory was now in fact around the corner; but the process of turning that corner was the
most arduous and painful experience of his life. In a dark hour
he wrote that now the troubles of a single day were worse than
the months of torture in the galleys. From October, 1559,
when the Protestants marched into Edinburgh and deposed
the queen regent, until about Easter of the following year,
it was impossible to tell what a day might bring forth, and
it was often a reasonable guess that it could bring forth only
disaster for the cause of the Reform.

That it was Knox's granite determination as a leader as
much as the rallying power of his eloquence as a preacher
that enabled him to win in the end and retire, as he did early
in 1560, from the political intrigues at which he had always
been so clumsy, is well demonstrated in his negotiations with
Sir James Croft, the Captain of Berwick. Not a little of his
strength lay in the fact that, being anything other than a diplomatist, he not only could give snubs but he could take them.
Perhaps his ability to take snubs was a sort of passive insolence. It was not that he was insensitive. We have seen how
bitterly he resented the levity of the queen regent's scorn. We
have also seen how, in a practical situation, his blundering
forthrightness could seem to be an almost intolerable liabil-
ity for his cause, for he trod on all toes, having indeed, it appeared, a preference for royal toes. But that very forthrightness had an advantageous side, for when he received snubs
that would have put others off their game, Knox could let
them roll very lightly off his back. To try to put Knox off with
a snub was like attacking a crocodile with a peashooter.

Knowing that the Protestants were holding the capital so

flimsily that the enemy could destroy them at any moment with its little finger, Knox wrote to Croft. In characteristically ponderous language he outlined a proposal that, though it was impossible for England to send official help, now that it had a treaty with France to respect, it might nevertheless send money and encourage Englishmen to volunteer in the Scottish Protestant cause. To Croft, who had of course already thought of this, it was no doubt irritating to have such an obvious idea expounded to him as though it would never have occurred to anyone but Knox. Taking the opportunity of satirizing Knox's preachiness, he affected to sermonize in reply, to the effect that it was very wicked of the Reformer to propose such an unscrupulous dishonoring of the spirit of the English treaty with France. How could a wise man like Knox suppose, he asked, that England could do such a thing? Pleased with his efforts, Croft told Cecil how he had snubbed Knox, and Cecil was delighted, but told Croft to act according to Knox's proposal. Meanwhile, Knox, no doubt well aware that Croft's tongue had been in his cheek, and that he was only indulging in a little private sarcasm, wrote back that Croft's attitude was quite reasonable, but it was nevertheless a pity he could not have English help.

English money was soon forthcoming, and the Protestant cause seemed strengthened by the desertion from the enemy camp of Maitland of Lethington, the queen regent's own secretary. Maitland took over the administrative work of the Congregation, relieving Knox for his proper role as prophet. Nevertheless, for one reason or another, Maitland's administrative experience did not seem at first to help. Everything went wrong for the Protestants. The queen regent's spies intercepted the English money, and there was mutiny among the Protestant troops. On November 5 some five hundred Protestant soldiers assisted in an ill-advised assault on the Leith garrison, and, abandoning their artillery, were forced to retreat in panic back to Edinburgh, whither the French pursued them, slaying all, men and women, who stood in their way. The Protestant leaders made valiant bids to mitigate the disaster. Lord James and Arran, hearing that the French were making to intercept a food convoy, led out the cavalry to try to disperse them, but the French forces were too well deployed, so that it was only with luck that the retreating army survived at all. Their casualties were heavy, and there were mass desertions in the ranks. As the mob saw the Protestants now getting the worst of it, they jeered at them as the retreating Congregation, Knox among them, hastened along the road toward Stirling on a cold winter's night.

In all this, nothing grieved Knox more than the raillery of the mob that had turned against the Protestants in their hour of need. Using the slogans the priests had taught them, bystanders in the streets shouted names at the Protestants; they called them traitors and heretics, and even threw stones at their heads. Knox had little reason, in his later policy, to trust a mob that could be as easily incited against him as by him. " God move their hearts to repentance," was his prayer.

The following day in Stirling, his prayer took the form of the eightieth psalm, on which he preached a magnificent sermon: "Thou makest us a strife unto our neighbors: and our enemies laugh among themselves. Turn us again, O God of hosts, and cause thy face to shine; and we shall be saved." There were three reasons why God had allowed his servants to be exposed to the shame of defeat. First, God wished his people to have a taste of his wrath on the traitors in their midst; secondly, God wanted his people to recognize how helpless they were without divine aid; thirdly, God desired to furnish later generations of his people with a testimony to both the devil's malice against God's elect and God's own marvelous ways of providing deliverance. It was tempting to suppose that God had been deaf to the prayers of his own people. It was a natural thought. Only by the power of the Holy Ghost could a man resist the temptation to think that thought. In hours such as these, the reprobate among them would fall by the wayside; only the elect would be sustained. Already defections had occurred in plenty. Would there be more? If so, the sooner the better. For God desired a wholly consecrated people to whom to give victory. In his wisdom *he* knew who would be loyal and who would betray the cause. *They* could not know unless God made it plain to them. And God was making it plain. Now, in the bitterness of their adversity, they would all see who were really on God's side and who were only his fair-weather friends. Knox cited the defeats of the Israelites. Why had God allowed them to be defeated? To purify them, until only the elect remained. When they had been few in number and without military strength, God had not visited them with adversity. But they had come to trust too much in mere human might. When a great man had come over to their side they had rejoiced at the number of spears he would add to their armory, or the political influence he would bring to their cause. They should have hearkened, rather, unto God's Word. Nevertheless, if they would now all turn to God in sincerity, their cause would triumph and their faith redound to the glory of God.

It is often imagined, among those who misunderstand the old doctrines of predestination and election, that these must impair men's zest for action, making those whom they influence feel they may sit down and take their ease, leaving all to God. The absurdity of such a notion of the practical effect of these doctrines may be seen from this sermon of Knox's. For it was these very doctrines that he used so effectively to boost the flagging morale of his supporters and whip up their courage and zeal, no less than to ensure their long-suffering and perseverance.

From this time onward the political side of the revolution was left to Maitland. Knox was thus freed for the role for which he was best fitted, the role of prophet. During the last few months before victory, there were some who professed to think Knox too much an extremist to lead the cause. But was it really his extremism that they distrusted? Was it not, rather, the religious aura with which he invested everything? Maitland seemed a better man for the task of handling the final stage of the revolution. He did not talk incessantly of Israel and the wrath of God, of repentance and the overthrow of idolatry. He appealed to Scottish patriotism, a lower but often livelier sentiment in the hearts of the masses. The Lords of the Congregation, he urged, were now fighting for the freedom of

Scotland from French domination. An able diplomatist, Maitland saw that this had always been a good tune to play, and it was a particularly good tune at the moment, for it could not only appeal to the hearts of Scotsmen, but please the English queen as well — both very useful ends in the conduct of the last phase of the revolution.

Knox retired to St. Andrews to devote himself to prayer and the study of the Bible.

Lord James and his now miserably attenuated army waited there to resist as far as they might an enemy invasion. They had not long to wait. Early in January, 1560, the enemy invaded Fife with evident designs on St. Andrews. With Arran, Kirkcaldy, and the little remnant force, Lord James fought with great courage. Knox tells us that for three weeks there was fighting daily, often from early morning until late at night, in the bitter cold and lashing rain of a winter storm. In all that time they did not take off their clothes, their armor, or even their boots. Knox preached. Even in the midst of such a battle he found opportunity to rebuke. Arran, he complained, kept himself too much aloof from the men. He should remember Jehoshaphat, who went out and in among his soldiers. Arran resented the reproach. A shallow man, he could hardly have seen the point of it. Was it not just another instance of the prophet's interminable preachifying? It was all very well for Knox to keep bringing out his Old Testament heroes, but had not Arran more pressing business to do?

Yet what more practical point could Knox have made just then? Nothing was more needed than upholding the soldiers' morale. The paid infantry were a sorry bunch ("ciphers," Knox called them), ready to run away at the least sign of defeat. On the little band of cavalry — two hundred horse — depended the slim chance there might be of a successful resistance. In those days, the art of keeping up the morale of an army was not consciously recognized, as it is now, to be an integral part of warfare. There were then no military academies to teach officers such techniques, and in any case Knox had, of course, no military training. But in this aspect of military science he was ahead of the commanders because he knew his Bi-

140

ble. Is it too much to suppose he was for the same reason often wiser than the professional diplomats of his day?

It was nevertheless with a sorrowful heart, he tells us, that he watched the heroism of the few in conducting a battle in which their defeat was, short of a miracle, inevitable. The sermon in which he had sought to uphold the morale of the soldiers had been on the danger in which Christ's disciples found themselves when they were in the midst of the stormy sea and he on the mountain. Knox had told his hearers that they should not faint, but should row with all their might against the storm until Christ should come. For, he had said, he was as convinced that God would deliver them out of their trouble as he was certain that it was the gospel of Christ he was preaching to them that very day. Yet now his own heart trembled as he prayed. The enemy was probably about ten times stronger in numbers, and it was approaching St. Andrews. Kirkcaldy's own house had been destroyed, and he had vowed vengeance on D'Oysel, the commander of the French forces, saying that though he might not have it in the present battle he should have it later, be it on French soil.

D'Oysel, however, was overconfident. He proceeded in a leisurely fashion. The queen regent was delighted with the progress he had already made. " Where is John Knox's God now? " she was reported to have asked mockingly. So D'Oysel was in no hurry to lose his Frenchmen in battle when he could hope to crush the Protestants with less bloodshed and a more spectacular display of might. But on January 24, as his men marched along the coast, they noticed English sails. The English fleet had seized a few ships, enough to cut the French communications. Within an hour of reaching St. Andrews, D'Oysel's men were compelled to turn. Fleeing toward Stirling, they suffered great hardship for lack of victuals, and within a week they were back at Leith, whence they had started.

The Protestants, now greatly encouraged by the miraculously timely arrival of the English ships and the abatement of the storm that had for so long made fighting unusually difficult, did their best to harass the retreating enemy, for many now wanted to have a whack at it under the conditions of equality they hoped presently to obtain. Kirkcaldy cut the Bridge of Tullibody, to delay the enemy's retreat, and it was only by tearing down the roof of a parish church that the French were able to improvise a bridge and make their way back. Their greatest need, however, was for food, yet few dared to stray from the main road to seek it, knowing that whatever the common people might be thinking or not thinking about the Protestant Reformation, they did not like French soldiery on principle. Knox tells us that one Frenchman, probably an officer, wearing a red cloak and gilt helmet, entered the cottage of a poor woman to obtain food. The woman, in accordance with the code of the Scottish peasantry in dealing with strangers, immediately offered him such bread as she had already prepared. But when the Frenchman, not content with it, and despite her tearful pleadings not to leave her household to starve, proceeded to make off with her children's dinner, she took the opportunity, while he was bending down, of tipping him up by the heels and ducking his head in her tub, where with the assistance of some others who came to help her, she succeeded in holding him down until he died. " God so punishing his cruel heart," writes Knox, "who could not spare a miserable woman in that extremity."

If the sight of a few English sails could cause such havoc among a numerically powerful enemy, what could not be done with really adequate English support? Despite his retirement from such affairs, Knox could not resist penning a letter to Railton, a Berwick official, making a final appeal for English help. Meanwhile, Châtelherault and other Protestant nobles were wasting time. They had made no serious effort to come to the aid of their harassed brethren at St. Andrews. While the enemy was in retreat at Stirling, Châtelherault could have taken him at an advantage and had done nothing. The English had now actually sent a fleet, which was lying in the Firth of Forth without as much as a welcome. Thanks to Maitland's efforts, representatives of the English Government wanted to confer with the Scottish Protestant leaders with a view to a treaty, and Châtelherault and his nobles were delicately squabbling over the location of the proposed meeting. All this was too much for a thundering prophet, retired from politics or no. There was plain speaking to be done. " To speak the matter plainly," Knox growled, " wise men do wonder what my Lord Duke's friends do mean." Knox knew very well what he was doing. It turned out afterward that Châtelherault, vacillating once more, had written the French king a cringing letter on January 25, begging pardon for his past misdeeds and promising loyalty to France; then, when the Scottish Protestant victory seemed more promising, he supported the Protestants again and ended by denying the writing of the letter. A fairweather friend indeed.

As usual, the Knoxian thunder was effective. By the middle of February, the Lord James, with Ruthven, Balnaves, and others, sailed from Pittenweem in Fife to Berwick, where on February 27 a bond of mutual defence against the French was signed. The English were to enter Scotland in full force to drive the French out of Leith. The Scots bound themselves to give similar assistance to England should the latter country ever be invaded by the French, and in token of their sincerity they agreed to send hostages to England to remain during the marriage of the Queen of Scots to the French King Francis II, and one year thereafter. This was an important point in the eyes of the English, who were still afraid of the traditional alliance between Scotland and France. It was psychologically difficult for Englishmen, however well disposed to the Scots, to forget the traditional enmity or to suppress the old, widespread sentiment that Shakespeare, writing forty years after these negotiations, expressed in the words he put into the mouth of England's Henry V on the eve of the Battle of Agincourt:

> " We do not mean the coursing snatchers only,
> But fear the main intendment of the Scot,
> Who hath been still a giddy neighbor to us;
> For you shall read that my great-grandfather
> Never went with his forces into France,
> But that the Scot on his unfurnish'd kingdom
> Came pouring, like the tide into a breach,
> With ample and brim fulness of his force.
> (Act I, Scene 2)

Less benevolent Englishmen were more inclined to express themselves as Shakespeare makes Westmoreland, in his advice to Henry, express the medieval English feeling toward the Scots, the feeling that persisted down to Shakespeare's own day:

> " For once the eagle England being in prey,
> To her unguarded nest the weasel Scot
> Comes sneaking, and so sucks her princely eggs,
> Playing the mouse in absence of the cat,
> To tear and havoc more than she can eat."
>
> *(Ibid.)*

So the English representatives were well pleased by the Scots' undertaking to send hostages. The Scots also promised to uphold their allegiance to their rightful sovereigns, provided that these should rule in accordance with the ancient laws and liberties of the land. Though the treaty was in no way explicitly founded on religion, it was, for Protestants on both sides of the Border, a very promising one, and from the time of its signing, political and military events moved swiftly. By the end of March an English army of nearly two thousand horsemen and five thousand infantrymen advanced from Berwick and met Châtelherault and the Scottish Protestant nobles at Prestonpans. On April 1, Mary of Guise, now dying, begged asylum and entered Edinburgh Castle. Deserted by all but two of her nobles, Seton and Bothwell, she was the most friendless woman in Scotland.

There was heavy fighting around Edinburgh that April of 1560, heavy fighting on both sides. When the English besieged Leith they met considerable resistance, and on Easter Monday their trenches were raided by the enemy, now under Bothwell's command. The French might at any moment appear with reinforcements. France, however, was in trouble. The Guise family there had followed the persecuting policy of the now dead French King Henry II; yet the Huguenots were giving endless trouble in several parts of the country. Dauphiné and Provence were near rebellion. There had even been an attempt to seize the persons of the Guises, which the latter revenged by ferocious reprisals. England and Spain were alike

144

interested in keeping French ambitions well within bounds. It was no time for France to be sending armies to the distant north. It had enough to do at home. So Bothwell went off to Europe in search of help from other countries: Germany, for instance, and Denmark. Meanwhile, the dying queen regent made her last bid for peace. A French bishop arrived as commissioner from the young Scottish sovereigns; but the negotiations he hoped to make came to nothing, and on June 10, Mary of Guise died of dropsy. In spite of her outstanding ability, patience, and other virtues that go to make a good ruler, she had thoroughly failed, and her failure was due as much to her perfidies as to the alienation of her own supporters by her persistence in pursuing a policy of subservience to France that no Scotsman could stomach. There is no doubt that without the extraordinary unwisdom of her policy Protestantism, humanly speaking, could hardly have convinced the minds of Scotsmen as fully as it did. The Scottish Reformation is, therefore, in no small measure, however indirectly, in her debt.

Knox, who had been back in the pulpit of St. Giles's since April, watched her end pitilessly. To him even her virtues had been tainted, almost more odious to him than her vices. Her crown, he said, was as seemly as a saddle on the back of an unruly cow. Nor did even her death temper his disdain. Years afterward he related what he had seen at the siege of Leith, when the Scots and English were suffering heavy casualties at the hands of the French. The French, he alleged, " stripped naked all the slain, and laid their dead carcasses before the hot sun along the wall, where they suffered them to lie more days nor one." Mary of Guise, Knox continued bitterly, when she saw this sight, hopped with glee, saying, " Yonder is the fairest tapestry that ever I saw: I would that the whole fields that is betwixt this place and yon were strewed with the same stuff." In the pulpit Knox had denounced her words as an insult to God's own image, in whom all men are made, and prophesied that God would execute His judgments upon her.

What death brought to Mary of Guise we cannot know; what is certain is that it brought Scotland peace. Within a week of it a truce was arranged, to be concluded by Cecil, who had come from London for the purpose, on July 6. But for the absence of any reference to religion, it could hardly have been more pleasing to Knox and his supporters. Both French and English were to evacuate Scotland, and in August a Convention of the Estates of the Realm was to meet and pass an act canceling everything that had been done since March 6, 1558. The Government of Scotland was placed in the hands of a Council of Twenty-four, seven to be chosen by the king and queen of Scotland and seventeen by the Estates of the Realm. The Scottish king and queen renounced all claim to the use of the arms of England. Bishops, abbots, and others would have the right to present to the Estates claims for injury to persons and property, and would also have protection against further losses.

The Treaty of Edinburgh, by which these arrangements were made, was signed on July 6 and proclaimed on July 8. On July 15, the French forces sailed from Leith and the English marched homeward. The political aim of the revolutionaries had been achieved. The young queen, when she arrived, would be required to exercise her sovereignty according to the ancient laws of Scotland. There would be no more absentee rule. National independence had been asserted. Was not that enough?

Not quite. For while John Knox was preaching on the nineteenth, at the National Thanksgiving Service at St. Giles's, the young Queen of Scots in France was receiving from her ambassador at Rome a Golden Rose from Pius IV, the newly elected Medici pope, and she and her feeble-minded husband were being exhorted by the same Lord Pius, *Pater Patrum,* not to suffer such a realm as Scotland to " go to perdition "! Knox's Thanksgiving Sermon is not recorded. Could he have known the pope's words when he preached it, the loss of the record would be even more regrettable. It might have been a unique document even for that age of invective.

At the Thanksgiving Service the Reformation preachers were in full force, and the question on the lips of all was: What of the religious settlement? For after all, it was for this that the revolution had been started. Fine indeed it was to

146

hear the national prophet preaching the Word on the triumphant occasion of Scotland's solemn thanksgiving for the successful assertion of its independence. But who was to establish the Reformed religion? Who was to put down the idolatry of Antichrist?

Who but John Knox?

15 Under the Treaty of Edinburgh, the old ecclesiastical hierarchy was to receive protection. But what, precisely, was there to be protected? Let us make a brief inventory of the Roman episcopate in Scotland in 1560, the shepherds to whose care the pope, in Rome, entrusted his Scottish sheep, that these might not " go to perdition."

There were thirteen Roman dioceses in Scotland. Of these, four were officially vacant. Of the remaining nine, one had as its bishop a layman, Lord Robert Stuart, one of the late King James's bastards, who had joined his half brother Lord James in October, 1559, in defense of the Protestant side. Of the remaining eight, two of the consecrated bishops, Hamilton of Argyll and Adam Bothwell of Orkney, had been converted to the Reformed religion, while Hepburn of Moray was on the point of conversion. That left five, one of whom, Beaton of Glasgow, had fled to Paris with the French forces and had never come back. For practical purposes, therefore, nine of the thirteen dioceses of Scotland were vacant. Of the four remaining nonvacant sees, Dunblane was filled by Chisholm, a repulsive old man with a large family of bastards for whom he had amply provided out of the patrimony of the Church, and Aberdeen was filled by Gordon, a more notorious figure still. It may fairly be said, indeed, that the sees of Aberdeen and Dunblane were worse than vacant. So only two members of the episcopate remain to be accounted for: Crichton of Dunkeld, a mediocre but respectable figure, and the primate himself, Archbishop Hamilton of St. Andrews, yet another royal bas-

147

tard, whose cruelty and cunning made him a fitting successor to the infamous Beatons. Such was the state of the Roman episcopate in Scotland when Parliament met in August, 1560. When Pius summoned his Scottish bishops to a session of the Council of Trent early in the following year, there were still only five to whom the summons could be addressed. Plainly, there was more wrong with the old religion in Scotland than the pope could cure with a Golden Rose and an aspiration that the eighteen-year-old Queen of Scots and her half-witted, sixteen-year-old husband should save the realm from perdition.

On August 1 the Scottish Parliament met to save Scotland by other means. Determined to see that all was done according to the established principles of law, the Protestant majority refrained from launching into the religious question until their opponents had been given the opportunity of voicing certain objections about procedure, the discussion of which took a whole week. Meanwhile, Knox had begun a course of sermons on Haggai, concerning the rebuilding of the Temple. Through his efforts and those of his colleagues in the ministry, a "supplicatioun" was signed by nobles and others requesting Parliament to deal summarily with the old religion and what was left of its hierarchy. The Roman clergy were declared to be unworthy of "honour, authoritie, charge or cure within the Kyrk of God," and were to be deprived forever of vote in Parliament on the ground of false doctrine and the impiety of the papal claims.

Attendance was without precedent in Scottish history. Some lairds came who had not in living memory exercised their right to sit. Indeed, their right was questioned until it was shown that it went back as far as the reign of James I early in the preceding century. Such was the temper of the majority that there was from the first little doubt how the discussion of the religious settlement would go. It would go ill for the old religion.

When the supplication concerning religious settlement was at last considered, it was decided that in the first place representatives of the new religion should be called upon to draw up a statement of Christian doctrine and discipline that might be fully considered by the Estates. No task could have been more after Knox's heart. For years he and his friends had been discussing these matters daily; they had prayed about them and meditated on them. They had, moreover, kept in touch with their Protestant brethren on the Continent, and were familiar with the current theological discussions. They had already for the most part made up their minds about what they considered the essentials, and how these could be expressed with special reference to the Scottish situation. Among the numerous Protestant confessions of faith and statements on Church order that they already had before them were those prepared the previous year by their Huguenot brethren in Paris. The task assigned to Knox and his colleagues — Winram, Spottiswoode, Willock, Douglas, and Row — was completed within four days. The new Confession of Faith was presented to Parliament and transmitted to the Estates according to the accepted canons of procedure. Opportunity was given for the supporters of the old religion to state their case as the Confession was read and voted upon, article by article. The Reformation ministers were present in order to answer theological or other objections that might be offered, and needless to say they were only too eager to be called upon. But in fact the objections that were raised were so few and so halfhearted that there was scarcely any need for the presence of the preachers. Archbishop Hamilton, together with Bishops Crichton and Chisholm, lodged their dissent, as did also three [37] of the nobles. But the overwhelming majority ratified and approved the Confession with evident delight. Randolph, who had been against the discussion, at that stage, of a question so likely to prove explosive, wrote to Cecil on August 19 that he had never in his life seen business of such great importance transacted with such efficiency and approved with such good will.

A week later, three acts were passed in one day, all of paramount importance in future Scottish history. The first, the

[37] Possibly five.

most fundamental of all, totally abolished the jurisdiction of the pope in Scotland. The second condemned all doctrine and practice contrary to the essential principles of the Reformed faith. The third specifically forbade the celebration of Mass within the bounds of Scotland, under penalty of confiscation of goods for the first offense, exile for the second, and death for the third. These penalties were tokens of the seriousness with which Parliament viewed the corruption that had come to be inextricably associated, in Scotland, with the Mass. They were, nevertheless, maximum penalties intended chiefly to deter philandering with the "Scarlet Woman," papal Rome. They were not punishments that were likely to be inflicted in any but exceptional cases. Many crimes had savage penalties attached to them that were very seldom enforced in fact.

Before the dissolution of Parliament, Knox and the other ministers were instructed to draw up a detailed program setting forth how they proposed to organize the Reformed Kirk. This was a much more onerous task than that of preparing the doctrinal Confession. The results of the ministers' labors, which lasted many months, were eventually presented in the Book of Discipline. During the preparation of this volume, however, the nobles were busy with plans of their own that were far from pleasing to Knox. It was evident that they were bent on imitating their English counterparts who, under Henry VIII, had enriched themselves by looting the ancient patrimony of the English Church. Knox well knew the danger of such greed. Many of the nobles were halfhearted in their concern for true reform; they were eager, rather, to feather their own nests while there were still plenty of fine feathers for the taking. Trusting the Lords less and less, he became increasingly convinced that the real hope of the Reformation lay with the preachers. On the other hand, the Lords were also intriguing along other lines that were more congenial to him. But these intrigues were fruitless. Especially hopeless was the attempt to get the recent acts of the Scottish Parliament ratified by the young sovereigns in France; yet in the absence of such ratification the Reformed religion in Scotland could not be deemed to be securely established, appearances notwithstanding. The Lords were also urging Elizabeth to marry Arran. This would have been a welcome alliance, since it would have provided Scotland with a Protestant king. But though Elizabeth spoke graciously enough about the proposal, it was clear that Arran would not be an acceptable suitor. England had, indeed, got all she wanted out of the treaty; for the moment, at any rate, it was no longer possible to do business with her. Maitland's intrigues were so complicated and interminable that even if there had been any prospect of their success, this would have come too late for Knox. Knox was impatient. Ever sensitive to what was going on in Continental Europe, he knew there was no time to waste: not only must the Protestant gains be consolidated; the Reformed Kirk must be made impregnable to attack by the forces that everywhere conspired to undermine and eventually overthrow it. As Knox labored on the Book of Discipline he was carefully preparing for the Kirk, he must have had many misgivings. He had to work with one eye on the Book and the other trained on the far-flung political scene.

To add to the public cares that troubled him at this time, Knox had suffered the anguish of personal bereavement. His wife, Marjorie, died in December. Though seeming, as do many Lowland Scots, to lack demonstrativeness as a lover, Knox had a deep affection for his wife, who had evidently been a most constant helpmeet to him in these stormy years. She was in every way different from her husband; yet perhaps she was as exceptional in her own way as he was in his, having just the virtues he lacked, and needing just his kind of massive strength to nurture them. Calvin had been charmed by her, calling her *suavissima,* and indeed only such gentle sweetness as was hers could have been powerful enough to hold as it did the enduring affection of so stormy and dominating a personality as John Knox. Calvin, who had lost his own wife in 1549, wrote Knox a tender letter of condolence. Knox was left with two young children. His mother-in-law, Mrs. Bowes, would no doubt come to look after these little boys for him; but the solace this thought brought was offset by the irksomeness of having to endure her curious melancholia that seemed to feed on rather than be subdued by her son-in-law's efforts to raise her spirits. Meanwhile he must care for the boys as best he could. Nathaniel was three and a half; Eleazer only two years old. From every point of view, therefore, the loss of Marjorie must have been a very bitter sorrow indeed for the Reformer, who probably needed her wifely affection more than even he knew.

The same month brought news of a miracle on the political scene. The intriguing politicians seem to have worked all along on the assumption that Francis would outlive his wife Marie Stuart. By the sudden death of Francis that month, the whole prospect was changed. Knox was delighted by the news, and did not disguise his pleasure. The sickly young king had died of an abscess in the ear — the ear, Knox growled, that " never would hear the truth of God." The Protestants had good reason to rejoice, knowing that it meant the end of Guise control of France, so that whatever might be the policy of the young queen — and what this would be kept everyone guessing — she would not have the might of France behind her that her mother, the regent, had enjoyed and used to such ill advantage to Scotland's health. If only the young queen could be won over to sympathy, at least, with the cause of the Reform in Scotland, the prospects would be rosy indeed. With this in mind, Knox now became party to an extraordinary project, one that shows how even a man of his innate common sense can let enthusiasm for a cause run away with sober judgment.

Knox had been as much disappointed as had the Lords by Elizabeth's rejection of Arran. But perhaps, thought Knox in a grand, wild moment, Providence had a better plan still. What if a marriage could be arranged between Arran and the now widowed girl of eighteen who was Queen of Scots? It was a bold thought, for Marie Stuart was likely to be the most sought-after among the royal ladies of Europe. Arran, however, was very well pleased by the idea. Probably he and Knox were the only two men in Scotland capable of hoping for its success: the former because he was a fool; the latter because he was intoxicated by his ardor for the cause of Reform. But after all, no one really knew anything of the young widowed queen's character or outlook. She had been away from Scotland since childhood and had been brought up in the court of France. One might and one did guess at the kind of influence which that court would have exercised upon her in her impressionable years. But, in the absence of reliable knowledge about her, one had to act only on reasonable assumptions; for instance, that a sheltered young girl who had inherited the throne of a realm she had never seen since the age of six would welcome advice from any of the country's leaders, whether she acted on it or not. At any rate, within a month of the death of her husband, Marie received a secret letter from Arran making overtures whose intent was clear enough. Marie's reply was certainly no less unambiguous. She definitely rejected the proposal.

It was an ominous indication that the young queen had a mind of her own and would not hesitate to express it on her return to Scotland to take the throne. Maitland was glum. Knox, from his pulpit, gravely warned his hearers that they must not indulge in a false sense of security. There was good reason for his anxiety. The Confession of Faith had been passed by Parliament. But the Kirk, not yet legally organized, was in a chaotic state. There was, for example, no systematic provision for the sustenance of its ministers. From what Knox could gather from conversation it appeared likely that the proposals he and his colleagues were about to present for the organization of the Kirk would have a stormy reception even among his sympathizers. And the mysterious shadow of the Great Unknown, the young queen who would presently be arriving in Scotland, fell darkly over the already gray prospect. Whatever else happened, the Kirk must be organized as quickly and as thoroughly as possible before Marie landed on Scottish shores, and to this aim Knox now devoted his skill, his energy, and his prayers.

On January 15, 1561, Parliament met, chiefly to consider the Book of Discipline that Knox and the other ministers had prepared. It was a splendid piece of work, showing the unmistakable mark of Knox's genius and vision. Conceived as the antidote to the disorder of the past, its motif was discipline, orderliness. By means of its program, the nation would be re-born. But Knox, for all his practical sagacity, and the frequency with which his supporters had let him down, was still inclined to imagine that in an emergency, at any rate, men pledged to the Lord's side would be angels in purity and strength. Disposed to believe that since the vast majority seemed to be inclined for Reform, they would be ready to make all the sacrifices needed for its full realization, Knox demanded the highest positive motives as though he were asking for no more than the observance of simple, negative rules. One is reminded of the story of the notoriously severe Dr. Keate of Eton, who is alleged to have preached a sermon to the boys in College Chapel on the text " Blessed are the pure in heart," and to have concluded it by glaring at his youthful audience with the words, " Now, boys, mind, you've got to be pure in heart: any boy I catch not being pure in heart I'm going to flog."

The Reformed Kirk was to be organized on democratic lines. No congregation would have an unwelcome minister foisted on it. Each congregation would have the right of freely choosing its own pastor. Yet the pastor was to be no mere employee of the congregation, which, though it could hire him, could not fire him. On the contrary, it was held bound to reverence its pastor as the servant and ambassador of Christ, obeying his commands, *if Scriptural,* as if it were God himself who was speaking. As a temporary measure, in view of the paucity of trained and experienced candidates for the ministry, a class of men was created to fulfill the functions of ministers, *faute de mieux.* These were the " readers," whose chief function was the reading of common prayer and the Scriptures; only when they were fully trained and properly ordained, however, were they to be allowed to preach the Word or administer the sacraments. Some ten or twelve " Superintendents " were to be selected for the extension of the Kirk's work throughout the realm.

Taking it for granted that the entire patrimony of the ancient Church was to be available for distribution according to fair and just principles, the framers of the Book provided that each pastor was to receive sufficient emoluments not only for his own needs, but for those of his wife and children, so that he should be assured of an honest, independent income, however modest, and his family provided with some sort of pension in the event of his death. The readers, being only unqualified substitutes, were to be paid less. Each congregation was to be self-supporting, as far as possible, and was to be responsible for its own poor. Able-bodied beggars were to be compelled to work for their living; other indigent persons were to be provided for at the expense of the congregation.

The plan included the eventual division of the entire country into self-supporting parishes; each congregation would eventually have a pastor of its own choice whom it would obey as the minister of God's own Word and sacraments. Into this neatly mapped-out parochial arrangement Knox and his colleagues fitted the ambitious system of national education that came in fact to be one of the most notable achievements of the Reformation, without which it could hardly have worked at all in the long run. To each parish was to be attached a school where every child would have at the least four years of schooling in the subjects then accounted essential for literacy. Such elementary schools were to be at the expense of the parish, which would pay the teachers, and the poor of the parish would be educated free of charge, so that attendance could be made compulsory on all. No father, it was insisted, " of what estait or condition that ever he be," should be allowed to employ his children " at his awin fantasie," but all obliged to have their children educated both in learning and in moral virtue. In the larger towns there were to be secondary schools, candidates for which were to be carefully selected from the most promising boys in the elementary parish schools. Likewise, from among the best products of the secondary schools were to be selected the candidates for the universities, who would be prepared for the Church, the law, or the practice of medicine. By this time Scotland had already three universities [38]: St. Andrews, Glasgow, and Aberdeen. None of

[38] The fourth, Edinburgh, dates only from 1583, eleven years after Knox's death. Though a scheme for a college in Edinburgh was projected

them, however, was yet very adequate, and they compared ill with some of their counterparts abroad. Knox outlined suggestions for the necessary improvements.

None of these educational projects was, strictly speaking, new. The Roman Church had for long endeavored to establish elementary schools of a kind throughout the land, and the secondary school envisaged in the Book of Discipline was, of course, the successor of the cathedral school of the Middle Ages. Knox's conception of education was in certain respects still quite medieval. Yet the system he inaugurated differed from its forerunners in its capacity for development. Most of all it differed in its actual effect. For the illiteracy in Scotland in 1560 gave place eventually to a surprisingly widespread literacy. While it is true that Knox and his friends envisaged a system that would have been even more hidebound than its medieval predecessor, the new system was inspired by motives that could not fail to liberalize and humanize it in the long run. The Reformers insisted on universality as a fundamental principle in their system of national education. This very universality, when it became effective, could not but mitigate the rigidity of the original framework. That the original framework was medieval is, after all, only what we should expect: Knox and his associates were born and bred in the Middle Ages. That they should have insisted on universal education, in a country as backward as Scotland was, is remarkable enough. Education could hardly be liberalized until it was first universalized.

At any rate, the democratic tradition of Scottish education did become one of the greatest glories of the country, making Scotland for long conspicuously literate compared with some of its neighbors. Scots peasants, moreover, though rough in speech and simple in life, did learn to think for themselves to

by Robert Reid, Bishop of Orkney, before the Reformation, the effective foundation of the College of Edinburgh out of which the university developed was a post-Reformation enterprise. See A. Logan Turner, *History of the University of Edinburgh* (Edinburgh, Oliver and Boyd, 1933), pp. 1–16, for further information concerning the relation of its beginnings to the circumstances and aims of Knox's Kirk.

an extent not so general among their English counterparts, and in striking contrast to the Irish peasantry. From the nineteenth century it became fashionable among the upper classes in Scotland to send sons to Oxford and Cambridge, and the standards of the Scottish universities suffered as the two English universities rose to new splendor; nevertheless the educational standard of the country as a whole remained very good. For long it was proverbial, so much so that southern imagination sometimes exaggerated it. Such was the reputation of the Scots in the nineteenth century that the story is told of a Scottish professor who, by way of a practical joke on two Cambridge dons who were visiting him at his country house, set the scene accordingly, playing on English credulity of the Scottish educational legend. When the Cambridge dons arrived they found the gate of the estate locked and a miserably clad yokel leaning on it, with a vacant look on his face, who, in reply to their question, replied in a rough voice but in fluent Ciceronian Latin that he would open it for them. Expressing the hope that they were enjoying their visit to Caledonia, the yokel added an elaborate Euclidean account of the direction of the house. At the door of the house itself they were confronted by a drab-looking old servant who in a matter-of-fact tone received them with a finely turned Greek ode. The visitors felt inclined to flee in terror of meeting a university professor in a country in which even the peasants spoke the language of Cicero and the menials that of Xenophon. Their host, when he appeared, kept them for long wide-eyed before he revealed the hoax: the menial and the yokel had been, of course, distinguished classical scholars in disguise.

There was really little objection in principle to the Book of Discipline. But it affected men's pockets. The elaborate program was to be financed, Knox assumed, out of the patrimony of the old Church. A Church which, as we have seen, had absorbed half the wealth of the country, could surely yield enough even for the grand scheme of social and educational reform that Knox was proposing. But how, precisely, was the money to be appropriated? So complicated were Rome's finances in Scotland that it was evidently going to be a very difficult thing to secure the cash. Much of the ecclesiastical wealth was already in the hands of powerful nobles and other influential laymen. These had a vested interest in retaining it and would be exceedingly reluctant to disgorge the revenues they possessed. Moreover, there were special charges on the available wealth, great as this seemed to be. For instance, what was to happen to the clergy of the old order who would be deprived of their livelihood? In many cases these would be incapable of training for the Reformed ministry even when their hearts were ready for such a course. Were they just to be allowed to starve? It seemed that that would be against human decency let alone Christian charity. The arrangement of finances presented an exceedingly difficult problem, and Knox and his associates not unnaturally left it to others to work out the details. No less unnaturally, these others, finding their purses affected, took the view that the whole program was too expensive.

Then there was the question of the punishment of public offenders. From the earliest times the Christian Church had exercised the right of excluding from its fellowship persons guilty, after Baptism, of certain crimes such as murder and adultery. Before the time of Constantine, such persons, at first deemed altogether incapable of true penitence and therefore ineligible for readmission to the Fold, later came to be regarded as readmissible on proof of genuine repentance and the public acknowledgment of this before the whole congregation. Knox longed to revive that ancient rigor. The Roman Church had so slackened its penitential discipline in Scotland that it had lost respect and influence. So it had come about that " neather was virtu richtlie praysit, neathir vice seveirlie punisched." Knox wished to revive primitive piety, while adapting it to the needs of his own day. To the secular authorities he left the punishment of capital crimes such as murder. But other offenses, such as fornication, drunkenness, swearing, and the oppression of the poor, were to be dealt with by the Kirk. In some cases it might suffice to give a private warning or rebuke to the offender. In others, however, something more drastic was needed, especially where there was great public

158

scandal. The offender might be brought before the minister and his session, as a court of the Church, and a day appointed for him to make public confession of his wrongdoing before the whole congregation, begging the congregation's prayers, and that they should receive him back among them. If his contrition seemed to be inadequate, other steps might be taken, such as an appeal to his conscience by his friends, and long prayer. If, however, the offender proved stubborn, he must be excommunicated, and excommunication in the Reformed Kirk was to be taken very seriously indeed, for it meant that no human being except the offender's wife and family was allowed to have any communication with him. The sentence of excommunication was to be so widely published that no one could plead ignorance of it. He was to be the subject of universal boycott: no one might sell to him or buy from him, and any children born after the sentence were to be excluded from the grace of Baptism. In these ferocious penalties was to lie the force of the most terrible judgment of the Kirk. It was a thoroughly medieval program, answering very well to the disciplinary ideals of the Roman Church, which had been too corrupt to realize these ideals until the Reformation made it too weak to do so. True, Knox's system, when it was eventually put into force in a modified form, did prolong the Middle Ages in Scotland: but in the long run it was self-emancipating. It inherited the power of the most democratic elements of the medieval tradition, elements that had been hitherto inadequately realized. In contrast, Loyola's Society in Spain, whose aims were being developed about the same time, deliberately revived the *least* democratic elements in the same tradition.

The Book did not meet with the approval of the nobles and gentry whose coffers had been enriched by the old religion and who, though they liked the new, were not all prepared to sacrifice the spoils. But though Parliament did not pass the Book, its ideals profoundly influenced the various authorities in the nation. Sometimes, indeed, these were overzealous in applying the principles Knox had set forth. For instance, the Town Council of Edinburgh, which had already in the summer of 1560 issued a warning against harlotry to brothel keepers and others, arrested a notable personage in one of the old medieval guilds, sentencing him to be carted through the town and banished for the crime of adultery. There was strong feeling against the severity of the sentence, and Knox himself interceded on his behalf. Then, in April, against the express prohibition of the Council, some of the young bloods of the town revived the traditional Robin Hood games organized by the craft apprentices. These games had been the occasion of such gross licentiousness that they had been discountenanced even in pre-Reformation times. To show their zeal, the Town Council sentenced one of the ringleaders to death. A deputation went to Knox to get him to urge clemency as he had done before, but Knox declined to intervene on this occasion. The deputation shouted that he would repent of it, to which Knox replied to the effect that he was not in the habit of repenting obedience to his conscience. However, the mob came to the rescue by taking the matter in its own hands. They broke into the Tolbooth prison and set the condemned lad free.

Despite these tribulations, Knox was steadily gaining ground. He had immense personal influence. The Town Council had fixed his salary at three hundred pounds a year, a handsome allowance at a time when you could buy a whole carcass of mutton for ten shillings.[39] Knox had stirred their consciences, too, about the educational program, on which they were disbursing large sums of money. They were also bestirring themselves about the poor, and on March 24, 1561, they ordained a compulsory levy for this purpose, and appointed official collectors to make it. The innumerable dues that had gone to the pockets of the more fortunately placed clergy of the old regime were being appropriated for the systematic extension of the schemes Knox had outlined. Wine was being taxed to help to meet the liabilities the Town Council had assumed for the promotion of Reformation principles, notably

[39] The total household expense of the king of Scotland for the month of July, 1512, was not much over five hundred pounds. A cowherd's wage for the year about this time was: a shirt, a pair of shoes, and three shillings. A soldier's pay, including maintenance, in the year 1560, was four pounds a month.

the sustenance of a trained ministry for the Kirk, the education of youth, and the relief of the poor. So though not yet on a national basis, Knox's policy was succeeding in the capital.

By August, nothing could stand in the way of its ultimate triumph throughout the whole realm — nothing except, perhaps, the queen of the realm, and on the nineteenth of that month her ships anchored in the Firth of Forth. The weather was bad. According to Knox it was the worst in living memory. But since he took it as a sign from God of the " sorrow, dolour, darkness and all impiety " of the impending rule of the nineteen-year-old queen he had made up his mind to dislike, his meteorological observations may be less than accurate. The sun, he tells us, did not shine for two days before her arrival or two days after it, and on the day of her coming there was a fog so thick and dark that one could hardly see "the length of two pair of butts." It was also pouring rain.[40]

Cannon in Leith fired to announce the arrival of the Queen of Scots. But there was fear in her young heart as she thought of the enigmatic prophet of whom she had heard much, the enemy of her mother and of Holy Mother Church. She had made up her mind to dislike him. Both she and Knox, indeed, were thoroughly prepared for their antagonism. But, on the other hand, she was determined to win Scotland's heart. To win Knox was beyond her aspirations; but there would surely be other gentlemen, less prophetic and austere, who would be vulnerable to her undoubted charm; as vulnerable, at the least, as had been the gentlemen at the court of France.

16

" It cam with a lass and will gang with a lass."
So, it was said, King James V had murmured on his deathbed when, having lost both his sons, he was informed of the birth of his daughter, Marie Stuart. For the Scottish crown

[40] This is a more notable phenomenon in the neighborhood of Edinburgh than some who are unfamiliar with the regional variations of the Scottish climate may suppose. The annual rainfall of New York State is nearly double that of Edinburgh.

had been brought into the Stuart family through Marjorie Bruce, daughter of Robert Bruce, who had married Walter Stuart. The king's dying prediction, we shall see, was fulfilled.

The Reformed religion was not, at the time of the queen's arrival, as well engrafted into Scottish life as Knox would have wished. Nevertheless, it was already in a very advantageous position. Parliament had wholeheartedly endorsed its doctrinal principles, and though the Lords had balked at the Book of Discipline because of the financial difficulties this involved, the Reformed Kirk had been very well established in the capital. The actual organization of it throughout the whole land could not in any case have been accomplished without considerable delay. For one thing, there were only some eight preachers for over a thousand parishes.[41] But if Knox could keep the control he now had of Edinburgh, the rest would follow.

On August 24, at Holyrood, Mass was said in the royal chapel. There had been a protest, but the door was held against the protesters. The following day, the Queen of Scots issued a proclamation commanding her subjects to make no alteration or innovation in the state of religion, and neither to molest nor trouble any of her servants. To modern ears this sounds, in the circumstances, a pacific, reasonable order; even generous and charitable. The country was to have the *status quo* in religious matters, while the devotional life of the royal household was to be the private affair of the queen. The Lords felt it was reasonable. Knox was, however, of another opinion. He believed, as he put it later, that " her liberty should be their thraldom or it were long." Knox knew from what he had seen in other countries that in the sixteenth century such arrangements about religion did not last. The Germans had resorted to the principle *cujus regio, ejus religio,* that is, in religion the principality would follow the prince, so that when a prince was Lutheran his domain would be Lutheran, and when he was not, so it would not be. Knox knew well that in dealing with Rome he was dealing with a totalitarian institution, that Mass in Marie's household could not remain her pri-

41 Six years later there were 269 ministers and 659 readers and other such substitute ministers.

vate affair. How soon would she be preparing to restore the old religion? She was, after all, the daughter of Mary of Guise and the niece of the Cardinal of Lorraine. It was to be war to the death.

Next Sunday, the thirty-first, the eloquence of his protest resounded through St. Giles's. Better ten thousand armed foes than one Mass; better that the queen should have brought back the hated French troops than that she should have included, as she did, a French chaplain in her retinue. So vehemently did he express himself that even some of his sympathizers wondered whether he was not going too far. Maitland certainly thought so. It was at this time that Randolph wrote south: " John Knox thundereth out of the pulpit, so that I fear nothing so much that one day he will mar all. He ruleth the roast, and of him all men stand in fear." But he admitted Knox could put more life into his audience in one hour than " five hundred trompettes."

There were others in St. Giles's that day, however, less sympathetic. Among these, probably, were palace spies. Knox, they reported, was evidently a force in the realm that could not be ignored. They advised the queen to see him.

So it was that within two weeks of the queen's arrival, John Knox received her summons to appear at the palace. He was now forty-eight, but a very old forty-eight. The extraordinary strain of his life had begun to tell on him. Though not as small as Calvin, he had always been on the short side, and now he had settled with age into a squat, neat little man. Age had also made him more punctilious in dress and general appearance; never gay or elegant, of course, but almost old-maidishly tidy and precise. Indeed, if he could step out of his century and into our own, clothes, beard, and all, we should be more likely, if asked for our guess, to put him down as a French *avocat* than as a Scottish revolutionary. He was a little over-dignified, no doubt; yet it was a " who dare meddle with me " kind of dignity rather than mere stuffiness. Like many great men of humble origin, he was a little too *maniéré,* and in the presence of his sovereign, when he felt he must be on the defensive, he was probably more pompous than usual.

163

After all, for both Knox and young Marie Stuart an inter-view was embarrassing. They were both highly intelligent; therefore both knew well the immense gulf that lay between them; each knew well also that the other was terrified yet must not show it. It was awkward for a young queen to feel she was putting an elderly man " on the carpet " (for Knox looked older than he was and would seem to her even older than he looked), when it would have been more gracious to have asked for his advice as a people's leader. Nor could even Knox, for all his dislike of petticoat government, have relished the prospect of lecturing a young girl come to a difficult posi-tion, when in happier circumstances he might have had a more chivalrous role to play. Moreover, it is always embarrass-ing to meet for the first time the progeny of your old enemy, not least when the progeny is charming, talented, and beau-tiful.

The Queen of Scots made a bad beginning. By nature she was gentle and flexible, friendly and affectionate; but she was also, inevitably, the spoiled darling of the French court in an age that taught its princesses to be imperious. Brought up to regard herself as before all else a queen, she felt that her first duty toward Knox was to impress this fact upon him as a prelude to showing him the charm of her royal clemency. Knox likewise made a bad beginning. Early in the morning, as he prepared for the audience to which he was summoned, pac-ing up and down the study of his house in Trunk Close, within a few minutes' walk of the palace, he braced himself for the morning's encounter by reflecting that he was the ambassador of God himself. Probably Knox was by nature quite a chival-rous man; certainly he was eager to show the queen he was no boorish tub thumper. But he must stick to his guns; he must " flatter no flesh," however beautiful the flesh might be. The more charming young Marie Stuart turned out to be, the more he would be on his guard; the more inflexible and dignified.

Apart from two servants standing near the window at the end of the audience chamber, Lord James Stuart was the only person present besides Knox and the queen. The latter began by reminding Knox that he had taken part in the downfall of her mother and that he had once written a book against the authority of queens. Knox was immediately on his dignity. He had taught the Word of God to the people and had preached against idolatry. But the Word of God led subjects to obey their princes. Yes, he had written the book she mentioned, and would recant it if his arguments could be refuted; but he did not think any learned man in Europe could refute them. Ruffled when the young queen insisted that he had written not only against Elizabeth but against the principle of female rule itself, he advised her not to be troubled by what had never harmed her.

Had Marie Stuart known the full case against Knox she could have checkmated him in one more move. Instead, she changed the subject. God had commanded subjects to obey their princes, she said; yet Knox had incited the people to adopt a religion other than that which their sovereign had ordained. The prophet warmed to this. Now he was on much safer ground. Religion, he replied, was a special case. Its authority was not derived from princes. Otherwise the Hebrews ought to have accepted Pharaoh's religion, and Christians should have followed the religion of Caesar Augustus. The queen pointed out that the early Christians and others to whom Knox referred did not raise their sword against their princes. A good point, but Knox flashed back a clever reply:

" Yet, Madam, ye cannot deny but that they resisted: for those that obey not the commandments that are given, in some sort resist."

Already Marie Stuart was learning, with all the receptivity of youth, how to be as inflexible in argument as her opponent. She stuck to her point.

" But yet," she repeated, " they resisted not by the sword? "

Knox was cornered this time. He must contrive some sort of answer if he, who had held congregations spellbound by the seeming rigor of his argumentation, was not to be beaten in the first round by a girl of nineteen. He spoke stiffly, so as to disguise his annoyance.

" God, Madam, had not given unto them the power and the means."

Fortunately for Knox, Marie could not finish him off there; for all her ability, she was too young and inexperienced in debate.

"Think ye," she went on, letting her opponent easily escape, "that subjects, having power, may resist their princes?"

Knox sighed inwardly, relieved at his escape, and went on to his usual sermonizing tactics.

"If their princes exceed their bounds, Madam, and do against that wherefore they should be obeyed, it is no doubt but they may be resisted, even by power. For there is neither greater honor nor greater obedience to be given to kings or princes than God has commanded to be given unto father and mother. But so it is, Madam, that the father may be stricken with a frenzy, in the which he would slay his own children. Now, Madam, if the children arise, join themselves together, apprehend the father, take the sword or other weapons from him, and finally bind his hands, and keep him in prison till that his frenzy be overpast; think ye, Madam, that God will be offended with them that have stayed their father to commit wickedness? It is even so, Madam, with princes that would murder the children of God that are subject unto them. Their blind zeal is nothing but a very mad frenzy; and therefore, to take the sword from them, to bind their hands, and to cast themselves in prison till that they be brought to a more sober mind, is no disobedience against princes, but just obedience, because it agreeth with the will of God."

The young queen's face clouded with passion, as though she were ready to burst into tears. Knox was certainly clever. He sounded most respectful, yet he was, she felt, insulting her. How could she reply to such arguments? Perhaps she had heard something like them before; but this man Knox was twisting them to suit his own purpose.

Seeing her dismayed look, Lord James intervened, gently inquiring what it was that had offended her. At length, ignoring Lord James and addressing Knox, she resorted to a feminine thrust of sarcasm:

"Well then, I perceive that my subjects shall obey you, and not me; and shall do what they list, and not what I command:

166

and so I must be subject to them, and not they to me."

Pleased with the success of his argument, and touched, perhaps, by her weak impotence in face of it, Knox grew more conciliatory:

"God forbid," he said, "that ever I take upon me to command any one to obey me, or yet set subjects at liberty to do what pleaseth them. But my travail is that both princes and subjects obey God. And think not, Madam, that wrong is done unto you when ye are willed to be subject unto God: for it is he that subjects people under princes, and causes obedience to be given unto them; yea, God craves the kings that they be as it were foster fathers to his Church, and commands queens to be nurses unto his people. And this subjection, Madam, unto God, and unto his troubled Church, is the greatest dignity that flesh can get upon the face of the earth, for it shall carry them to everlasting glory."

He was enjoying himself now, for the queen had given him an opportunity to instruct her. But she was not to be led astray. After all, was not this strange religion he was upholding a heresy? What right had he to lecture her as though he were the pope himself?

"Yea," she rejoined, "but ye are not the Kirk that I will nourish. I will defend the Kirk of Rome, for I think it is the true Kirk of God."

This was exactly the retort Knox wanted to enable him to go on. She must be weaned from her enslavement to Rome and submit instead to the plainly revealed Word of God.

"Your will," he declared, pleasantly enough, "your will, Madam, is no reason; neither doth your thought make the Roman harlot to be the true and immaculate spouse of Jesus Christ. And wonder not, Madam," he hastened to add, seeing her astonished anger, "that I call Rome a harlot; for that Church is altogether polluted with all kind of spiritual fornication, as well in doctrine as in manners. Yea, Madam, I offer myself further to prove that the Church of the Jews that crucified Christ Jesus was not so far degenerated from the ordinances and statutes which God gave by Moses and Aaron unto his people when that they manifestly denied the Son of God,

167

as that the Church of Rome is declined, and more than five hundred years hath declined, from the purity of that religion which the apostles taught and planted."

What could she say to that? Was it not a matter of opinion? And between the opinion of this horrid man and that of her own family, she naturally had no difficulty in choosing.

" My conscience is not so," she said.

" Conscience, Madam, requires knowledge; and I fear that right knowledge ye have none."

Now he was arrogant in her eyes. He was talking to her as a French priest would talk to an illiterate peasant. She smiled to hide her resentment.

" But I have both heard and read," she said.

" So, Madam, did the Jews that crucified Christ Jesus read both the Law and the Prophets, and heard the same interpreted after their manner. Have ye heard any but such as the pope and his cardinals have allowed? And ye may be sure that such will be speaking nothing to offend their own estate."

What manner of man was this? He was no mere rebel or heretic; he was setting himself up against the pope and the cardinals. She who had inherited the Crown of Scotland and had come to win Scotland back to French civilization was being asked to choose between Holy Mother Church and this long-winded little man. Was not he self-opinionated to the point of absurdity? She wondered what was passing through the mind of Lord James Stuart. She must impress him. She must be polite, extremely polite.

" Ye interpret the Scriptures in one manner," she said, " and they interpret in another. Whom shall I believe? And who shall be judge? "

Knox glowed with righteous glee. Now he could expound the objectivity of Reformed Kirk doctrine. His royal pupil, he saw, was intelligent, so intelligent that at first she had almost tripped him up. Now she was in a more receptive frame of mind, it seemed. Plainly it was time to give her a full account of the nature of Protestant doctrine and of its assent-compelling force. His long, silky beard moved as he cleared his throat.

He tried to look her straight in the eyes, but hers were down-cast.

"Ye shall believe God," he declaimed grandly, "God that plainly speaketh in his Word: and further than the Word teaches you, ye neither shall believe the one nor the other. The Word of God is plain in the self; and if there appear any obscurity in one place, the Holy Ghost, which is never contrarious to himself, explains the same more clearly in other places: so that there can remain no doubt but unto such as obstinately remain ignorant.[42] And now, Madam, to take one of the chief points which this day is in controversy betwix the papists and us: for example, the papists allege, and boldly have affirmed, that the Mass is the ordinance of God, and the institution of Jesus Christ, and a sacrifice for the sins of the quick and the dead. We deny both the one and the other, and affirm that the Mass as it is now used is nothing but the invention of man; and therefore is an abomination before God, and no sacrifice that ever God commanded.

"Now, Madam, who shall judge betwix us two thus contending? It is no reason that either of the parties be further believed than they are able to prove by unsuspect witnessing. Let them lay down the Book of God, and by the plain words thereof prove their affirmatives, and we shall give unto them the plea granted. But so long as they are bold to affirm, and yet do prove nothing, we must say that, albeit all the world believed them, yet believe they not God, but receive the lies of men for the truth of God. What our Master Jesus Christ did, we know by his Evangelists: what the priest doth at his Mass, the world seeth. Now, doth not the Word of God plainly assure us that Christ Jesus neither said, nor yet commanded Mass to be said at his Last Supper, seeing that no such thing as their Mass is made mention of within the whole Scriptures?"

[42] Cf. the Roman doctrine of invincible ignorance. Also the Scots Confession of Faith, 1560, Art. XVIII: "For this is ane thing universallie granted, that the Spirite of God, quhilk is the Spirite of unitie, is in nathing contrarious unto himselfe."

Poor Marie Stuart. She had been taught to leave such matters to priests, as she left fighting to soldiers. She knew passages of Scripture as they came into the poetry of the Church's worship; but she had never learned to handle the Bible itself as this man Knox was doing. She was out of her depth. If only her uncle were here, or some of the learned priests she had known in France.

" Ye are oure sair [43] for me," she said at length, " but if they were here that I have heard, they would answer you."

But she had given in to him; she had admitted that she had no means of arguing about her religion, since she depended in such matters wholly upon the clergy of her faith, and indeed on the small minority of these who were specialists. It was not that she had not read. In her library were many books relating to the theological discussions that were rending Europe at the time. But they had not helped her to defend her faith against even the least incisive argument from Scripture. Knox eagerly took up her implied challenge.

" Madam, would to God that the learnedest papist in Europe, and he that ye would best believe, were present with your Grace to sustain the argument; and that ye would patiently abide to hear the matter reasoned to the end. For then I doubt not, Madam, but that ye should hear the vanity of the papistical religion and how small a ground it hath within the Word of God."

It was his way of being fatherly and kind. He wanted her to be instructed, and he was prepared that her instruction should be conducted by any learned priest of her choosing, provided that the priest should be constantly interrogated by himself. There was no arrogance in his confidence in matching his own learning against that of the most erudite man Rome could supply for the occasion: Knox believed, rather, that any tolerably intelligent man who knew his Bible thoroughly could confound Rome's best doctors as the boy Jesus confounded the Jewish doctors in the Temple when he was twelve years of age. For the Bible, he believed, gave a man not only the most

---

[43] Too sore; that is, too difficult.

important *kind* of learning, but moral integrity in the use of it, and it was by this integrity that the simplest man could blow the specious arguments of even a learned doctor sky-high. But to Marie Stuart, who could not understand his attitude, Knox's words seemed the height of presumption. He was setting himself up, it seemed to her, to be above the most learned man in the Roman Church. Was not this arrogance bordering on insanity?

"Well," she said, a touch of threatening in her voice, "ye may perchance get that sooner than ye believe."

Knox was sensitive to threats. He had spent his life under their shadow, and had at last, for the time, triumphed. The hint of a threat was enough to elicit the worst from him. Waspishly, he turned on the young queen with biting sarcasm.

"Assuredly, if ever I get that in my life, I get it sooner than I believe," he retorted. "For the ignorant papists cannot patiently reason, and the learned and crafty papist will never come in your audience, Madam, to have the ground of their religion searched out; for they know that they are never able to sustain an argument, except fire and sword and their own laws be judges."

Perhaps she had never thought of that. There seemed to be something in what he was saying. But she was irritated, sensing the futility of the conversation. It was almost noon, when it was her custom to dine. She was hungry as well as very tired of the whole interview.

"So say ye," she said weakly. She was on the point of finding a means of closing it and dismissing Knox with as much regal dignity as she could contrive, when he continued:

"But I can believe that it has been so to this day. For how oft have the papists in this and other realms been required to come to conference, and yet could it never be obtained, unless that themselves were admitted for judges. And therefore, Madam, I must yet say again that they dare never dispute but where themselves are both judge and party. And whensoever that ye shall let me see to the contrary, I shall grant myself to have been deceived in that point."

Fortunately for the young Queen of Scots, dinner was an-

171

nounced. Knox had touched on the most damaging criticism he could have made of papalist ways. In dealing with Rome it was impossible to argue, because Rome always insolently claimed to be the final judge in any debate to which Rome was a party. Rome would not, because she could not, debate except on her own ground, in her own house. It was like going to hell to argue with the devil: how could you win?

But Knox could not finish his sermon without the benediction. As he respectfully took his leave, he declaimed with immense dignity:

" I pray God, Madam, that ye may be as blessed within the Commonwealth of Scotland, if it be the pleasure of God, as ever Deborah was in the Commonwealth of Israel."

It was a magnificent conclusion. Deborah was the exception to the Biblical sanction against feminine rule. By his mention of the Commonwealth of Scotland, moreover, he was affirming its proud independence, which, all well knew, he had done more to restore than any other man alive.

So ended Knox's first audience with his sovereign. He had held his ground; but she had annoyed him as much as he had exasperated her. There is little doubt that what annoyed him was her grace and charm, and it annoyed him for an excellent reason. The support of the nobles was essential to Knox's work, and by this time he knew their weaknesses outside in. He was afraid, and very reasonably afraid, that the beautiful young Queen of Scots, in captivating their hearts, would lure them away from what he believed to be the truth of God. For he was very well aware that she would be making it her business to win back the nobles to her side, and he was sensitive to the fact that, for all his own power and eloquence, she had qualities that, even apart from the allure of her femininity, appealed to nobles and gentry, qualities he knew he did not and certainly could not hope to have. So when he was asked later what he had thought of the queen, his verdict was severe. " If there be not in her a proud mind, a crafty wit and an indurate heart against God and his truth, my judgment faileth me." It seemed that his judgment had indeed failed him at this point, because of his fears of the witchery of her charm on those to whom he must look for the support of his cause.

Knox's fears, however, quickly proved well grounded. Many of the Lords were quietly enchanted, one by one. Each new victim at first protested against the queen's Mass, then gradually was charmed into silence. The common people, on the other hand, were not seduced. They heard the preachers inveigh against the queen, while she remained aloof, beyond the people's reach, symbolizing old fears. But there was more than this in the minds and hearts of the people. By this time, many had learned to appreciate the spiritual as well as the political independence that had been won for them by Knox and his colleagues. Their hopes for the future had blossomed again after a century of despair, and Marie Stuart in Holyrood, they believed, was the one impediment to these hopes. On her entry in public they burned in effigy a priest saying Mass. It was their way of expressing their national independence. Had not John Knox said he would rather have all the French troops back in Scotland than one single Mass? The magistrates of Edinburgh were on the people's side. They issued a scurrilous-sounding proclamation requiring all " monks, friars, priests, nuns, adulterers, fornicators and all such filthy persons " to leave town. The queen was being publicly insulted by her own subjects, with the connivance of the magistrates of the capital and other important towns. At Stirling the mob drove the priests violently out of the choir in her presence, and when she wept at the sight there was no one who dared come to her support. At Perth she wept again on seeing a pageant specially prepared to insult her. Her tears came to be taken as a sign of her weakness; so also was her mirth. The Lords who had been captivated by her charm tried to console and encourage her as best they could; but in their hearts they pitied her. Indeed, it was her obvious need for their protection that evoked their natural chivalry. The most poignant element in the tragedy of Marie Stuart was already, as always, its inevitability. Seeking to capture the hearts of her people with a Roman benison behind a French charm, she could not have failed to alienate them as she did. By the time of the next General Assembly of the Kirk in December, the rift between nobles and people was obvious.

The former seemed to have veered toward the queen's side while the people were championing Knox. Maitland even went so far as to say that the General Assembly could not meet without her consent. Knox knew which card to play here. " If the liberty of the Church," he said, "should stand upon the queen's allowance or disallowance, we are assured not only to lack assemblies but also to lack the public preaching of the evangel." So it was agreed that the Assembly could meet freely as long as the queen's interests were represented.

Such was now Knox's power. But he had to reckon with the cupidity of the nobles. When the preachers proposed that the queen should be asked to ratify the Book of Discipline, Maitland laughed out loud. Who would pass a Book of Discipline that disciplined their own pockets — sometimes to the extent of more than half their fortune? It was stolen property, no doubt, that they wanted to retain for their own pleasure; but men are often more reluctant to relinquish stolen goods than property lawfully obtained. The consequence of the nobles' reluctance was that the Kirk was financially hampered. Until a settlement was reached, the preachers had to earn their bread in secular avocations, which was contrary to Knox's conception of a ministry wholly dedicated to the preaching of the Word, the administration of the sacraments, and the care of the flock.

But a settlement of a kind was provided; for though the Lords had no mind to yield up all their plunder, and had also been bewitched by the charm of the beautiful young queen, their consciences had been in some measure irrevocably touched by Knox. Just before Christmas, the queen's Council approved an act that appropriated to the Crown a quarter, or, should that prove inadequate, a third, of the old ecclesiastical patrimony, for the benefit of "the common affairs of the country." As much of that sum as was necessary for the " sustentation " of the ministers of the Reformed Kirk was to be applied to this end. For many years thereafter, this was the sole financial provision for the Kirk. To Knox, the arrangement was far from satisfactory. It meant, he said, that two parts of the ecclesiastical endowments were to be gifted to the devil, and the third divided between the devil and God. The devil would soon demand three parts of the third. For the servants of the devil, said Knox dryly, this would be a fine arrangement, were it not that there is a judgment hereafter, and then heaven or hell forever.

17 Throughout the course of the year 1562, Knox impatiently watched the court mark time. There was no proper settlement for the Kirk; the *status quo* was upheld in all things wherever possible. It looked almost as though the queen were not ruling at all, but, rather, watching. What was she watching for?

Knox could well guess. It was easy to see the direction of her glance: her eyes were turned southward toward England. She was holding Scotland as a card in her hand, while her eyes were set on the English Crown.[44] If Elizabeth would recognize her as heir presumptive, then one day Marie Stuart could reign over both realms. No wonder she seemed to be watching rather than ruling.

In principle, Knox had always been favorable to friendship with England. But what the Queen of Scots had in mind would certainly be something very different from the alliance he had often dreamed might one day come about. Knox felt proud of the purity of the Reformed Kirk in Scotland. He considered the English Church, with its toleration of some of the paraphernalia of the old religion, tepid in reform. Yet in itself this was, in his eyes, no obstacle to alliance. The real obstacle was that in an alliance engineered by a royal court that planned to have Marie Stuart on the throne of both Scotland and England, the Churches of both lands would be no more than pawns in the game, the ultimate object of which would cer-

---

[44] Marie's claim to the English throne depended upon the invalidity of the annulment of the marriage of Henry VIII and Catherine of Aragon. Were this held invalid she was the indisputable heiress to the throne of England. Elizabeth I succeeded by act of Parliament.

tainly include the destruction of the work for which he had labored so hard and suffered so much, and above all the restoration of the " filthy abomination " of the Mass. Knox had not forgotten England's Mary Tudor. Scotland's young Mary, safe on two thrones, could wreck the whole Protestant cause and, it seemed to him, hand over two realms to Antichrist.

Meanwhile, he preached and wrote and organized the Kirk as best he could in the absence of a proper settlement. All was not dismal for Knox during these anxious months. He believed that, however the nobles might be bewitched by the queen, he might still be able to count on many of them if it came to a showdown. Lord James, for instance, seemed to lack the zeal he had once shown for the cause of Reform; yet Knox knew he was reliable at heart. The previous year, Lord James had been created Earl of Mar, and announced his betrothal to Agnes Keith, sister of the Earl Marischal. Knox married them in St. Giles's on February 8. In his sermon he acknowledged the services the bridegroom had in the past rendered to the Reformed Kirk, and with a touch of humor he reminded him that if he should slacken in his zeal now, his wife would get the blame for it.

We tend to think of Knox as God's warrior rather than God's man of peace. His efforts at peacemaking were, indeed, sometimes sadly unsuccessful. It was one of these efforts which, about this time, brought him perhaps the most embarrassing personal humiliation of his life. Knox had for long been obliged to look to Arran as one of his main supporters, though Arran had been always a weak-minded young man. Neither he nor his family, the Hamiltons, were favorites of the queen. Among the " young company " she had brought from France were the three youngest Guise uncles, the son of the Constable Montmorency, and the Earl of Bothwell. A feud had arisen between the Hamiltons and the queen's favorites, and after some scandalous scenes a pitched battle between the two parties had been narrowly averted at Christmastide, 1561. On the pretext that the feud had become embarrassing, the Earl of Bothwell, accompanied by a rich burgess, called on Knox one evening to inquire whether he might take upon himself the

176

task of securing a reconciliation. At first Knox was suspicious of the proposal. He knew Bothwell was unscrupulous. Still, was not this an excellent opportunity to show the Kirk's power for good? To reconcile foolish enmities was, after all, surely a task befitting an ambassador of the Prince of Peace. So he undertook to arrange the desired reconciliation. On Tuesday, March 24, Bothwell and Arran formally embraced each other at the Hamiltons' house at Kirk-o'-Field, just beyond the south wall of the city, and Knox suitably addressed them. The following day they duly attended church together. But many who heard of the reconciliation sniggered. It sounded melodramatic.

The following day, just after Knox had finished his sermon and was settling down to his correspondence, Arran, in a frenzy of excitement, and accompanied by the town clerk and an advocate, burst in on him, complaining wildly that he had been betrayed. Bothwell, he alleged, had proposed the murder of the queen's favorites and the kidnaping of the queen, so that, with her imprisoned in Dumbarton Castle, he, Bothwell, and Arran should together rule the country. It was all a wicked plot, he sobbed, to get him arrested for treason. Arran's demeanor suggested that he had gone out of his mind. Knox, after listening gravely to his weeping and raving, pointed out that he had no reason to fear anything so long as he had not actually agreed to take part in the alleged plot, and the best course for him was to think no more about the matter. But Arran could not keep quiet. He wrote to the queen and then fled to his father's house where he was locked up. Having escaped, he was handed over by Lord James to the queen, who put both him and Bothwell in custody. It was a bitter blow to Knox. Not only had he been made to look foolish. This would not have mattered much. What did matter was that his chief remaining supporter among the great nobles had been disgraced as a suspected traitor. Nothing could have been more embarrassing.

But Knox was too busy to indulge in self-recrimination. The only minister in Edinburgh at this time, he was extremely overworked. At last, in April, he got an assistant, John Craig, who relieved him of half his preaching duties. All summer he fought for a settlement, going on with his protests against the queen's failure to implement the expressed wishes of Parliament and the manifest will of the people. His sermons poured forth the old warnings; but against the *vis inertiæ* of the royal court they seemed impotent, while his fulminations against the Mass as the fount of all impiety were beginning to look unpleasantly like monomania. Knox was, indeed, at this time, thoroughly tired out. He was frustrated and in a difficult position. If only he had not known too well the ways of sixteenth century diplomats, he might have rested on his oars. But he knew, and he was bitterly opposed to the whole policy of the court. He distrusted suavity because he had suffered and seen men suffer the results of it. He wanted peace and quiet meditation, but his conscience forbade the indulgence of such desires. He delivered a course of sermons on his old favorite passage of Scripture, the seventeenth chapter of The Gospel According to Saint John, Christ's last meditation. Would that he, John Knox, could pass the rest of his life in quiet meditation on this passage, which, more than any other, had inspired the work of his life. But perhaps, as he came to the fourth verse of that great chapter, his conscience pricked him. Dare he yet expect personal solace and peace for his anguished soul? In that verse he read the words of Christ to the Father: " I have finished the work which thou gavest me to do." Christ had finished His appointed task; but had John Knox finished his? He dared not feel it was so.

Perhaps, indeed, the task he had set himself was an impossible one. He had seen a vision of the City of God on earth. He had wanted to plant the heavenly Jerusalem on Scotland's hills. But if all this were to be more than an idle dream, obstacles must be met. The fundamental obstacle was that, as he had discovered, you cannot build Jerusalem as a sort of pleasant suburb of Babylon. If you do, Babylon will destroy Jerusalem. So Knox had asked for a settlement that would not be defeated. He had seen the roots of Scotland's misery and he had proposed an excellent, practical scheme for the betterment of affairs. One of the worst features of misrule had been that the government of Scotland was, even for sixteenth century conditions, ridiculously overcentralized. Knox had shown the way to decentralization, and much more besides. It was an experiment in democracy; but Scotland, like every infant democracy, needed to be nurtured. The peasants were not yet sufficiently trained to build Jerusalem, and the gentry were not yet sufficiently interested. Knox's proposed settlement had been hardheaded. Defeated in Parliament by the cupidity of the nobles, it was now held in abeyance by court intrigue. Yet if Knox could have got the settlement he wanted, and a reasonable measure of good will from the queen and her Council, he could have established a Scottish democracy that would have been the political wonder of the world, for it would have been free from the more tyrannical elements that inevitably disfigured the system that eventually had to be devised in default of a timely settlement. There was really little, if anything, of the tyrant in Knox. He was, rather, by nature an imaginative visionary; but he was so afraid of the dreamer's temptation to live on his dreams that the process of translating them into practice at all costs had become an obsession with him. So it was that in 1562 he reached the point where he was obliged to compromise with his own vision or lose all Jerusalem to the Babylon that was determined to devour her. If he could not get the settlement that was needed, he would make his own settlement. Some of its results would be uglier than he had wished. But what else could he do? He had spent all his life in negative criticism of the misrule of Scotland; at last he had been given an opportunity to be positive. He had risen to the occasion magnificently, with a scheme that was an able combination of the loftiest ideals and the most down-to-earth understanding of the practical difficulties involved in their realization. And he had been thwarted by the folly and selfishness of those in high places. Politically, the people were not yet ready for his democracy, while the upper classes selfishly feared it.

Officially, Knox, in the summer of 1562, was still loyal to the Government. He disliked its policies, or lack of them; but so do we all dislike many things our Governments do, however loyal we may be. By August, however, it had come to Knox's ears that there was real mischief afoot. A Jesuit, De Gouda, had come to Scotland in June with a brief from the pope. It was rumored that he had boasted to Lord James that he could restore the Mass. It was evident that, with Marie Stuart on the throne, the remaining partisans of the old religion were getting more cocky. Knox made a tour of the Ayrshire country, and on September 4, Glencairn and seventy-seven gentlemen of that district signed another " band." Meanwhile, the queen went on an expedition of a different kind. Huntly, a noble who adhered to the old religion, had proved treacherous. He had been implicated in a plot to murder Lord James and Maitland. His son, imprisoned, had escaped and refused to give himself up. The queen traveled north to impose order on the household of these recalcitrants. It was a successful expedition. Old Huntly died in the fighting and his son was captured and executed at Aberdeen. Lord James came out of all this with the earldom of Moray added to his possessions.

The queen returned to Edinburgh in November. Her court was enjoying a celebration; news of banqueting, dancing, and all sorts of frivolities at the palace troubled Knox, who interpreted the celebrations as rejoicing at the expense of the cause of Reform. He preached vehemently against some of the nobles who had called themselves weary of his endless tirades. Then, on December 13, he broke into open denunciation of the queen herself. Preaching on the text " Understand, O ye kings, and be warned, ye that judge the earth," he asked who were these princes of the world who, amid the persecution of God's saints, amused themselves in " fiddling and flinging." The allusion to fiddling conveyed echoes of Nero, who had fiddled while Rome burned.

The queen could not overlook that sermon. Another summons came to Knox's house, requiring him to present himself at the palace the following day. Knox duly appeared before the queen. But this time it was no private or near-private audience that had been arranged for him. It was as though he were on trial, or almost so. Lord James was present, with Maitland and Morton and many of the queen's ladies and attendants, when she received Knox in her bedchamber. He was charged with having spoken irreverently of the queen in order to make her appear odious and contemptible to her people. What had he to say for himself?

"Madam," replied Knox, "this is oftentimes the just recompense which God giveth the stubborn of the world, that because they will not hear God speaking to the comfort of the penitent, and for the amendment of the wicked, they are oft compelled to hear the false report of others to their greater displeasure. I doubt not but that it came to the ears of proud Herod, that our Master Christ Jesus called him a fox; but they told him not how odious a thing it was before God to murder an innocent, as he had lately done before, causing to behead John the Baptist, to reward the dancing of a harlot's daughter. Madam, if the reporters of my words had been honest men, they would have reported my words, and the circumstances of the same. But because they would have credit in court, and lacking virtue worthy thereof, they must have somewhat to please your Majesty, if it were but flattery and lies. But such pleasure (if any your Grace take in such persons) will turn to your everlasting displeasure. For, Madam, if your own ears had heard the whole matter that I entreated; if there be into you any sparkle of the Spirit of God, yea, of honesty or wisdom, ye could not justly have been offended with anything that I spake."

Knox proceeded to give an account of the sermon, which he said he could do fairly well from memory, since he had preached it only the previous day. He explained that he had begun by extolling the office of kingship; that not only had he insisted on the dignity of the place to which God has called rulers, but he had reminded his hearers of the obedience that was due to them as God's lieutenants. Only then had he gone on to observe that most princes do in fact shamefully abuse their authority. For while murderers and other malefactors are welcomed at thrones, God's saints are banished and exiled. Princes *ought* to be learned in God's law.

"But," he went on, approaching the delicate point, "God's law they despise; his statutes and holy ordinances they will not

181

understand; for in fiddling and flinging they are more exercised than in reading or hearing of God's most blessed Word; and fiddlers and flatterers (which commonly corrupt the youth) are more precious in their eyes than men of wisdom and gravity, who by wholesome admonition might beat down into them some part of that vanity and pride whereinto all are born, but in princes take deep root and strength by wicked education.

" And of dancing, Madam, I said that albeit in Scripture I found no praise of it, and in profane writers that it is termed the gesture rather of those that are mad and in frenzy than of sober men; yet I do not utterly damn it, providing that two vices be avoided: the former, that the principal vocation of those that use that exercise be not neglected for the pleasure of dancing; secondly, that they dance not, as the Philistines their fathers, for the pleasure that they take in the displeasure of God's people. For if any of both they do, so they shall receive the reward of dancers, and that will be drink in hell."

The appositeness of the doom he predicted for the dancers is better appreciated if we bear in mind that it was the custom to play the dance tune right through before each dance so that the first couple should have time to take their drink. Knox was no killjoy. His protest was like the protest that a moralist of today might make against, say, war profiteers riding their Cadillacs over the bodies of a million dead heroes. The protest would not be against driving a car, even an expensive one, but against driving it with mockery in one's heart, mockery of those who had fought and suffered and died for their country.

Knox concluded by challenging anyone to speak up who had heard the sermon and dared claim that he had said more than he now reported. The queen glanced around, but the faces of her courtiers were discreetly expressionless and their tongues silent. She paused for a moment. Knox had not said anything against the throne itself. He had been thundering against her personally. She could not quite follow his argument. No matter. He disliked her, of course; evidently it was because of her religion. She must show clemency. And this time it was not quite so difficult, because for the first time, in a curious sort of way, she found herself almost liking him. Through the exaggerations of her informers she had been led to expect a rebellious man. She could have dealt with that, she thought, remembering how she had subjugated the Huntlys a month or two before. But Knox was not a rebel. He was obsessed with certain ideas against her religion; because of his prejudices he could not be expected to like her. Perhaps if she showed special generosity in her demeanor toward him, as it was now for the moment in her heart to do, he would cease to cause unrest in the realm. There was an unexpected sweetness in her voice as she said: " Your words are sharp enough as ye have spoken them; but yet they were told to me in another manner."

Knox was motionless; but inwardly his heart rejoiced. He had made his point. The danger was over. Perhaps, he thought, he had touched her young conscience.

" I know that my uncles and ye are not of one religion," the queen continued, " and yet I cannot blame you albeit you have no good opinion of them. But if ye hear anything of myself that mislikes you, come to myself and tell me, and I shall hear you."

She was being friendly now. Her magnanimity was worthy of a queen. But Knox, having cleared himself of the suspicion of treason, was set on making the most of his opportunity. She was his sovereign. He had acknowledged that. But he would show her the dignity of his own calling as God's minister.

" Madam," he said, " I am assured that your uncles are enemies to God, and unto his Son Jesus Christ; and that for maintenance of their own pomp and worldly glory that they spare not to spill the blood of many innocents; and therefore I am assured that their enterprises shall have no better success than others have had that before them have done that which they now do. But as to your own personage, Madam, I would be glad to do all that I could to your Grace's contentment, provided that I exceed not the bounds of my vocation. I am called, Madam, to a public function within the Kirk of God, and am appointed by God to rebuke the sins and vices of all. I am not appointed to come to every man in particular to

183

show him his offense; for that labor were infinite. If your Grace please to frequent the public sermons, then doubt I not but that ye shall fully understand both what I like and mislike, as well in your Majesty as in all others. Or if your Grace will assign unto me a certain day and hour when it will please you to hear the form and substance of doctrine which is proponed in public to the churches of this realm, I will most gladly wait upon your Grace's pleasure, time and place. But to wait upon your chamber door, or elsewhere, and then to have no further liberty but to whisper my mind in your Grace's ear, or to tell to you what others think and speak of you, neither will my conscience nor the vocation whereunto God hath called me suffer it. For albeit at your Grace's commandment I am here now, yet cannot I tell what other men shall judge of me, that at this time of day am absent from my book and waiting upon the court."

It was the height of audacity. The queen hated him again. He was asking her to wait upon him.

"You will not always be at your book," she said mysteriously, turning away from him.

As he left the queen's bedchamber, there was a prophet's abbreviation of a grin on his dignified countenance. He heard some of his critics whisper ominously that he looked too cocksure. He stopped short.

"Why should the pleasing face of a gentlewoman affray me?" he asked sharply. "I have looked in the faces of many angry men, and yet have not been afraid above measure."

Then, leaving the palace, he went home, well satisfied with his own eloquence. No wonder that Randolph wrote that in his dealings with the queen, Knox spoke "as if he were of God's privy council, that knew how He had determined of her in the beginning, or that he knew the secrets of her heart so well that she neither did nor could have one good thought of God or of His true religion."

18   The following Easter, some of the Roman priests had celebrated Mass, defying the law. The Protestants decided that since the queen and her Council were evidently going to do nothing about the matter the time had come for them, the Protestants, to execute the law themselves. Something would have to be done, for if the bolder priests said Mass at Easter with impunity, it would not be long until even the more timid ones would be saying it on ferial days. Several priests were apprehended in Ayrshire, charged with idolatry and threatened with the Biblical punishment for that offense, death. Other priests were known to be hiding in woods and glens.

The queen sent for Knox again. They talked for two hours before supper. She begged him to use his influence to promote religious toleration. Let those have their Mass who liked to have Mass. The words sounded as fair to Knox as they do to a modern ear. But he was too close to the situation to be deluded by their sweetness. The Scots were in the position of the Israelites whom Moses had found worshiping a foreign idol, the Golden Calf. If Moses had let them have their way who wanted to dance and sing and worship their idol, Israel would have been lost. Because they could not have both Yahweh and the Golden Calf, Moses had had to stand in the gate of the camp and shout, "Who is on the Lord's side?" That was what Knox must do now, for Scotland could not have both Reformation and the Mass. It must have one or the other, and if it had the Mass, even one Mass, it would soon be back to Beaton-rule and slavery again. Knox knew what he was dealing with. There could be no tolerance of intolerance, and it was the intolerance of papalism that he had spent his life fighting against. That was why he had not rested until Parliament had made the Mass illegal. The queen had promised to uphold the laws of the realm as she found them. Very well,

185

would she execute the laws? If she did not, others would.

"Will ye," she asked, "allow that they shall take my sword in their hand?"

"The Sword of Justice, Madam, is God's," replied Knox, "and is given to princes and rulers for one end, which, if they transgress, sparing the wicked, and oppressing innocents, they that in the fear of God execute judgment where God has commanded, offend not God, although kings do it not; neither yet sin they that bridle kings to strike innocent men in their rage. The examples are evident; for Samuel feared not to slay Agag, the fat and delicate king of Amalek, whom King Saul had saved. Neither spared Elijah Jezebel's false prophets, and Baal's priests, albeit that King Ahab was present. Phinehas was no magistrate, and yet feared he not to strike Cozbi and Zimri in the very act of filthy fornication. And so, Madam, your Grace may see that others than chief magistrates may lawfully punish, and have punished, the vice and crimes that God commands to be punished. And in this case I would earnestly pray your Majesty to take good advisement, and that your Grace should let the papists understand that their attemptates will not be suffered unpunished. For power, by act of Parliament, is given to all judges within their own bounds, to search for Massmongers, or the hearers of the same, and to punish them according to the law. And therefore it shall be profitable to your Majesty to consider what is the thing your Grace's subjects look to receive of your Majesty, and what it is that ye ought to do unto them by mutual contract. They are bound to obey you, and that not but in God. Ye are bound to keep laws unto them. Ye crave of them service: they crave of you protection and defense against wicked doers. Now, Madam, if ye shall deny your duty unto them (which especially craves that ye punish malefactors), think ye to receive full obedience of them? I fear, Madam, ye shall not."

The queen went off to supper in a huff. Knox, with his Biblical twist to the well-established medieval doctrine of the sovereignty of the people under God, had touched a sore point. He had delineated the constitutional limits to the exercise of her queenly authority. After supper, however, she reconsidered the matter. An idea had come to her. Next day she was to go hawking near Kinross; she would ask Knox to meet her there early in the morning, and she would try yet another approach. Perhaps the very stubbornness of Knox had excited her feminine desire to conquer him by her charm. She believed she had detected his weakness. At any rate, next morning when he presented himself she greeted him almost as a parishioner seeking advice from her priest. First, talking in a casual, friendly way, she showed him a little ring on her finger with a pointed diamond. Ruthven, one of her councilors, had given it to her. It was supposed to be a charm against poisoning, she added with a smile. She confided that she did not like Ruthven. He was a dealer in enchantments of that kind. It was Maitland, she said, who had got him put on her Council.

Knox, on the defensive, snubbed her by saying that he did not care to discuss Ruthven, seeing that he was not present. But the queen was determined not to let Knox annoy her by his snubs. She continued to chat pleasantly, bringing the conversation round to his forthcoming visit to Dumfries. She had heard that he was going there to elect one of the superintendents of the Kirk.

Gravely, Knox replied that it was true there was to be such an election, and he was going to Dumfries on that account. But, she went on, it had come to her ears that the man proposed for the office was Alexander Gordon, formerly Bishop of Galloway and titular Archbishop of Athens. Was it not so?

"He is one, Madam, that is put in election," replied Knox, emphasizing the elective character of offices in the Kirk.

"If ye knew him as well as I do," said the queen, growing more confidential than ever, "ye would never promote him to that office, nor yet to any other within your Kirk."

She could well claim to know Gordon. He was her own cousin, being the son of a bastard daughter of James IV.

Knox felt he must defend Gordon as best he could.

"What he has been, Madam," he said, "I neither know nor yet will I inquire; for, in time of darkness, what could we do but grope and go wrong even as darkness carried us? But if he fear not God now, he deceives many more than me. And yet, Madam, I am assured that God will not suffer his Church to be so far deceived as that an unworthy man shall be elected, where free election is, and the Spirit of God is earnestly called upon to decide betwix the two."

So the Kirk claimed infallibility too, she mused. But aloud she said only: "Well, do as ye will, but that man is a dangerous man."

Knox kept his own counsel. What the queen was saying was probably only too true. Perhaps it would be better to steer clear of Gordon after all. But of course he must not admit to her that she had caused him to change his mind. He made to take his leave, but the queen went on talking. Now she was consulting John Knox on a matter of great importance in the realm, as though he were the Cardinal Primate of Scotland. Lady Jane Stuart, the natural daughter of James V, was married to the Earl of Argyll. She was a sort of problem child, Lady Jane. She had forsaken her husband to come to the royal court. But on the other hand, Argyll's treatment of his wife was not what it might be. The queen did not think Knox would approve of the way Argyll had been treating Lady Jane.

Knox was listening carefully now. Yes, he knew about that sad affair. (Well the queen knew he knew, or she would hardly have broached the question.) He had been consulted about it before the queen's coming to Scotland, and had reconciled the unhappy pair. To the best of his knowledge they were now in amity.

"Well," said the queen sorrowfully, "it is war [45] than ye believe. But do this mekle [46] for my sake, as once again to put them at unity; and if she behave not herself as she ought to do, she shall find no favors of me."

The queen went on to beg Knox not to tell Argyll that she had been talking about the matter. She could trust Knox, of course.

Knox may have been justified in his boast that he flattered no flesh; but this did not make him completely invulnerable to

[45] Worse.   [46] Much.

the flattery of others, if only it were clever enough. The queen's subtle blandishments had proved irresistible. Much pleased, he was about to take his leave when the queen drove a master stroke. That affair they had been discussing the previous night about the lawbreakers who had been saying Mass at Easter and had so far gone unpunished: she had resolved to take Knox's advice and have them brought to justice. He could depend on that.

Knox could hardly believe his ears. This was more than he could have hoped for. Could it be that the Spirit of God had turned her heart after all? It was wonderful news.

In his grandest manner he expressed his warmest felicitations:

" I am assured then," he said, " that ye shall please God, and enjoy rest and tranquillity within your realm; which to your Majesty is more profitable than all the pope's power can be."

Knox saw that Gordon was not elected. Nor was he long in writing to the Earl of Argyll to remind him of his duty to his wife. Keeping his word to the queen, he did not, of course, mention the source of his information that the marriage was once again going badly. He contented himself with observing that the Earl's behavior toward his wife was offensive to many godly persons. (Perhaps he was even beginning to hope that the queen might be included among these.) Lady Argyll's complaint, he wrote, was " grievous, that ye altogether withdraw the use of your body to her." Naturally, Argyll did not relish the rebuke, though he remained on terms of friendship with its author.

The queen kept her promise to bring the offenders to trial. They included John Hamilton, the old primate of Scotland himself, together with forty-seven others, charged with celebrating Mass. On May 19, the day before Parliament was due to meet, they were all tried and put in ward. John Hamilton was committed to ward in Edinburgh Castle. Argyll, as Hereditary Justice General, was among the judges.

Parliament did not actually meet until May 26. When it did, there were scenes of great pomp and splendor. The queen rode in state to the Tolbooth. She made a flowery speech. "The voice of Diana!" her admirers whispered. The ladies were resplendent, their dresses gaily decorated with tassels. Knox was displeased and protested against such frivolities, for he thought they were unbecoming on an occasion of such gravity. People regarded his protests merely as signs of his usual censoriousness and did not take them seriously. But Knox was serious. Later he wrote vehemently that such "styncken pride of women" as was seen at the Parliament had never been seen before in Scotland. He thought Parliament far too solemn an occasion for the display of pretty clothes.

It was not really the pretty clothes, however, that irked Knox in that Parliament. It was the fact that once again it did not do anything about the Book of Discipline. The reason given was, of course, that the time was not yet ripe. Not yet ripe! Had not Knox waited for three years already? Yes, but it happened, he was told, that the Queen of Scots would soon be getting a husband and would then be asking favors of Parliament. *Then* would be the time to get her to ratify the Kirk's position. To put a better face on their proceedings, however, they made a few minor enactments.

Before Parliament was dissolved on June 6, Knox preached before the nobility. He spoke of the extraordinary mercy of God toward the realm of Scotland, and of their no less extraordinary ingratitude for it. He recalled the terrible sufferings of the saints in their struggle for victory. Why would not they ask the queen? "The queen, say ye, will not agree with us. Ask ye of her that which by God's Word ye may justly require, and if she will not agree with you in God, ye are not bound to agree with her in the devil." Why, some were even talking as though the Reformed faith was not legally established in Scotland after all. Finally, he flung out against the proposed marriage of the queen. Of course there would be plenty of suitors, for kings and dukes "strive all for the best game." But it would be a papist she would marry, and if the Lords should ever give their consent to bring such an infidel (and, he reminded them, "all papists are infidels"), then they would be doing all that lay in their power to banish Christ Jesus from the realm. They would bring God's vengeance upon the country, a plague upon themselves, and small comfort to their sovereign.

This sermon drew angry protests even from Knox's friends. But Knox meant every word of it. He had heard rumors that Maitland was trying to bring off a match between the Queen of Scots and Don Carlos of Spain. That would have been the last straw. But while many sympathized with Knox's feelings against the rule of Scotland by foreigners, few could approve the forthrightness of his words. There were others, of course, less friendly to Knox, who quickly conveyed the news to the palace that he had spoken openly against the proposed marriage of the queen. One of these " placebos," [47] as Knox called them, was Robert Douglas, Provost of the Collegiate Church of Lincluden, who proposed that Knox should be immediately called to give an account of his behavior.

Knox was ushered into the queen's presence shortly after dinner. Erskine of Dun, now a superintendent in the Kirk, was allowed to accompany him. The queen was in a towering rage. The interview was to be the most dramatic in Scottish history, and in the course of it Knox made the most famous reply of his life.

19   The Queen of Scots had never been in such a rage in all the twenty-one years of her life.

Her own intrigues had not been going well. The interview with Elizabeth for which she had hoped had not come off. In France, even the Huguenots had united with their compatriots against England. Maitland, his head ever buzzing with old ideas of new diplomatic maneuvers, had proposed that Marie Stuart should marry the Spanish Carlos. On May 10, 1563, the Cardinal of Lorraine had spoken on behalf of his niece at a

---

[47] " Placebo " was the form equivalent to the modern " aye " at a public meeting; hence, a " placebo " was a " yes man."

session of the Council of Trent, and the Most Reverend Fathers had expressed their pleasure at the great filial devotion of the Queen of Scots to the Holy Apostolic See, praying that God would " give her force both to extend the boundaries of her kingdom and to carry afar the name of the Catholic religion." The cardinal, moreover, had another suitor in mind for Marie. An envoy from France had accordingly suggested to her the name of the Archduke Charles of Austria. Above all, her own heart was torn. Barely twenty-one years old, yet two and a half years a widow, she could hardly look on the question of her marriage with the dispassionate eye of a Maitland or the calculating glance of her uncle the cardinal. But she was ambitious too. When, a hundred years later, the Duc de la Rochefoucauld wrote that one often passes from love to ambition, seldom from ambition to love, perhaps he had forgotten Marie Stuart. She had never been allowed to separate these motivations.

As she waited for Knox to enter, a scene from the past moved quickly across her mind. At fifteen and a half, dressed in a blue velvet robe covered with silver lilies and precious gems, and on her head a diamond coronet worth many great fortunes, she had been conducted by the French king to the altar of Notre Dame de Paris. Opposite the great west door of that cathedral, a vast amphitheater had been erected; a gallery was hung with blue velvet and adorned with golden lilies. Before the door she could see, in her memory, the papal legate, the Cardinal Archbishop du Bellay, with the prelates of France. She remembered how bands had played music to charm vast waiting crowds; how the halberdiers had kept guard for the arrival of the royal pair. The splendor had been intentionally spectacular. For over two hundred years no dauphin had been married on French soil, and the triumphant Guises wanted to show everyone that they had virtually brought Scotland within the hegemony of France. After High Mass, the bridegroom, just fourteen years of age, had received homage as king consort of Scotland. A bilious boy, weak, timid, and as unhandsome as his bride was beautiful, he had led her, with the heavy gold crown of Scotland now suspended over her head, to dinner at the Archbishop's palace, after which the royal procession had made its way through the thronged streets, receiving tremendous ovations from the delighted crowds, to the old palace of the Tournelles. Not even Paris had seen such magnificence. That evening there had been a ball. As the girl queen danced a stately pavan, a courtier had to carry her train behind her, for it was seven and a half yards long. And during the ball, a fantastic show entranced the guests: singing girls, hobbyhorses caparisoned in gold, white ponies drawing pagan gods, and six galleons with sails of gold, each carrying a masked prince. As these galleons passed the marble table at which the princesses sat, the princes leaped out in turn and gallantly " captured " the princess of their choice. Young Francis, of course, had somewhat nervously carried off his own lady, the precocious and exceedingly intelligent Marie. Nurtured in the atmosphere of French court profligacy, he had evidently been well aware, despite his absurd youthfulness and timidity, of the attractions of his future wife, whom he had been taught to regard as God's gift to him, while she, dazzled by the glory of his surroundings, had no doubt seen Francis through a haze of splendor and strength that were certainly not his own.

All that was gone. The court in which she now found herself was so austere that even its feeble attempts at gaiety, could not but make her think wistfully of a warmer land and of those splendid scenes of the past. She longed for love and wondered how to mix it with ambition as, she believed, a queen must do. The prodigal splendor of the past seemed a dream now; she wanted to make it a reality, to relive all her emotions at a deeper level. And here was this little man, whom she had tried to conciliate even at the expense of humbling herself before his evidently insatiable arrogance; here was this meddlesome little peasant preacher turned prophet now interfering in — of all things! — her marriage. She could hardly wait for him to enter the room.

"I have borne with you in all your rigorous manner of speaking," she began, "both against myself and against my uncles; yea, I have sought your favors by all possible means. I

193

offered unto you presence and audience whensoever it pleased you to admonish me; and yet I cannot be quit of you. I avow to God, I shall be once revenged."

She burst into tears, then into an uncontrollable fit of sobbing. She wanted to go on speaking, but the sobs choked her and the hot tears that had scalded her eyes were on her pretty cheeks again as soon as she tried to dry her sad face.

Knox looked on unmoved, his silky beard uncannily still. So she had thought, had she, that he would be satisfied with opportunities for her admonition? He had wanted much more. He had wanted a settlement for the Kirk; money to support his preachers and extend the Kirk's work, increasingly hampered by the severe winter that had reduced the land to near-famine while the royal court fiddled and danced. He had wanted, indeed, nothing less than the orderly socialization of Scotland under the banner of the Kirk of Jesus Christ, Very God, crucified, risen . . . whose Kingdom should have no end. And what had this weeping child who was Queen of Scots given him? Pretty flatteries, idle words, empty tokens of good intentions for the Kirk. They had meant nothing, these tokens, these flatteries, these words; nothing but a fresh sign of Guise perfidy. Well might she weep, she who, while neglecting the rights of the Kirk of God in her realm, had caused a scandal even in her own court by allowing the amorous, erotic French poet Chastelard to be discovered in her bedroom one hapless night in February, ten days before his execution. Knox did not stop to consider precisely how much truth there had been in that scandal. That the daughter of Mary of Guise should so behave was only as he would have expected.

But now the queen's sobs had subsided and she was looking at him with deep hurt in her swollen eyes. He began in his accustomed, tedious style, and was soon reminding her that he flattered no flesh when she cut him short.

" But what have ye to do with my marriage? " she asked, her voice trembling with rage and hurt.

Knox smothered an impatient gesture. Could she not even wait to hear his argument?

" If it please your Majesty patiently to hear me," he went

194

on, " I shall show the truth in plain words. I grant your Grace offered unto me more than ever I required; but my answer was then, as it is now, that God hath not sent me to await upon the courts of princesses . . . but I am sent to preach the evangel of Jesus Christ to such as please to hear it; and it hath two parts, repentance and faith. And now, Madam, in preaching repentance, of necessity it is that the sins of men be so noted that they may know wherein they offend; but so it is that the most part of your nobility are so addicted to your affections that neither God's Word, nor yet their commonwealth, are rightly regarded. And therefore it becomes me so to speak, that they may know their duty."

Had Marie Stuart been less perturbed just then, she might have wondered whether it could possibly be that Knox was, in his way, jealous of the nobles for having stolen her from him. But she did not. She was too outraged by his insolence. Peasant-born renegade priest that he was, who within her own short lifetime had been a miserable captive, chained to an oar of a French galley — how dare such a man meddle in her marriage?

" What have ye to do with my marriage? " she repeated insistently. Her past clemency had been wasted on such a man. She must give him a sharp reminder of the obscurity of his birth, to bring home to him the absurdity of his interference in a queen's marriage, so she added waspishly: " Or what are ye within this commonwealth? "

" A subject born within the same, Madam," he flashed back. In this later famous retort lay the very essence of the meaning of his revolution. A ruler was placed in a position of immense trust and authority by God himself; but the humblest subject of the ruler had for that very reason the duty as well as the right to be concerned that the ruler's rule was in accordance with God's law. This duty was not least evident to subjects who had learned the law of God directly from God's Word in his Kirk that is the " company and multitude of men chosen of God, who richtly worship and imbrace Him be trew faith in Christ Jesus, quha is the only head of the same Kirk, quhilk alswa is the bodie and spouse of Christ Jesus, quhilk Kirk is catholike, that is, universal, because it conteinis the Elect of all ages, of all realmes, nations and tongues, be they of the Jewes, or be they of the Gentiles, quha have communion and societie with God the Father, and with his Son Christ Jesus, throw the sanctificatioun of his haly Spirit." [48] Knox was speaking not only for himself. He was speaking for everyman under God. He would not be put off by her veiled reference to his lowly birth. He went on:

"And albeit I neither be Earl, Lord, nor baron within it, yet has God made me (how abject that ever I be in your eyes), a profitable member within the same: Yea, Madam, to me it appertains no less to warn of such things as may hurt it, if I foresee them, than it does to any of the nobility; for both my vocation and conscience crave plainness of me. And therefore, Madam, to yourself I say that which I speak in public place: Whensoever that the nobility of this realm shall consent that ye be subject to an unfaithful [49] husband, they do as much as in them lieth to renounce Christ, to banish his truth from them, to betray the freedom of this realm, and perchance shall in the end do small comfort to yourself."

Marie Stuart burst into tears again. Erskine tried to mollify her in his gentle, kindly way, praising her beauty and charm and telling her how every prince in Europe longed to win her love. But the girl went on crying. Knox waited gravely as a father waits for the tears of a justly punished child to give place to a chastened demeanor.

"Madam," he continued, "in God's presence I speak: I never delighted in the weeping of any of God's creatures; yea I can scarcely well abide the tears of my own boys whom my own hand corrects, much less can I rejoice in your Majesty's weeping. But seeing I have offered unto you no just occasion to be offended, but have spoken the truth, as my vocation craves of me, I must sustain (albeit unwillingly) your Majesty's tears rather than I dare hurt my conscience or betray my commonwealth through my silence."

[48] *Confession of Faith,* 1560, Article XVI.

[49] That is, unfaithful to God, infidel, as Knox accounted those who in face of the Reformation stubbornly adhered to the corrupted old religion.

The queen indignantly commanded Knox to leave her presence and await her pleasure in the antechamber. Erskine remained with her, and he and Lord John of Coldingham, who was then admitted, both stayed with her for the better part of an hour. Knox seemed particularly satisfied with all that he had said and done. The queen's ladies were sitting about in the anteroom. He took the opportunity of giving them a more everyday sort of homily on the side. They were exquisitely dressed; they had spent much time on the adornment of their bodies. Very fine: they looked beautiful. But how much time had they spent on their souls?

"O fair ladies," he said, with a not unkindly smile that quickly changed to a look of great solemnity, "how pleasing were this life of yours if it should ever abide, and then in the end that we might pass to heaven with all this gay gear. But fie upon that knave Death, that will come whether we will or not! And when he has laid on his arrest, the foul worms will be busy with this flesh, be it never so fair or so tender; and the silly [50] soul, I fear, will be so feeble that it can neither carry with it gold, garnishing, targeting, pearl, nor precious stones."

The ladies were entranced by the directness of his words. No wonder, they thought, he was such a name in the land. What strength there was in that voice of his! They felt as though he had taken them up one by one and shaken them over the jaws of hell; all in their pretty dresses too. A wonderful experience. They were quite sorry when Erskine came out and told him he might go home for the present. Erskine and Lord John had persuaded the queen to take no further action in the meantime, however otherwise her heart might be directing her.

So Knox went back to his house in Trunk Close. He was now convinced that Scotland's only remaining hope was a second revolution. The only question was how soon it must be. He longed for a season of quiet and peace, for he was sick of the endless strife. But there could be no peace with Marie Stuart or her court. Disappointed, in varying measure, with the

[50] Weak.

nobles of Scotland on whom he had relied, he would now turn
to the people. The form the second revolution would take he
did not yet know. It was in God's hands. It might be that the
people must rise against their sovereign with the might of the
sword. It might be that God had another plan.

Shortly after giving Knox this audience, the Queen of Scots
left for the west country.

20 The Laird of Pitarrow, comptroller to the queen,
was at sermon in St. Giles's on Sunday, August 15,
when a messenger from the palace came over to him and whispered something in his ear. The Laird's face clouded. Perhaps the report was exaggerated; even so, if it were true at all
it was bad enough.

It was true. The queen had, of course, taken the Mass with
her on her travels to the west: a chaplain naturally formed
part of her entourage. In Protestant eyes that was deplorable
enough; but it was only what was expected. What had not
been expected was that, in her absence from Edinburgh, Mass
had continued to be celebrated at Holyrood. Now, it trans-
pired, a crowd had forced a way into the Holyrood chapel and
were brawling there. It was said that the priest was in danger
of his life.

Two of the ringleaders, burgesses of Edinburgh, were cited
for trial on October 24. Knox decided this was as good an occasion as any for his second revolution. On October 8 he sent
out letters to key places throughout Scotland, spreading news
of the forthcoming trial of two Protestant burgesses, and summoning all who were concerned to preserve the Kirk against
the evident danger. Some of them might be inclined to think
the matter of insufficient account to warrant their leaving
their homes; others might be timid about offending the " upper powers." Knox expressed the hope, however, that " neither
flattery nor fear shall make you so far to decline from Christ

Jesus as that, against your public promise and solemn band, ye will leave your brethren in so just a cause. And albeit there were no great danger, yet cannot our assembly be unprofitable; for many things require consultation, which cannot be had unless the wisest and godliest convene." It was a summoning of the whole Kirk to rise to its own defense.

One of the letters came into the queen's hands. Was not this treason? she asked her councilors. While some of the nobles went to Knox to remonstrate with him, the queen postponed the trial of the burgesses. Knox would listen to neither pleading nor warning. He was in for serious trouble, they said. He replied he had nothing to fear: he had done nothing wrong. Nothing wrong! Had he not summoned the queen's lieges? Was not that treason? Knox pointed out that it had been done before. Ah, yes, they said; but that was before the queen had come to her realm: it was different now. Men had borne with Knox in the past; he would find they would not bear with him in the future, unless he bowed to the queen. Knox reported that he had never set himself up against the queen's Majesty except in the service of God. Nor had he any fears that what was right in the past might not be right in the future. " My God," he told Maxwell, " is unchangeable."

Maitland and Lord James had no desire to let the affair reach the stage of a public trial. They wanted to keep on as good terms as possible with both the Kirk and the Queen. These were the two great powers in the land. How much better it would be, they felt, if the whole matter could be hushed up. They told Knox they had gone to great pains to mollify the queen, but that she was very angry. And after all, they urged, he was in the wrong. If he would only just admit his fault, they could patch things up. Knox said he would make his own defense at the proper time and in the proper place. But what defense could he have? they asked. Knox replied that since he was evidently already guilty in their eyes, it would hardly do for him to lay his defense before them now. No, there must be a public trial.

The nobles, tired of his lofty speeches, decided there was nothing for it but to let him stew in his own juice. Writing

199

eight years later, a year before his death, Knox felt these nobles were never the same to him again. On the other hand,
there were visits from sympathizers. One of these, John Spens
of Condie, an advocate, wanted to see the documents in the
case. Spens, who was evidently a gentle sort of man, expressed
great relief when he had read them. Rumors had made him
fear that Knox had done something wrong, something discreditable to the Reformed Kirk. He was delighted to find, to
the contrary, that there was no truth in the gossip about him.
Of course he would be put on trial; but God would not fail
him. God would come to his assistance. Such was the confidence that the preachers of the Reform had instilled into their
people — confidence in the care of God for each one of his
children. Well had they taught them that God was " a very
present help in trouble."

The queen was enjoying another sort of confidence in the
action she was about to take against Knox. Far away, the
Council of Trent, at last closing after no fewer than eighteen
years of intermittent talking with a view to the crushing of
Protestantism and the revival of the power of the Roman
Church, had been toying for months with the idea of excom-
municating English Elizabeth and recognizing the Queen of
Scots as the rightful queen of England.[51] With the Queen of
Scots married to a Spanish prince it might not even be neces-
sary for disaffected Englishmen to be incited to assassinate
Elizabeth. In any case, the strength of England's sea power
was not yet fully known, though it was soon to assert itself.[52]
It was hoped that England could be frightened into accepting
Marie Stuart for its queen, so setting the scene for a relatively
peaceful restoration of papal power throughout both England
and Scotland. And now that the Queen of Scots had caught

[51] *Supra*, n. 44.

[52] Marie Stuart's execution by Elizabeth in 1587 made it certain that
Spain would attack England, and England, united to resist such attack, defeated Spain's " Invincible Armada " the following year, so completely that
this, Spain's first serious attempt to conquer England, was also its last. It
was also the end of the hopes of the papacy (though not the end of its
dreams) of re-establishing the power of the Roman Church in the world
by the use of force.

Knox napping, she could quickly convict him of treason and, so disgracing him, destroy the Reformed Kirk whose socially prominent supporters she had already done her best to alienate from his leadership.

Between six and seven o'clock in the evening, on the appointed date, a few days before Christmas, John Knox arrived at Holyrood, accompanied by such a large body of sympathizers that they crowded the inner close of the palace, and even the stairs right up to the door of the room where the trial was to take place. A chair was reserved for the queen at the head of the Council table. On the right, in virtue of his precedence, sat Châtelherault; on the left, Argyll. The other nobles at the table were Lord James Stuart (Earl of Moray) and Glencairn, Marischal, and Ruthven; also seated at the table were the various officers, Pitarrow (the queen's comptroller), Knox's friend John Spens the advocate, and the Lord Justice Clerk. Old Maitland of Lethington was among the other persons present in the room but not seated at the Council table.

The queen entered ceremoniously and was seated with Maxwell standing behind her on one side and Maitland on the other. The queen, immensely enjoying herself, saw Knox standing bareheaded at the other end of the table. Suddenly she burst out laughing. Some of the courtiers dutifully joined in. It was a polite gesture.

" But do you know what I am laughing at? " she asked. " That man once made me weep, and never wept a tear himself. I will see if I can make him weep."

Maitland began: " The queen's Majesty is informed that ye have travailed to raise a tumult of her subjects against her, and for certification thereof there is presented to her your own letter subscribed in your name. Yet because her Grace will do nothing without a good advisement, she has convened you before this part of the nobility, that they may witness betwix you and her."

The queen interposed that Knox should be required to acknowledge his handwriting. Knox was shown the letter. Yes, he acknowledged that the signature was his. Playfully, he added that it was unnecessary for him to read the text of the letter that had been written by the scribe, because he had such confidence in the latter that he had just signed blank sheets and let the scribe copy out the text of the letter in each case.

"More than I would have done," said Maitland gravely.

"Charity is not suspicious," rejoined Knox, laughing quietly in his beard.

"Well, well," the queen interrupted, "read your own letter, and then answer to such things as shall be demanded of you."

She was impatient to have Knox convicted. Taking the letter, Knox assumed his most rhetorical air, a deliberate caricature, almost, of himself reading Isaiah in St. Giles's.

The queen commanded John Spens to make the formal accusation. He did so in a quiet, gentle voice. What a mild man he was, thought Knox admiringly, for though he was no mild man himself he could admire the quality in others. No sooner had the letter been read than Marie Stuart looked round the table and asked: "Heard ye ever, my Lords, a more despiteful and treasonable letter?"

Nobody spoke. Then Maitland, adopting his most skillfully resonant voice and fatherly tone, said: "Master Knox! Are ye not sorry from your heart, and do ye not repent that such a letter has passed your pen, and from you is come to the knowledge of others?"

Knox assumed a puzzled look. Would the Lord Secretary be so kind as to tell him what it was he was to repent. He could not very well make an act of contrition without knowing the offense for which he ought to be contrite.

"Offense!" exclaimed Maitland. "If there were no more but the convocation of the queen's lieges, the offense cannot be denied."

"Remember yourself, my Lord," enjoined Knox, "there is a difference betwix a lawful convocation and an unlawful. If I have been guilty in this I have oft offended since I came in Scotland: for what convocation of the brethren has ever been to this day into which my pen served not? Before this no man led it to my charge as a crime."

It was an echo of Christ's words in the Bible Knox knew so

well: " I sat daily with you teaching in the temple, and ye laid no hold on me." But Maitland, using the argument that had been offered to Knox before in private conference, pointed out that times had changed:

" Then was then and now is now," he said. " We have no need of such convocations as sometimes we have had."

Knox replied that he could see no difference, except that the devil used to go about unmasked and now wore a light disguise. He had formerly come in open tyranny and oppression; now he took the trouble to put on the cloak of justice. Essentially, there was no difference. Knox was just about to plunge into another of his endless disquisitions, when the queen, more impatient than ever, cut him short and asked the Council whether they were not trifling. He had made convocation of her lieges without her authority. Was not that treason? Lord Ruthven shook his head. No, it was not quite as simple as that, he informed her. After all, Knox made convocation of her lieges every day when he brought them to prayer and sermon. Something more would have to be proved.

" Hold your tongue," snapped Marie sharply. " Let him make answer for himself." It was bad enough cornering Knox without having her own Council behave as though they were pleading for him. Whose side were they supposed to be on, anyway?

" I began, Madam," said Knox, " to reason with the Secretary, whom I take to be a far better dialectician than your Grace is, that all convocations are not unlawful; and now my Lord Ruthven has given the instance, which, if your Grace will deny, I shall address me for the proof."

What was he up to? thought the queen. Was not he just taking his last opportunity to throw his common insolence in her face before being proved guilty?

" I will say nothing against your religion," she said, " nor against your convening to your sermons, but what authority have ye to convocate my subjects when ye will, without my commandment? "

" I have no pleasure to decline from the former purpose," said Knox grandly. " And yet, Madam, to satisfy your Grace's two questions, I answer that at my will I never convened four persons in Scotland; but at the order that the brethren has appointed, I have given divers advertisements, and great multitudes have assembled thereupon. And if your Grace complain that this was done without your Grace's commandment, I answer, so has all that God has blessed within this realm from the beginning of this action. And therefore, Madam, I must be convicted by a just law, that I have done against the duty of God's messenger in writing of this letter, before that either I be sorry, or yet repent for the doing of it, as my Lord Secretary would persuade me. For what I have done, I have done at the commandment of the general Kirk of this realm; and therefore, I think, I have done no wrong."

" Ye shall not escape so," cried the queen. She turned to her councilors. " Is it not treason, my Lords," she asked, " to accuse a prince of cruelty? I think there be acts of Parliament against such whisperers."

Some nodded vaguely. Knox returned to his point: " But wherein can I be accused? "

The queen showed him a passage in his letter in which he had written that the two burgesses were being tried only in order to prepare the way for the queen " to execute cruelty upon a greater multitude."

" Lo, what say ye to that? " she asked triumphantly.

There was whispering at the table. Some wondered whether Knox should have such an invitation to worm his way out of the charge once more. Taking advantage of it, he inquired formally of the queen:

" Is it lawful, Madam, to answer for myself? Or shall I be damned before I be heard? "

" Say what ye can," she answered, " for I think ye have enough ado." [53]

Knox began by appealing to the Protestant sentiments of the nobles.

" I will first desire this of your Grace, Madam, and of this most honorable audience, whether if your Grace knows not,

[53] That is, " you will have a hard enough job."

that the obstinate papists are deadly enemies to all such as profess the evangel of Jesus Christ, and that they most earnestly desire the extermination of them, and of the true doctrine that is taught within this realm? "

The queen said nothing. But one of the Lords spoke up: " God forbid that either the lives of the faithful, or yet the staying of the doctrine, stood in the power of the papists: for just experience has told us what cruelty lies in their hearts."

This was precisely what Knox had hoped the Council would admit.

" I must proceed then," he went on, " seeing that I perceive that all will grant that it were a barbarous cruelty to destroy such a multitude as profess the evangel of Jesus Christ within this realm, which ofter than once or twice they have attempted to do by force, as things done of late days do testify, whereof they, by God and his providence, being disappointed, have invented more crafty and dangerous practices, to wit, to make the prince party under cover of law: and so what they could not do by open force, they shall perform by crafty deceit. For who thinks, my Lords, that the insatiable cruelty of the papists — within this realm, I mean — shall end in the murdering of these two brethren now unjustly summoned, and more unjustly to be accused? I think no man of judgment can so esteem, but rather the direct contrary, that is, that by this few number they intend to prepare a way to their bloody enterprises against the whole. And therefore, Madam, cast up when ye list [54] the acts of your Parliament. I have offended nothing against them; I accuse not in my letter your Grace, nor yet your nature of cruelty. But I affirm yet again, that the pestilent papists, who have inflamed your Grace without cause against those poor men at this present, are the sons of the devil; and therefore must obey the desires of their father, who has been a liar and a murderer from the beginning."

Knox looked as though he could go on for hours. One of the Lords stopped him.

" Ye forget yourself; ye are not now in the pulpit," he cautioned him.

[54] When you please.

"I am in the place," replied Knox, now thoroughly warmed to his subject, "where I am demanded of conscience to speak the truth; and therefore I speak. The truth I speak, impugn it whoso list. And hereunto, Madam, I would add that honest, gentle, and meek natures by appearance, by wicked and corrupt councilors may be converted and alter to the direct contrary. Example we have of Nero, who, in the beginning of his empire, we find having some natural shame; but after that his flatterers had encouraged him in all impiety, alleging that nothing was either unhonest nor yet unlawful for his personage, who was emperor above all others: when he had drunk of this cup, I say, to what enormities he fell the histories bear witness. And now, Madam, to speak plainly, papists and conjured enemies to Jesus Christ have your Grace's ear patent at all times. I assure your Grace they are dangerous councilors, and that your mother so found."

Maitland smiled. Knox was preaching himself to his doom. They had heard enough. It was time to stop him. He whispered softly to the queen. Let the Lords now consider and pass judgment. But Marie had been irritated by Knox's cleverness in turning the blame on the councilors. He was treating her as though she were an irresponsible child in the hands of wicked statesmen. She would have one more thrust at him, before he was convicted. His words were fair enough, she observed, in speaking before the Lords; but what about the time he had made her weep? Knox went carefully over the whole conversation he had had with the queen on that occasion, as far as he could remember it. Once again Maitland whispered to the queen. Then he told Knox he might return to his house — adding acidly, "for this night."

Knox had to have the final word.

"I thank God and the queen's Majesty," he said. "And, Madam, I pray God to purge your heart from papistry, and to preserve you from the counsel of flatterers; for how pleasing that they appear to your ear and corrupt affection for the time, experience has told us in what perplexity they have brought famous princes."

When he had gone, the Lords were required to vote whether

Knox had offended the queen's Majesty. The vote was unanimous. Every man at the table said he was not guilty of the charge. The queen left. Maitland and others raged at the way the voting had gone. The queen returned to the table and the vote was demanded all over again. It was given exactly as before.

The queen was bitterly disappointed. She felt that her councilors had failed her. It was from this time that, changing her policy disastrously, she went on the road that led to her ruin. Distrusting her advisers, she turned to personal favorites. There was, for instance, an Italian *valet de chambre* at the palace, called David Riccio. He had been there for a year or two. She would use him. Within a year, after rapid advancements, the *valet de chambre* became French Secretary. Then, tired of both Knox and her own councilors, she married Lord Darnley in July, 1565. Riccio became her chief adviser. The following March, when she was six months pregnant, she was sitting one evening after supper with Riccio and the Countess of Argyll, when a band of armed men burst into the room and demanded that he accompany them. He ran screaming like a child behind the queen and clutched her skirt; but he was dragged off to a bedroom. Fifty dagger wounds, it is said, were found on his dead body afterward. Darnley, from motives of jealousy, had instigated the murder, with the ready help of a number of the nobles whom the queen had slighted. For a time there were many who, shocked by the murder, rallied to the queen's support. She was nevertheless on the way to the humiliation, abdication, and imprisonment of 1567, and the tragedy of twenty bitter years that ended with the executioner's ax. Perhaps, indeed, a vision of her tragic end had flashed before her when, many years earlier, she had worked a pretty device into her embroidery: " *En ma fin est mon commencement.*"

Her last encounter with Knox showed she was no match for him after all. Both intellectually and morally, he was at the height of his power. Long experience in handling audiences of varying kinds had given him an extraordinary skill in debate. Having come before the queen and Council on a charge of treason and with seemingly irrefutable evidence against him signed by his own hand, he left with his judges unanimously voting his innocence. Little wonder that when the General Assembly of the Kirk met on Christmas Day he was in excellent form. Insisting that the brethren must fully consider the question whether he had acted rightly or not, and vote on this question, Knox threatened that if they did not do so he would never again open his mouth as a public minister. Well might the court party have wished for the fulfillment of that threat, if only they could have believed in its possibility. The Assembly duly considered the question, of course, in accordance with Knox's wishes, and wholeheartedly endorsed the action he had taken. Knox took the opportunity of reminding them of what he had said five years before about the lawfulness, in certain circumstances, of withholding tithes. Unless those who had misappropriated the ancient patrimony of the Church and were spending it on their pleasure would yield it up, the common people would be justified if they stopped paying the tithes. This was a threat that no one could ignore. It could mean that the second revolution was to take the form of a popular uprising against the rich that might be exceedingly horrible to live through.

Meanwhile, though the queen continued perforce to recognize the Kirk, she did not give it the money.

21 On Palm Sunday, the twenty-sixth of March, 1564, a wedding took place that was the cause of much tongue-wagging in Scotland.

John Knox, now a widower of fifty, was married in church that day to the daughter of Lord Ochiltree, an old friend of his. The bride, Margaret Stuart, was not yet seventeen. Naturally, Knox's numerous enemies made the most of this event to discredit him. The marriage was denounced as "monstrous." There were fantastic stories that he had used magical arts to win the young girl, and in later generations it was even suggested that he had been trying to worm his way into the royal family, for Lord Ochiltree, a Stuart, was related to the queen, though very distantly. As a matter of fact, not only was the relationship too distant to be of any practical significance, but Lord Ochiltree, a pleasant, quiet man, was of little social consequence and so impoverished that he was obliged occasionally to borrow money from his son-in-law.

Whatever were the motives of this extraordinary marriage, they were certainly not those of an adventurer. Knox's first wife, Marjorie Bowes, had been dead more than three years, and for some time his mother-in-law had been looking after Nathaniel and Eleazer, Knox's two sons, who were both still under seven years of age. To Knox, Mrs. Bowes had always been just a little *de trop*. We have already seen that there was less romanticism in the sixteenth century on the subject of marriage than in our own times. But when all that is said, the marriage of a widower of fifty to a girl barely seventeen does seem intrinsically repellent. Even in Knox's day public opinion was offended. When William Farel, one of the Continental Reformers, a scion of an aristocratic family of Dauphiné, had married a girl under sixteen when he himself was nearly seventy, he had incurred Calvin's severe rebuke.[55] " Certain it is," wrote Calvin, " that our poor brother, Master William, has for once been so ill-advised that we must all be on his account in shame and confusion." So Knox's marriage, though less outrageous, was not congenial to the finer feelings of his own day. Politically, it was certainly not advantageous; emotionally it was no doubt otherwise for Knox. He had of late years lost many of his friends, and Ochiltree was one of the few who had, in his quiet way, stood by him through every trial. Moreover, notwithstanding the disparity of their ages, Margaret seems to have made Knox a very good wife. Though few details are known about their domestic life, it appears that Margaret discharged her duties with diligence and affection until the time of his death eight years later. She bore him

---

[55] At the time of Knox's second marriage, Calvin was dying. He died two months later, May 27, 1564.

three children, all daughters, Martha, Margaret, and Elizabeth. These all married in the course of time. Elizabeth, the youngest, married John Welch, a minister of the Kirk. The older biographies of John Witherspoon, one of the signatories of the American Declaration of Independence, claimed that he was descended from Knox through the latter's youngest daughter. While the evidence for this is insufficient, Witherspoon's alleged descent from Knox has not yet been satisfactorily disproved.[56]

After his marriage to Margaret Stuart, Knox took relatively little part in public life. He preached and administered the affairs of the Kirk, and he went on being effectively explosive. But his explosions were henceforward in some ways more withdrawn from the political arena. For more than a year he hardly exploded at all.

By about the time of his second marriage, Knox had had enough of political life. He had fought his fight, and on the whole he had been extraordinarily successful. He had not achieved all he had wanted for the Kirk; but since what he had wanted was nothing less than the New Jerusalem on Scottish soil, it was not difficult for so innately practical a man to accept the failures. Tired as he was, he would have gone on at the old pace; but he knew with the shrewdness of age that he had done all that for the present could be done. The rest must wait for hands and voices other than his. His conscience thus stilled, he was easily disposed to hope for a quieter life. For years he had known scarcely any privacy. He had seen too little of his children, and he had enjoyed too few of the pleas-

[56] The descent alleged in the older biographies of Witherspoon rested in part on mere conjecture. (See Blackader MS., Wodrow MSS., National Library of Scotland.) Readers interested in investigating this subject should consult a MS. (W772.5) by Jessie Laing Sibbet, in the library of the Presbyterian Historical Society of Philadelphia. On the other hand, there is no evidence, as far as I know, sufficient to disprove the alleged descent. Dr. Hugh Watt, Principal Emeritus of New College, Edinburgh, and a Knox scholar, who is still disposed to entertain the descent story, informs me that it is hoped that a complete list of Knox's descendants, as far as this may be compiled from the records at Register House, Edinburgh, may be prepared, possibly by the time of the quatercentenary of the Scottish Reformation in 1960.

ures of friendship, for the seemingly casual visits of friends too often turned out to mean troublesome business. Above all he was tired of duplicity and intrigue, though he had sometimes himself paid the intriguers back in their own coin. Now in the company of his young wife he felt he could enjoy what he had missed. After striving with royal courts he could appreciate her ingenuousness. Her artless laughter soothed him. Her simple, girlish earnestness in the regular family devotions filled with peace the heart of the man who had thirsted after righteousness.

The eighth General Assembly met on June 25, 1564. The rift between commonalty and nobles was more noticeable than ever. The courtiers now even refused to sit with the others. Maitland complained that Knox had modified his prayers for the queen. Now he was using the form: " Illuminate her heart, *if it be Thy pleasure.*" Was not this a suggestion that he was willing to fulfill the public duty of prayer for the sovereign, though in fact he believed she was past redemption? Wearily, Knox pointed out that all prayers should have the saving clause, " Thy will be done." He could not resist adding that the queen's behavior was not such as to induce in him any assurance that she was among the elect, though he could always pray, in case it might be so, present appearances notwithstanding. Maitland wanted Knox to say in what way the queen had rebelled against God as Knox had alleged. Knox said she had not listened to the gospel. Maitland reminded him of her willingness to be admonished. To be admonished, yes, replied Knox; but not to obey the admonitions. So went on the unprofitable argument. Some of the Protestant nobles had strayed so far that it had been heard said among them that perhaps the Mass was not really idolatry after all. There was much talking as usual; as usual nothing was settled. The court went back to its well-laden table; the preachers to their poverty and need.

After the queen's marriage to Darnley, by which time she was setting aside the advice of the Protestant nobles altogether and looking instead to men like Riccio and Bothwell, the preachers did not all merely live in poverty; some of them died of it — died in a few cases, it was said, of starvation in the streets. On July 28, at nine o'clock at night, three heralds stood at the Mercat Cross of Edinburgh, flourished their trumpets, and proclaimed that Darnley, "the rycht nobill and illustris Prince Henry, Duke of Albany," was to be styled, during his marriage to the Queen of Scots, "King of this our Kingdom." Infatuated by him, Marie had been unable to refuse him anything his foolish ambition craved, though without the assent of Parliament the designation was in fact illegal. Darnley, a tepid adherent of the old religion, was present at sermon when Knox preached on August 19, 1565. He sat on a chair opposite the pulpit, curious, no doubt, to hear the eloquence of the famous preacher. It had become almost a fashion in high society in Scotland to be admonished by Knox, and perhaps the nineteen-year-old Darnley wanted a taste of the fashionable pleasure. But Knox scarcely looked at him. The time for action was over for the present, he was saying; the night was coming in which no man could work. But beyond lay a "more vehement battle" for Scotland, and abroad a fire was lighted "that shall burn more than we look for." Meanwhile let the faithful recall God's "wondrous works." Let them hide in prayer while the fury of the world spent itself, knowing that in the end all cruel persecutors would receive their just reward and God's troubled people enter into his peace. With deep earnestness and all the skill that years of personal suffering and pulpit experience had combined to give him, he raised his throbbing voice:

"Come, my people, enter thou into thy chambers and shut thy doors after thee; hide thyself for a very little while, until the indignation pass over. Grant unto us, O Lord, to repose ourselves in the sanctuary of thy promise until that thou thyself appear to the comfort of thy afflicted and to the terror of thy enemies."

But there were occasional thrusts too, especially at rule by babes. Darnley could understand only a phrase here and there, and what little he understood he did not like. Wearied by the long sermon, he left in a huff and rode off to go hawking. That same afternoon Knox was forbidden to preach in Edinburgh at any time again while the king and queen were present at court. Knox replied with dignity that he would obey the Kirk's orders. The Town Council duly made formal protest against the ban.

Months passed. Knox preached, but his sermons were more meditative, less inflammatory. As the queen banished the Protestant nobles, he prayed for them, that God might comfort them. He called upon the faithful of all congregations to contribute more toward the terrible needs of the ministers and of the poor. He was commissioned by the Kirk's Assembly to order a General Fast. His first daughter, Martha, was born. He was commissioned by the Assembly to go on a preaching tour in the south; but he was back in time to hear the news of Riccio's murder on the night of Saturday, March 9. Marie was imprisoned in her room and the Protestant nobles took possession of the palace. The Earl of Moray (Lord James) came back to Edinburgh with his men. But Marie, having won Darnley's heart back, escaped to Dunbar with his help. Now hopelessly in the hands of ridiculously irresponsible advisers, she was able, nine days after the murder of Riccio, to stage a great display of military force in the streets of Edinburgh. Openly at war with the Kirk, she appeared to the imagination of the faithful in all the most lurid colors of Scotland's tyrants of the past. Knox fled to Kyle, Ayrshire, his wife's country, where he remained for some five months, employing his time on the great *History of the Reformation in Scotland* that he had already begun. Craig, his assistant, remained in Edinburgh to minister to the faithful.

About the end of the year Knox went, with the approval of the General Assembly, on a visit to England, and while he was absent from his native land political events moved rapidly. Darnley, whom Marie had named King of Scotland, was murdered by Bothwell in February, 1567. Within a few weeks, the Queen of Scots had married the murderer. Shortly afterward she was seized by some of the nobles at Carberry Hill and taken to Edinburgh, where outraged crowds in the street shrieked, "Burn the whore!" On June 16 the Queen of Scots was incarcerated in Lochleven Castle.

Knox returned in time for the meeting of the General Assembly on June 25. The nobles themselves were now divided into two camps, one the Earl of Moray's party and the other adhering to Argyll. The Assembly made an attempt to conciliate the divided Protestant Lords; but it was evident that so long as Marie Stuart was spared, there could be no peace in the land. Elizabeth sent Throgmorton to Edinburgh to ask Knox to urge "lenity." But Knox was preaching daily that the wrath of God on the land could be averted only by her being brought to justice and executed for her crimes. Throgmorton turned to the nobles in the hope that they could stop Knox and his colleagues from advocating such extreme measures and fanning the flame of hatred against the queen. Maitland tried; but Knox preached on as before.

When the General Assembly met again on July 26, it was unwilling to follow the course Knox demanded. The queen was deposed, however, and on August 22, Moray became regent for her infant son. Some of the preachers expected that at last something would be done for the Kirk. But by the end of the year any hopes they had cherished had worn thin. At Stirling, on December 17, the infant heir to the Scottish throne was christened and was solemnly received into the Holy Roman Church with all the pageantry and splendor associated with Rome's past tyranny. Charles IX sent a diamond pendant as a christening present; Elizabeth's gift for the occasion was a gold baptismal font.

On May 2 of the following year, 1568, Marie Stuart escaped from her captivity in Lochleven. The famous story of her escape from that castle stronghold does not quite belong to our narrative; yet all that pertains to her is in some sense a facet of the drama of Knox as well as a chapter of her own extraordinary life, the truth about which is more incredible than fiction. Her escape was accomplished despite elaborate safeguards. With the aid of an extremely intelligent lad of sixteen, Willie Douglas, she was enabled to walk through the door of the castle disguised as a servant, and her escort, having locked the castle door from the outside, rowed her across the lake, dropping the castle keys in the water as he rowed, so as to delay her anticipated pursuers. By that time, though not yet twenty-five, she had known all sorts of heights of joy and depths of sorrow. Now, having buried two husbands and lost two thrones, she was to give herself into the hands of the Protestant queen for whose throne she had intrigued. Then, in 1587, after twenty years of Elizabeth's amiable ambiguity, she who had been princess of the dream of almost every prince in Europe placed her head on the executioner's block, so ending one of the saddest dramas of all history.

Had Knox lived to see her end he would have shed no tear for her. Why was he so pitiless toward Marie Stuart? The Scotsman in him hated her Guise blood. But the violent language he used of her, bordering sometimes on indecency, sprang from no mere hatred of a beautiful young woman's lineage or race or even disposition. To Knox, Marie was a perfect, living symbol of the injustice that had once torn his young heart and opened his eyes to the unrighteousness of the old regime. It is more galling to be thwarted at the end of a race and cheated out of victory an inch from the finishing line than it is to be prevented from starting. Was it not Marie who, when victory was almost in his grasp, snatched it out of his hand, leaving him (but for his faith in God) with only its empty shell? Such, at any rate, were the facts as he saw them. He thought he had slain the dragon, yet in this child of Guise blood its tail rose up like a python to devour the slayer. God would protect him; yet the venomous offspring of the dead dragon was a lively reminder of the dragon's power, the power of Antichrist, the power of Rome, the tormentor of God's elect. Knox knew he hardly looked the part of Saint George. He believed his calling was greater. He believed in the possibility of social righteousness. That was one reason why the Old Testament so much appealed to him, for in it the rise of the ethical consciousness of a people is uniquely unfolded. Even before the doctrines of election and predestination had fully taken hold of him, he had passionately believed that men in fact varied enormously in their moral worth. More and more he saw them to be of two kinds: those whose worth was infinite and those who had no worth at all. That these latter, the worthless, should be so uniformly in the saddle, kicking the long-suffering backs of the infinitely worthy whose worth meant nothing to their persecutors — all this persuaded Knox that the old system itself was evil, so thoroughly evil that it could not be cured, but must be smashed. With poetic precision, Marie Stuart symbolized for Knox the whole edifice of Babylon: bewitching but unjust; gracious but trivial; beautiful but a whore.

In his last years, Marie became more and more an obsession for him. Against his own counsel, the Scots had in their folly spared her life. They had let her slip out of their fingers when it was their plain duty to make an end of her. Now he blamed England for learning nothing from Scotland's folly.

Moray's regency was short. He was assassinated on January 23, 1570. In his sermon the following day, Knox paid generous tribute to him, though he could not resist mention of that " foolish pity " that had spared the life of so wicked a queen. His own heart was sad. He now longed, as elsewhere he put it, to leave the world in the hands of God and take his own good night of it. As he told of the joy of the departed brother who was now at rest in Christ, he poured forth his grief for the tribulations of the Kirk he so loved. Yet in his obsession against Marie he was no mere old man harking back to past sorrows. For even in her abdication and exile she was still a force dividing the land. Maitland was for her. Even Kirkcaldy, one of Knox's oldest friends, with whom he had suffered in the galleys, was holding Edinburgh Castle in her name. And for all the obscene yelps of the mob at the time of her arrest, there were many among the common people who still looked upon her with affection. As the regency passed to Lennox and then to Mar, the futile agony of internecine strife continued. The Marian party, which included many of Knox's former supporters, feared and hated him.

In the fall of 1570, Knox had a slight stroke that temporarily affected his speech. He could neither walk nor write. Rumors spread like wildfire that he was a done man. He would never preach again. But within a week he was back in the pulpit, and by Christmas he was already involved in another foray. By the

216

following May, however, Edinburgh had become too hot even for him. He had refused to be silenced. One night a shot had been fired through the window at his accustomed place; he had escaped death only because he happened to be out of the room. His house was placed under guard. His friends besought him to leave the town for a while, but he refused.

On April 30, Kirkcaldy ordered all enemies of the queen to leave town within six hours. Knox intended once more to stay despite the ultimatum. Kirkcaldy was determined, however, that no harm should come to Knox. Partly, he had in mind, of course, the interests of the Marian party, for Knox was now so sacrosanct that it would cause the party incalculable injury if the prophet were killed, and this, in the present state of affairs, was quite likely to happen. But Kirkcaldy was also thinking, no doubt, of old times, and of the affection that he and others still had for Knox despite their resistance to some of his precepts. He told Knox, therefore, that if he did not leave town he would have to be held in custody in the Castle. He and Maitland requested Knox to go there for a talk. Accompanied by Craig and Winram, his fellow preachers, Knox went for the interview, which turned out to be a remarkably friendly one; almost convivial. Maitland was not well, and the interview took place in his bedroom, where he sat playing with a dog on his knee. Châtelherault and Kirkcaldy were present. Inevitably there was argument between Maitland and Knox. But the nobles were in a good humor: they had money and munitions from France. Prospects in this world looked brighter, they thought, and they were making themselves believe their prospects in the next were all right too so long as they behaved decently to God's prophet.

Knox, for his part, had mellowed a little. Already he had begun to understand that his last fight was to accept God's will that fighting for him was over. He had done the work that needed doing and must not expect to see its fruition in his lifetime on earth. Like Maitland he himself was a sick man. They had each gone their own ways in life, and the difference between these ways was well expressed in their final sally. Maitland, in explanation of his own behavior, spoke of " shifts to save us from great inconvenience." Knox replied that honest men had not thought them so. But for all that, there was no quarreling, for the prophet's thunder was growing faint.

22

Knox was physically a broken man when, leaning on the arm of his attendant and secretary, Richard Bannatyne, he left Edinburgh on May 5, 1571, to go to St. Andrews, where he lodged at the priory. He was accompanied by his young wife and their three infant daughters.

There is something peculiarly exhilarating about returning to the scene of one's college days. If there has been in them even only a thin strand of happiness, in retrospect it is magnified until the whole memory glows. So it must surely be even when the return is to scenes drab and dull in themselves. But St. Andrews has a curiously magical flavor. No less than Heidelberg or Venice, though in a different way, it is a haunted town. Girt by the cold North Sea that breaks on its sandy shores, it is now a fashionable seashore resort, a town of old gray buildings, many in ruins, among which the ghosts of the past seem to wander restlessly. No doubt in 1571 the appearance and feel of the town were very different from what they are today. And yet if, after tasting its flavor, we let our minds pause to identify the ghosts that make St. Andrews live so sharply in our own imagination, we shall find that they are mostly ghosts Knox knew only too well and much better than we do. It was now forty-three years since the burning of young Patrick Hamilton in the town had shocked the nation. It had been said that the smoke of that fire would blow into every house in the land, and so it had.

But as Knox leaned on Bannatyne's arm, looking out at the familiar scene at which he had arrived, it was rather, perhaps, the thought of Wishart's fiery trial that filled his mind. It was almost twenty-five years since that mild young scholar had fallen victim to the Cardinal Primate's fear-laden power. In

218

these twenty-five years had been crowded more events than Knox cared to remember. Marie Stuart had been but three years old. She had since risen to great worldly glory and fallen in abject shame. For Knox, that quarter of a century had been an endless struggle for the overthrow of Rome's tyranny in Scotland. Though the Jesuits had given the papacy hope of plotting for the recovery of its old power; though there were grim portents of troubles in plenty for Scotland in the years ahead; though he himself had not been able to convince all his compatriots, even his brethren in the Kirk, of the real significance of his work and the urgency of the measures he had called for — yet he could look out on the scene of his youth and feel he had done the work God had called him to do. He had established the Kirk by law. One day, despite its present trials, it would be spread over the whole country, the blessed Word of God preached in every parish, and the Bread of Life broken in the uttermost parts of the land. There were now people singing of the pope, as no man could have sung in the taverns in Patrick Hamilton's day:

> " The Paip, that pagane full of pryde,
>   He hes us blindit lang
>
> . . . .
>
>   Bot his abominatioun
>   The Lord hes brocht to licht;
> His Popische pryde, and thrinfalde crowne,
>   Almaist hes loist thair micht."

Here in what had been the ecclesiastical capital of Scotland, the very stones chanted the words to his heart. Here, surely, among these gray monuments of the past, in the hush punctuated by the breaking waves, God's prophet, his day's work done, could find rest at eventide.

But it was not to be so. The university was politically divided: two of the three colleges were for the queen. Knox continued to preach, and among his hearers, as before, were many enemies. Rumors were spread about him — some mere college gossip; others, more deliberate slander. Those who had an interest in the system he had overthrown had no scruple in defaming him. There was talk about his complicity in the murder of Riccio, though Knox's name, for all the queen's detestation of it, had not been among the seventy listed for investigation at the time of the crime. There were salacious innuendoes about his relations with his mother-in-law, Mrs. Bowes, a woman who had been over fifty and the mother of fifteen children when Knox first met her. There were even tales that in his youth he had committed adultery with his stepmother.[57] As he hobbled along the wind-swept streets of the town he could hear from a sheltered corner the excited whisper of a group of undergraduates irresponsibly repeating the gossip they had heard.

There were petty jealousies too. Even the minister, Robert Hamilton, who had succeeded Knox's old friend Goodman, in 1566, resented the great man's coming to St. Andrews. Indeed, the whole panorama of his stormy life among the great seemed to be kaleidoscoped at St. Andrews into a mockingly trivial caricature. Nor was Knox, in his old age, able to stand aloof from the petty strife any more than he had been capable of remaining inactive in the great national turmoils of the days of his prime. Unable to write two lines with his own hand, he took the utmost pains with his sermons, having them written out for him almost in full. Then, on Sundays, well wrapped up and with a staff in one hand and Bannatyne supporting him on the other side, he would pick his steps cautiously from the priory, where he lived, to the parish kirk of the town.

James Melville, then an undergraduate at St. Leonard's College in the university, has left picturesque testimony to Knox's preaching zeal in his last days. St. Leonard's was politically against the queen's party, and Melville was among those who

[57] Such calumnies increased in number and incredibility after Knox's death. In 1628, for example, Father Alexander Baillie charged him with having committed incestuous adultery after his second wife's death — a remarkable achievement, since that event did not take place until twenty years after the death of Knox himself. Father Baillie adduced proof of the levity with which Knox regarded this vice by attributing to him the exact words that Sanders, a writer against English Protestantism, had already put into the mouth of Sir Francis Brian in a conversation with Henry VIII.

loved Knox with all the fervor of a young man. Armed with a pen and a " little book," he would go off on Sundays to hear the prophet preach. Notetaking, he tells us, was easy in the first half hour, when the preacher was moderately and dispassionately expounding God's Word. Then, as Knox came to the application of his text, the message began to thrill him so much that his hand trembled so that he could not take notes properly. Finally, as the excitement reached its climax he found that he " could nocht hald a pen to wryt." Knox was continuing to preach, despite his infirmities, with all the old earnestness and some of the old fury in denouncing those whom he believed to be holding up, in their own petty and selfish interests, the coming of God's Kingdom.

But most charming of all the pictures Melville draws is that of the old man coming on occasion to rest awhile in the college yard, where he would call some of the freshmen and bejants [58] over to him and plead with them to learn of God and of God's great work in Scotland, urging them to be faithful to the cause of the Reform, to use their time well, " lern the guid instructiones," and " follow the guid exemple of our maisters."

Among those who listened to Knox at this time was the Earl of Morton. Morton was to be proclaimed regent on the day of Knox's death, and soon thereafter to recapture, with English help, Edinburgh Castle, which had been holding out for the queen. But though one of the most inveterate of Marie Stuart's enemies, Morton was no friend to either the old religion or the new. Nominally on the Protestant side, he was a greedy and unscrupulous man, and he was now trying to bring back bishops so that he might appropriate a large part of their emoluments for his own purse. Nearly a year before, the former Archbishop of St. Andrews had been hanged, and John Douglas, rector of the university, was nominated in his place. Anticipating Knox's opposition, Morton came to St. Andrews to see that Douglas was duly inaugurated. It would be convenient, he felt, to have bishops in Scotland when the two king-

[58] A bejant at St. Andrews is a sophomore.

doms would be united as he hoped. The two kingdoms were to be indeed united under one crown thirty years after Knox's death; but the whole history of Scotland for almost a century thereafter was to be a tale of incessant bitterness and strife between bishop and presbyter, until at length presbyter prevailed. As Morton expected, Knox, though he had a personal affection for Douglas himself, warmly opposed the plan and adamantly refused to have any part in the inauguration.

Much of the rest of Knox's time was spent in completing his magnum opus, the *History of the Reformation in Scotland,* for which he continued to collect original documents and any other materials he could find, bearing on the events he knew so well because, inevitably, he had played the leading part in them. In one of his letters he signed himself " lying in St. Andrews half dead." Though " without great corporal pain," he was " daily looking for an end of the battle." In his extraordinary zeal for the cause of Reform it did not seem even to occur to him to question that it was better to wear out than to rust out. In his rage against those who seemed to him to be trying to spike the guns of God, he denounced the plotters in Edinburgh Castle as " traitors and murderers." Neither of the two political parties pleased him, however. Both were, in their own ways, unrepentant of their oppression of " the poor Kirk of God." His prayers were more than ever for . . . the Kirk . . . the Kirk . . . the Kirk.

A truce between the political parties in Edinburgh was concluded at the end of July, 1572, and thereupon Knox's old flock begged him to return. Nothing could have pleased him better at the time; yet he demurred: they must not expect him to modify his protestations against unrighteousness. When assured, however, that he might speak as he had always spoken, he came back, settling this time in the residence near the Netherbow that is now shown to visitors as " Knox's house." By this time he was exceedingly feeble. By making the journey in stages, he was in Edinburgh by the last Sunday of August, preaching again in St. Giles's. His voice was now so weak that he had to be given a little pulpit in a corner of the nave, and even so he was probably audible to very few. On September

7 he wrote to his successor, Lawson of Aberdeen, to hurry lest he come too late. Only a few days afterward came grim news from Paris. A massacre of Protestants, begun on the Feast of Saint Bartholomew, August 24, was spreading. Instigated by Catherine de Médicis, the killings were destined to continue until October 3. Despite the refusal of some of the provincial governors of France to authorize the massacre within their provinces, it eventually wiped out fifty thousand Protestants by the sword, and at the order of Pope Gregory XIII, bonfires were lighted all over France to celebrate the slaughter. On the first day in September, Knox preached again. His voice was now very faint; but even Knox's whispers were thunder. Among his hearers was the French ambassador, Du Croc. In his now hoarse whisper Knox told him to go back and tell the king of France he was a murderer. Du Croc, horrified and affronted, complained to the Scottish nobles, and the nobles shrugged their shoulders. No one, they explained, could stop the mouth of John Knox.

After inducting Lawson to St. Giles's on Sunday, November 9, Knox returned to his house for the last time. In his bedroom in Edinburgh, he lay down to prepare for death. A fit of coughing left him very weak, so that by Thursday he could no longer read the Bible aloud as was his daily custom. Into his bedroom came his old friends, bidding him farewell. For each he had a blessing and an admonition. He sent a message to Kirkcaldy to remind the latter of his old constancy in the cause and to warn him that if he did not repent he would die miserably.

Soon he was overtaken by considerable pain and his mind grew confused. He made to get up to preach and had to be restrained. He called his elders and deacons and told them that his fight had been for God. He had had no vested interest in what he had preached and taught. He had opposed men only in their rebellion against God. About this time, Maitland had lodged a complaint with Knox's kirk session, charging Knox with having called him an atheist and an enemy to God and urging the session not to believe everything Knox said as though he were an oracle, for he was as vain as the rest of men. To the astonishment and discomfiture of the session, the dying man alluded to Maitland's complaint. He did not deny he was subject to vanity as are other men; but he had preached the Word, and that Word left no doubt that the wicked would be destroyed. With death now approaching, his certainty of this was no less lively. He bade them read the Ninth Psalm, which they did, and left with tears in their eyes:

" The wicked shall be turned into hell, and all the nations that forget God. For the needy shall not alway be forgotten: the expectation of the poor shall not perish for ever. Arise, O Lord, let not man prevail: Let the heathen be judged in thy sight. Put them in fear, O Lord: that the nations may know themselves to be but men."

Soon he could speak only in the brief phrases of a dying man. He asked insistently that the Bible be read aloud to him. He wanted to hear the fifty-third chapter of Isaiah. He called for more psalms, and even Calvin's sermons. But above all he kept telling the friends around him to read to him from The Gospel According to St. John, his beloved seventeenth chapter, " the place where I cast my first anchor."

To that bedroom, hushed but for the murmured reading of the Book and his own occasional dying phrases, came the greatest nobles of the land. One by one, they passed before him, the rich men who had listened to his words and given him power to set up his Kirk, though they had not always felt able to accept the uncompromising precepts he had given. Glencairn was there, of course, and Lindsay; Boyd, Ruthven, and even Morton, who was just elected, though not yet proclaimed, regent of Scotland. Hourly they awaited the death of the prophet, who on his deathbed seemed holier than ever before.

On November 23, in the afternoon, when all except his attendants were, as he would have wished, at sermon, he felt death near and enjoined those who stood by to " see the work of God." But death did not yet come. After some restless hours, he spoke suddenly again — words that told of great interior victory:

" I have been in meditation these last two nights," he murmured, " of the troubled Church of God, the spouse of Jesus Christ, despised of the world but precious in his sight. I have called to God for her, and have committed her to her Head,

224

Jesus Christ. I have been fighting against Satan, who is ever ready to assault; yea, I have fought against spiritual wickedness in heavenly things and have prevailed. I have been in heaven and have possession, and I have tasted of those heavenly joys where presently I am."

Who could have written a better epitaph for the prophet than these impressive words, uttered on the edge of the valley he was about to enter, fearing no evil because he knew God would be with him? His rod and his staff would comfort him.

Slowly, he repeated the Lord's Prayer. Turning his gray-blue eyes glassily toward the bystanders, he asked quietly, " Who can pronounce such holy words? " Then he seemed to fall asleep, a sleep broken by mutterings: " The Kirk! . . . The Kirk! "

Monday morning dawned. He insisted on getting up. Putting on his doublet and his hose he crawled to a chair and sat down. He tried to get up and walk, but of course he could not even stand. After about half an hour he had to be helped back to bed. Toward noon he requested his wife to read him the fifteenth chapter of Saint Paul's first letter to the Corinthians. The awed young woman read in a trembling voice.

He muttered on. " Into Thy hands I commend my spirit. Into Thy hands . . ." But death would not come. About four o'clock in the afternoon, as the placid winter sun was setting over Edinburgh, he called again for his favorite chapter from Saint John. His wife and Bannatyne and various friends took turns in reading. They read for three hours. Then they stopped, because he did not seem to be listening any more. They let pass the usual time for prayers, so as not to disturb him. But at last, about half past ten, they knelt down and whispered the evening prayers — very softly, as one whispers in the presence of death. When they had risen from their knees, someone went over to his bedside and, hardly expecting a reply, asked him gently whether he had heard the prayers. Very slowly, Knox opened his eyes and seemed to be smiling as he answered:

" Would to God you heard them as I did. Praise God for the joyful sound! "

It was nearly eleven when he uttered a long, sobbing sigh.

Someone begged him to give a last sign that he was at peace. Unable to speak, now, he lifted his hand. It dropped at his side. Death had come at last. God's warrior had passed beyond the Church Militant.

In his will there was evidence enough of the truth of Knox's claim that he had made no worldly profit out of God's Kirk. "None have I corrupted, none have I defrauded; merchandise have I not made." More than half his total estate consisted of debts due to him. The rest was a small sum of money that would have left his family in dire poverty had not the General Assembly ordered that his stipend be paid to his young widow for a year after his death. The Regent Morton took care that his dependents were decently provided for.

To the south of St. Giles's, in those days, lay the churchyard, which disappeared about sixty years later when Parliament House and other buildings were erected on its site. To a grave [59] in that churchyard, on Wednesday, the twenty-sixth of November, they carried the body of the great man who had fought against spiritual wickedness in heavenly things and had prevailed. All the nobles in town attended the funeral. Among them was the Regent Morton. Noted for his sententiousness of speech, he uttered at the graveside the inevitable words:

"Here lies one who neither flattered nor feared any flesh."

But surely uppermost in the minds of the mourners as they turned homeward out of the cold was the thought that John Knox would never more denounce unrighteousness. And as at last the conversation turned to politics and the future of their country, there must have been few, even among those who had most resented his scorifying rebukes, whose hearts did not tenderly ache at the prospect of that everlasting silence.

[59] The exact site of Knox's grave is not known with certainty. But in the square between St. Giles's and Parliament House is to be found a very small slab of stone set in the ground, marking the traditional spot by the simple inscription:

I · K

1572

The initials stand, of course, for IOANNES KNOX. Ironically, the stone is now under the shadow of an equestrian statue of King Charles II.

APPENDIX
I

A. SOVEREIGNS OF SCOTLAND

JAMES V (1513–1542)

Born in 1512, only legitimate son of James IV, who was slain on the field at the Battle of Flodden together with the flower of the Scottish nobility and about one fifth of the entire Scottish army. During the infancy of James V, Scotland was ruled by regents. By the age of fifteen he was accounted fit to rule with the guidance of his mother.

MARIE STUART (1542–1567)

Born in 1542, succeeded to the throne six days after her birth; known to later historians as "Mary Queen of Scots." Abdicated in 1567; beheaded by order of Elizabeth I of England in 1587. During her infancy Scotland was ruled by the Regent Arran (the second Earl), and, from 1554 until 1559, by the queen regent, Marie de Guise, the mother of Marie Stuart.

JAMES VI (1567–1625)

Born in 1566, only child of Marie Stuart and her second husband, Lord Darnley. Assumed government in 1583; became, in 1603, by the Union of the Crowns, also James I of England. Educated by the Scottish poet and humanist George Buchanan, he developed scholarly interests and engaged in literary activities.

B. SOVEREIGNS OF ENGLAND

HENRY VIII (1509–1547)

Born in 1491, third child and second son of Henry VII and Elizabeth of York. Abolished papal jurisdiction in England in 1534, under the Act of Supremacy.

EDWARD VI (1547–1553)

Born in 1537, only child of Henry VIII by his third wife (Jane Seymour). During his short reign, power was in the hands first of Somerset, then of Northumberland.

MARY I (1553–1558)

Born in 1516, daughter of Henry VIII and his first wife (Catherine of Aragon). Known to later historians as Mary Tudor, and remembered also, because of her persecutions of Protestants, as "Bloody Mary."

ELIZABETH I (1558–1603)

Born in 1533, only surviving child of Henry VIII by his second wife (Anne Boleyn). Last English sovereign before the Union of the Crowns of England and Scotland in 1603.

C. SOVEREIGNS OF FRANCE

FRANCIS I (1515–1547)

Born in 1494, son of Charles of Valois and Louise of Savoy. Inclined at first to favor the cause of the Reformers, he later repressed Protestants.

HENRY II (1547–1559)

Born in 1519, second son of Francis I and Claude, daughter of Louis XII. Even more absolutist than his father, and more severe toward the Protestants.

FRANCIS II (1559–1560)

Born in 1544, eldest son of Henry II and Catherine de Médicis. Married Marie Stuart (Mary Queen of Scots) in 1558. A sickly boy of feeble understanding, he allowed France to be virtually governed by his uncles, Francis (Duc de Guise) and Charles (Cardinal de Lorraine), the elder brothers of Mary of Guise, queen regent of Scotland during the minority of Mary Queen of Scots.

CHARLES IX (1560–1574)

Born in 1550, third son of Henry II and Catherine de Médicis. His mother, Catherine de Médicis, had exercised power during his minority, and he submitted to her authority even after being proclaimed of age in 1563.

D. BISHOPS OF ROME

LEO X (1513–1521)

Giovanni de' Medici, born in 1475, second son of Lorenzo de' Medici. Excommunicated Luther in 1521.

ADRIAN VI (1522–1523)

Adrian Dedel, born in 1459 at Utrecht; became tutor to the Holy Roman Emperor Charles V.

CLEMENT VII (1523–1534)

Giulio de' Medici, born in 1478.

PAUL III (1534–1549)

Alessandro Farnese, born in 1468, member of circle of Cosmo de' Medici. Established Inquisition in 1542.

JULIUS III (1550–1555)
  Giovanni Maria del Monte, born in 1497.

MARCELLUS II (1555)
  Marcello Cervini, born in 1501. Reigned less than a month.

PAUL IV (1555–1559)
  Giovanni Pietro Caraffa, born in 1476. Under Paul III he had advised the reactionary measures then taken.

PIUS IV (1559–1565)
  Giovanni Angelo Medici, born in 1499.

PIUS V (1566–1572)
  Michele Ghislieri, born in 1504. Became a Dominican friar at the age of fourteen. In 1569 expelled Jews from the Papal States. Was a rigorist and a reforming pope. The first pope for many years to discourage nepotism, he made only one nephew a cardinal. His personal asceticism was in marked contrast to the habits of his predecessors. Canonized by Clement XI in 1712.

APPENDIX

II

WHEN WAS KNOX BORN?

Until 1904, the accepted date of Knox's birth was 1505. The traditional acceptance of this date was evidently due to a solitary statement in John Spottiswoode's *History of the Church of Scotland*. Spottiswoode (1565–1637) was Archbishop of Glasgow (later of St. Andrews) during the " First Episcopacy " in Scotland, and he wrote as such at the command of James VI.

The date of Knox's death was never, of course, in question, and if he had been born in 1505 he would have been sixty-seven when he died. The known feebleness of the last two years of his life made this seem credible enough. It was also known that Knox studied under John Major. Major taught at the University of Glasgow from 1518 to 1523, being described as Principal Regent of the " college and pedagogy " of that university. On June 9, 1523, Major was incorporated at the University of St. Andrews, which he left for Paris in 1526, returning to St. Andrews in 1531, where he spent the rest of his life.

A student was incorporated at Glasgow in 1522 under the name "John Knox," a name that was not, however, uncommon, so that this student cannot with any certainty be identified as the future reformer. It was difficult, on the 1505 hypothesis, to account for the definite statement of Beza that it was at St. Andrews that Knox studied under Major. It was not, perhaps, entirely impossible; but the kind of work Major would have been doing at St. Andrews when Knox, if born in 1505, would have been there, made the notion unplausible. The fact that the records of the University of St. Andrews show no student of the name "John Knox" is not conclusive either way, for there are discrepancies in these old documents.

In Hume Brown's life of Knox, published in 1895, it was revealed that a letter written by Sir Peter Young to Beza, dated at Edinburgh, November 13, 1579, states plainly that Knox died in the fifty-ninth year of his age (Hume Brown, *John Knox,* Vol. II, p. 322). This evidence, which in any case cannot be ignored, is weighty for various reasons. Curiously, it did not seem to shake Hume Brown's confidence in the traditional birth year, 1505. Hay Fleming, however, an eminent historian of Scotland, made an exhaustive study of the evidence and concluded with a strong conviction that Knox could not have been born in 1505. He maintained that the true date could be placed as 1513–1515.

Sir Peter Young's letter to Beza was crucial. But Hay Fleming also maintained there was reason to believe Spottiswoode's statement was due to an error in transcription or printing. On the positive side, moreover, several other considerations support the later date, not least that it fits the statement of Beza himself that Knox studied under Major at St. Andrews. The notion that he did so at Glasgow is ruled out, of course, for when Major was teaching there Knox would have been only a little boy. That Knox should have gone to Glasgow University is intrinsically not a particularly credible supposition, in the absence of strong supporting evidence, because a Haddington boy would be more likely to go to St. Andrews, which, founded in 1412 was more ancient, more important, and equally accessible. Again, the later birth date also makes the delay in his entry into public life much shorter: that he should have been forty-five, as the 1505 hypothesis implied, before publicly announcing his Protestant sympathies, is hardly credible in such a man. On the other hand, it seems difficult to believe that a man in his fifties could be as decrepit as Knox latterly was; nevertheless, both the extreme hardship he had suffered and a common psychological attitude in the sixteenth century toward aging make this less incredible than at first it seems. It is well known to modern physicians that some men's bodies are as senescent at seventy as are others at eighty or ninety. Knox's body might well have seemed broken with age in his late fifties; after all, he had never spared it.

On the whole, therefore, there seems good reason to distrust the old tradition and to place the date of Knox's birth, as most scholars now do, between 1513 and 1515. The arguments advanced by Hay Fleming may be found in his contributions to *The Scotsman* (May 27, 1904) and *The Bookman* (September, 1905).

APPENDIX
III

BIBLIOGRAPHICAL NOTE

Apart from the manuscript records of the period and the letters of Knox in national, ecclesiastical, and university collections in Edinburgh and elsewhere, the most useful single source book for those readers who might wish to pursue the further study of Knox's life is his own *History of the Reformation in Scotland*. The first, unfinished edition of this work was published in 1586–1587 and was suppressed and seized. In 1644, an edition was made by David Buchanan, since which time there have been many others, some elaborately annotated, others of a less scholarly sort. The modern student is fortunate in having easy access to an excellent edition that answers the needs of both specialist and general reader. Edited by Professor William Croft Dickinson, it was published in two volumes at Edinburgh by Thomas Nelson & Sons in 1949.

The first important biography of Knox, that of Thomas M'Crie, appeared early last century and passed through many editions. The first American one was published in 1813 by Eastburn Kirk at New York. This biography, for long the standard one, was written in the laudatory style of a literary tradition that is no longer fashionable. But though many readers would find it irksome on that account, it is still very much worth reading. It presents the historical evidence in a fair and scholarly way, though the interpretation is almost always in Knox's favor. The abundant notes contain much valuable and interesting material, and some of Knox's previously unpublished letters and other documents relating to him are included in a long appendix.

Between 1846 and 1864, a collection of the works of John Knox in six volumes, edited by David Laing, was published in Edinburgh for the Bannatyne Club, and in 1895 James Thin of Edinburgh issued a reprint of this collection. The first two volumes contain the *History;* the remaining four volumes contain various letters, writings, and sermons.

The same year, 1895, Hume Brown's biography of Knox was published in two volumes by A. and C. Black. This was also a very scholarly work, containing the results of a good deal of original research into the Continental European sources. A year later a biography by Taylor Innes appeared which captured the spirit of Knox perhaps better than had any previous work.

Andrew Lang's biography, published in 1905, was the first attempt to discredit the older tradition about Knox. Skeptical of Knox's impartiality in recounting the story of his own life in the *History,* Lang sought to produce a work that would correct the uncritical hero-worshiping tendencies of previous biographers. Lang's work is usefully provocative, perhaps not always quite fair, nearly always vivacious. Henry Cowan, in a life of Knox published about the same time, attempted, on the other hand, to popularize the story as this was known by those who had learned to read it through M'Crie's spectacles. There were also other, less ambitious, sketches. Of the many biographies of Knox published in the United States, I know of only one written by an American: it was by the Virginia-born Mrs. Terhune and was published in 1900. I have not been able to see a copy of this.

Mr. Edwin Muir's pleasantly written biography of Knox was published by Jonathan Cape in 1929. It owes much, as the author acknowledges, to Lang. But the purpose is a special one: to try to explain in contemporary terms how Scotland's prophet felt and behaved, on the assumption that his religious conviction was in fact a delusion. It is difficult to write a really good account of a man whose deepest convictions one can in no way take seriously, and Mr. Muir's life of Knox, for all its clarity, suffers from this fundamental shortcoming. Lord Eustace Percy's biography (Hodder & Stoughton, Ltd., 1937) shows no such lack of sympathy. It is a work of unobtrusive scholarship, commendable honesty, and delightful literary skill. It presupposes, however, a greater acquaintance with the historical background than the average modern reader is likely to possess.

INDEX

Aaron, 167

Aberdeen, 33, 52, 155, 180

Aberdeenshire, 114

Act of Supremacy (1534), 31

Agincourt, Battle of, 143

Alexander VI (Pope), 32

Ambrose, 99

Angus, 125

Angus, Earl of, 15

Anstruther, 124

Argyll, fifth Earl of (Archibald Lord Lorne): character of, 115; sent to offer Knox terms, 121; rebuked by Knox, 189; mentioned, 91, 122, 123, 127, 188, 201, 214

Argyll, Lady. *See* Stuart, Lady Jane

Armada, 200

Arran, James, second Earl of (Regent). *See* Châtelherault

Arran, James, third Earl of: character of, 115; resents Knox's reproach, 140; proposed for hand of Elizabeth, 151; embraces Bothwell, 177; mentioned, 41, 134, 135, 137, 152, 153, 176

Arthur's Seat, 86

Articles of Religion, Knox's influence in drafting English, 60

Auchterarder, 121

Augsburg, 76

Augustine, 19, 58, 99

Augustinian Hermits, 17

Avignon, 25

Ayrshire, 34, 36, 81, 122, 180, 185, 213

Babylonian Exile, 50

Baillie, Father Alexander: charges Knox with incestuous adultery, 220

Balnaves of Halhill, Henry, 52, 134, 143

Bannatyne, Richard, 218, 220, 225

Bannockburn, Battle of, 22

Basel, 77

Beaton, David (Cardinal): fights archbishop in Glasgow Cathedral, 38; assassination of, 40; strength of his fortress, 41; mentioned, 33, 34, 35, 36, 37, 123, 148, 218

Beaton, James (Archbishop of Glasgow): "pasquil" shown to, 83; flees to Paris, 147

Beaton, James (Archbishop of St. Andrews), 25, 27 f., 123, 148

Berwick, 54 f., 56, 60, 112, 134, 136

Beza, Theodore, 230

"Black Rubric," 60

Blackader MS., 210

Bodin, Jean, 99

Bonner, Edmund (Bishop of London), 70

Book of Common Prayer, English, 53, 54, 60, 72, 73, 74, 75, 105

Book of Discipline: provisions of, 154 ff.; mentioned, 150, 151, 153, 162, 190

Borgia, Cesare, 32

Borgia, Francis, S.J., 32

Boston Tea Party, 31

Bothwell, Adam (Bishop of Orkney), 147

Bothwell, James Hepburn, fourth Earl of, 144, 145, 176 f., 211

Cromwell, Oliver, 14
Cunningham, Alexander. *See* Glencairn, fifth Earl of
Cupar, 125 f.

Daniel, 43
Darnley, Henry, Lord, 207, 211, 212, 213
Dauphiné, 144, 209
David, 62
David I (King of Scotland), 86
Deborah, 101, 172
De Gouda, 180
Diana, 190
Dieppe, 66, 69, 92, 110, 111, 112
Dominican Friars, 26, 29, 82, 110, 118
Douglas, Gavin (Bishop of Dunkeld), 15 f.
Douglas, John. *See* Morton, Earl of
Douglas, John (preacher), 149, 221 f.
Douglas, Robert, 191
Douglas, Willie, 214
D'Oysel, 126, 132, 141
Dress, Knox's attitude on feminine, 88 f., 190, 197
du Bellay (Cardinal Archbishop), 192
Du Croc, 223
Dudley. *See* Northumberland, Duke of
Dudley, Andrew (admiral), 41
Dumbarton Castle, 177
Dumfries, 187
Dunbar, 127, 132, 213
Dunbar, Gavin (Archbishop of Glasgow), 38
Dundee, 34, 35, 50, 51, 52, 109, 114, 116, 117
Durham. *See* Tunstall, Cuthbert

Eck, 25
Edinburgh: Knox burned in effigy in, 88; Knox arrives in, 110, 112; mentioned, 14, 15, 36, 37, 50, 82, 87, 89 f., 91, 96, 107, 114, 127, 132, 137, 144, 155 f., 159, 161, 162, 180, 198, 212, 216, 221, 225
Edinburgh, Treaty of, 146, 147
Edward II (King of England), 32
Edward VI (King of England): death of, 62; mentioned, 32, 34, 59
Election, doctrine of, 35, 79, 94, 103 f., 138 f., 215
Elijah, 186
Elizabeth I (Queen of England): offended by *Blast*, 100; rejects Arran, 152; mentioned, 97, 110, 111, 112, 131, 151, 165, 175, 191, 200, 214, 215
Emden, 73
Erasmus, Desiderius, 25, 66, 71
Erfurt, 17
Erskine, Lord. *See* Mar, Earl of
Erskine of Dun, John: character of, 114; mentioned, 81, 117, 191, 196, 197
Euclid, 157
Excommunication: in Roman Church, 28; in Reformed Church, 159

Falkland, 123, 126
Farel, William, 209
Fénelon, 57
Fife, 16, 51, 140, 143
Fleming, Hay, 230 f.
Flodden, Battle of, 22 f., 50
Forth, Firth of and river, 50, 127, 161
Foxe, John, 98
Francis I (King of France), 41
Francis II (King of France): death of, 152; mentioned, 127, 135, 143, 192 f.
Francis of Sales, 57
Franciscan Friars, 118
Frankfurt, 72, 73, 74, 75, 76, 111, 113

Galleys: Knox sent to, 46 ff.; description of, 47; Knox released from, 52
Gardiner (Bishop), 70

liam: character of, 115; mentioned, 40, 46, 52, 131, 140, 141, 142, 216, 217, 223

Knox, Eleazer, 91, 152, 209

Knox, Elizabeth, 210

Knox, John: birth of, 14, 229 ff.; personal appearance of, in youth, 20 f.; comes under influence of Wishart, 30; preaches at St. Andrews, 43; sent to galleys, 46; released from galleys, 52; his love of England, 52 ff., 71 f.; licensed to preach in England, 54; style of preaching, 55 f.; declines English bishopric, 61; betrothed to Marjorie Bowes, 64; on female rule, 68, 98 f.; marries Marjorie Bowes, 78; on Eucharist, 80, 105; temptation of, 86 f.; birth of first son, 91; writes the *Blast*, 96 ff.; other writings of, 100 ff.; receives freedom of Geneva, 111; proclaimed outlaw, 117; fulfills his prediction, 124 f.; attitude toward mob vandalism, 128; mob turns against, 138; death of wife, 151; educational scheme of, 155 ff.; personal appearance of, in middle age, 163; first audience with Queen of Scots, 163 ff.; second audience, 180 ff.; third audience, 185 ff.; fourth audience, 191 ff.; last audience, 201 ff.; marries Margaret Stuart, 208; completes *History*, 222; death of, 225 f.; burial of, 226; *passim*

Knox, Margaret, 210

Knox, Martha, 210, 213

Knox, Nathaniel, 91, 152, 209

Knox, William, 13

Kyle, 213

Lausanne, 77

Lawson (preacher), 223

Leishman, Thomas, 81

Leith, 50, 51, 112, 132, 134, 141, 143, 144, 145, 161

Lennox, Earl of (Regent of Scotland), 216

Leslie, John, 40

Lever, Thomas, 74

Lincoln, Abraham, 10

Lindores Abbey, 126

Lindsay, Sir David (satirist), 16, 128

Lindsay, the Master of, 224

Linlithgow, 129

Lochleven, 213

Locke, Anne (Mrs.), 90, 91, 116, 134

Loire, 49

Lollardy, 24, 30, 34

London, 53, 146

Longniddry, 36, 50

Lorne, Archibald, Lord. *See* Argyll, fifth Earl of

Lorraine, Cardinal of, 85, 92, 109, 163, 191

Lorraine, Mary of. *See* Mary of Guise

Lothians, 14, 50, 51, 87, 119

Louvain, 25, 27

Loyola. *See* Ignatius

Luther, Martin, 16 f., 25, 30, 35, 52, 72, 73, 94, 162

Maitland of Lethington, William: takes political leadership of revolution, 139; diplomacy of 140; complexity of his intrigues, 151; mentioned, 115, 137, 142, 153, 163, 174, 180, 187, 191, 199, 201, 202, 203, 206, 207, 211, 216, 217, 223 f.

Major, John: Knox's teacher, 14; a conciliarist, 15; mentioned, 19, 25, 43, 229 f.

Mar, Earl of (Lord Erskine): regency passes to, 216; mentioned, 81, 91

Mar, Earl of (Lord James Stuart). *See* Stuart, Lord James

Marburg, 26

Marie Stuart (Mary, Queen of Scots): widowed, 152; arrives

237

in Scotland, 161; gives Knox first audience, 163 ff.; mocked by crowds, 173; her claim to English throne, 175; gives Knox second audience, 180 ff.; gives Knox third audience, 185 ff.; gives Knox fourth audience, 191 ff.; description of marriage in Paris to Francis II, 192; summons Knox for last time, 200 ff.; mentioned, 13, 32, 34, 51, 108, 120, 127, 135, 143, 146, 153, 162, 176, 177, 190, 198, 213 ff., 219

Marischal, Earl, 82, 176, 201

Martin V (Pope), 25

Mary, B.V., 21, 49

Mary of Guise (Queen Regent of Scotland): hears of Knox's preaching, 81; dislike of bishops, 82; mocks "pasquil," 83; regency passes to, 115; outlaws preachers, 117; goes to Dunbar, 127; Knox's infinite trust in her perfidy, 133; suspended from regency, 135; death of, 145; mentioned, 84, 96, 97, 106, 107, 108, 109, 112, 119, 120, 122, 123, 125, 126, 132, 133, 134, 135, 136, 137, 141, 144, 163, 194

Mary, Queen of Scots. See Marie Stuart

Mary Tudor (Mary I, Queen of England; "Bloody" Mary): proclaimed queen, 63; death of, 110; mentioned, 32, 69, 70, 73, 97, 111, 112, 176

Mass: prohibited by Perth authorities, 119; prohibited by Scottish Parliament, 150; mentioned, 21, 25, 38, 47, 49, 54, 60, 79, 80, 81, 86, 95, 117 f., 122, 162, 169, 173, 176, 178, 180, 185, 189, 198, 211

Matthew, Gospel According to Saint: Knox preaches on fourteenth chapter of, 69 f.

Maxwell, Sir John, 199, 201

Maxwell, William D., 80

Mayflower, 14

Melanchthon, Philip, 71

Melville, James, 40, 220

Mercat Cross, Edinburgh, 88, 107, 135, 212

Methuen, Paul (preacher), 109

Minorites, 15

Money, value of, in sixteenth century Scotland, 66, 160

Montaigne, Michel de, 99

Montmorency, 176

Montrose, 33, 34

Mont-Saint-Michel, 52

Moray, Earl of. See Stuart, Lord James

More, Thomas, 71

Morton, Earl of: regency passes to, 224; on Knox, 226; mentioned, 180, 221 f.

Moses, 10, 43, 44, 167, 185

Muhammad, 44, 65

Myln, Walter: burning of, 106; mentioned, 125

Nanak, 32

Nantes, 49 f.

Nero (Emperor), 70, 180, 206

Netherbow, Knox's house near, 222

Newcastle, 58, 59, 61

New York State, 161

Nîmes, 128

Normandy, 91

Northumberland, Duke of (John Dudley), 58, 61

Notre Dame de Paris, Marie Stuart's marriage at, 192 f.

Ochiltree, Lord, 208 f.

Oxford, 24, 74, 91, 157

Paip. See Papacy

Paisley, Abbot of, 33

Papacy: Scotland's relations with, 15, 24, 32; abolition of jurisdiction of, in Scotland, 150; mentioned, 25, 31, 33, 41 f., 43, 48, 49, 53, 61, 62, 67, 77, 80, 85, 95, 157, 167, 168, 200, 215, 219

Spens of Condie, John, 200, 201, 202
Spottiswoode, John (Archbishop of St. Andrews), 229
Spottiswoode, John (preacher), 149
Sprott, George W., 81
Stirling: Regent's armies block road at, 122; D'Oysel's forces flee toward, 141; mob drives out priests in presence of Queen, 173; mentioned, 41, 109, 110, 114, 117, 121, 134, 138, 141, 142, 214
Stirling Bridge, Battle of, 22
Stirlingshire, 119
Strassburg, 73, 74
Strozzi, Leo, 45
Stuart, House of, 25
Stuart, Lady Jane, 188 f., 207
Stuart, Lord James (Earl of Mar; Earl of Moray): character of, 114 f.; assassination of, 216; mentioned, 52, 81, 91, 121, 122, 123, 125, 127, 132, 137, 140, 143, 147, 164, 166, 168, 176, 177, 180, 199, 201, 213, 214
Stuart, Lord Robert, 147
Stuart, Margaret; marries Knox, 208; mentioned, 209, 210, 225 f.
Stuart, Marie. See Marie Stuart
Stuart, Walter, 162
Superintendents, 154

Tartas, 128
Tay, River, 50, 117, 125
Tertullian, 98
Throgmorton, 214
Tolbooth, 160, 190
Toronto, 114
Tournelles, palace of the, 193
Trafalgar, 71
Transubstantiation, doctrine of, 54, 86
Trent, Council of, 32, 42, 148, 192, 200
True Church, doctrine of the. See Church, True

Trunk Close, Knox's house at, 164, 197
Tullibody Bridge, 142
Tunstall, Cuthbert (Bishop of Durham), 70
"Twopenny Faith," 93
Tyrol, 32

Venice, 218
Virgil, 16

Wallace, William, 22
War of Independence, Scottish, 14, 23, 24, 48
Wars of Religion, Continental, 31
Washington, George, 10
Wedderburn, the brothers, 28
Welch, John, 210
Wesel, 73
Westminster, 62
Westmoreland, Earl of, 144
Whitelaw, 134
Whittingham, William, 73, 74, 75
Willock, John (preacher), 149
Winchester, Paulet, Marquess of, 70
Winram, John, 39, 149, 217
Wishart, George: reads Greek Testament, 33; preaches in Dundee, 35; arrest of, 37; trial of, 38; character of, 39; burning of, 39; mentioned, 30, 32, 34, 36, 40, 42, 43, 48, 49, 81, 123, 129, 218
Witherspoon, John (President of Princeton), 210
Wodrow MSS., 210
Wycliffe, John, 24

Xenophon, 157
Ximenes, 85, 93

Young, Sir Peter, 230

Zürich, 68, 73, 74
Zwingli, Huldreich, 35, 73, 80